Gustav Mahler
and The Courage To Be

This is one of a Series of Books
Studies in the Psychology of Culture
by the same author:

Gustav Mahler
and
The Courage To Be

by

David Holbrook

Sometime Fellow of King's College,
Cambridge,
Assistant Director of English Studies,
Downing College, Cambridge

VISION

Vision Press Limited
11-14 Stanhope Mews West
London SW7 5RD

ISBN 0 85478 243 5

Printed in Great Britain by
Clarke, Doble & Brendon Ltd
Plymouth
MCMLXXV

For my love

'Men will have to work a long time at cracking the nuts that I'm shaking down from the tree for them.'

Gustav Mahler, *Briefe*

Here the impossible union
Of spheres of existence is actual,
Here the past and future
Are conquered, and reconciled . . .

T. S. Eliot, *The Dry Salvages*

Contents

Acknowledgements

I should like to express my gratitude to a number of people who have helped me with this book. Wilfrid Mellers has been very encouraging, writing to a number of publishers, encouraging them to publish what is really a very deep disagreement between himself and me, about art, the baby's cry, and consciousness, which has gone on beneath a good deal of co-operation and dialogue. Peter Franklin of York University was also most helpful, and so was Mr Jack Diether. M. Masud R. Khan, Editor of the *International Library of Psychoanalysis*, has been most encouraging, in a general way, over my studies of the psychology of culture, while Colin Wilson lent me some books and made suggestions. Alan Ridout, Professor at the Royal College of Music and composer, also read the manuscript and made useful suggestions. None of these colleagues, of course, bears responsibility for my errors.

The music examples are from books published by: Universal Editions Ltd; His Masters Voice; Editions Eulenberg; Boosey and Hawkes; the Bruckner and Mahler Society and Mr Diether; and Messrs Dent.

Work on the final stages of the book was much helped by a grant from the Elmgrant Trust at Dartington and by my part-time appointment at Downing College, for both of which forms of assistance I am grateful.

D.H.

1

Introduction: What is the Point of Life?

The night looks softly down from distances,
Eternal with her thousand golden eyes,
And weary mortals shut their eyes in sleep.
To know once more some happiness forgotten.

See you the silent, gloomy wanderer?
Abandoned is the path he takes, and lonely,
Unmarked for distance or direction.
And oh! no star illuminates his way,

A way so long, so far from guardian spirits!
And voices versed in soft deceit sound, luring:
'When will this long and futile journey end?
Will not the wanderer rest from all his suffering?'

The Sphinx stares grimly, ominous with question,
Her stony, blank gray eyes tell nothing, nothing,
No single, saving sign, no ray of light:
And if I solve it not, my life is forfeit.

This is a sketch-poem by Gustav Mahler, 1883, for *Songs of a Wanderer*, translated by Gabriel Engel. It is quoted by Jack Diether in 'Mahler and Psycho-analysis', *Psycho-analysis and the Psychoanalytical Review*, Winter 1958–9, U.S.A.[1] Diether also discusses this poem (which Mahler did *not* set to music) in an article on 'Mahler Juvenilia' in *Chord and Discord*, Vol. 3, No. 1, p. 68. The last line surely means 'If I cannot find meaning in my life, I am confounded, I am faced with nothing but my nothingness?' Diether discusses another moment where Mahler failed to complete a piece, having 'no star to guide him' . . . 'No idea how to get back (or resolve the thing anyhow) in one line' (p. 67). But Mahler adds words of his own, almost indecipherable.

[1] See Appendix 4, Mahler's Poems, in Henry-Louis de la Grange's official Biography, Vol. 1.

Gustav Mahler and The Courage To Be

Auf ihrem Grab blaue Blüm'lein blühen,
Umschlingen sich wie sie einmal,
Dem Reif sie nicht welken, nicht dorren . . .

As Diether says, 'If there were in his soul "no single saving sign, no ray of light" he could not manufacture one to order—neither then nor later.' Yet in his music, I believe, he did create such light and signs.

*

The work that follows is an attempt to apply certain insights from recent psychoanalytical theory and existentialism to the criticism of a work of music. My reason for embarking on this, although I am a literary rather than a musical person, is that I believe we have nothing in literature as profoundly concerned with fundamental problems of existence as Mahler's later work, while in music criticism, apart from some superb work by Jack Diether, we do not yet have sufficient recognition of Mahler's achievement. Nor in literary criticism do we have sufficient recognition of the problems of existence which confront us— and which could be tackled as Mahler tackled them, if we understood him better. (We may compare, for instance, the triviality of dealings with death in the work of Ionesco, Pinter, Beckett, etc.)

I have discussed object-relations psychology at length elsewhere. All that needs to be said here is that from this psychology I believe there has emerged a 'philosophical anthropology' which confirms a great deal of what existentialist philosophers from Martin Buber to Ludwig Binswanger have told us: chiefly that man's primary need is to find himself *confirmed* in the 'creative reflection' of meeting or 'relationship', so that he can feel his existence has meaning. It is to this that the 'schizoid diagnosis', based on the earliest problems of the growth of identity, now draws our attention, while it endorses the convictions of existentialism, both Christian and humanist. Buber sees 'confirmation' ultimately as a manifestation of God—and to him *'Thou God seest me'* is perhaps the ultimate confirmation. But in the work of others, from Husserl to Binswanger, 'encounter' between the self and others as the basis of the relationship between ourselves and the universe is also the basis of our quest for meaning. Mahler's achievement was to find a sense of being confirmed in an invulnerable sense of meaningful existence in a Godless universe. As Jack Diether has said, Mahler was 'the first musical existentialist' and 'perhaps the only total one to date'. In his music, says Diether, quoting Nietzsche, we truly hear 'the bowels of existence' speak-

12

ing to us. The symbolism of his quest centres in the imagery of *seeing and being seen*—blue eyes, blank grey eyes, a thousand golden eyes, and 'everywhere and ever shines the blue horizon', symbolizing the creativity to which one belongs.

A profound connection between the sense of meaning and the need for 'confirmation' is made by Martin Buber, in his essay 'Distance and Relation', in *The Knowledge of Man*. He compares man's existence with that of the animals, and concludes that 'An animal does not need to be confirmed, for it is what it is unquestionably', but

> it is different with man. Sent forth from the natural domain of species into the hazard of the solitary category, surrounded by the air of a chaos which came into being with him, secretly and bashfully he watches for a Yes which allows him to be and which can come to him only from one human person to another. It is from one man to another that the heavenly bread of self-being is passed.
>
> p. 71

It is this 'Yes' for which Mahler's protagonist awaits, in *Das Lied von der Erde*:

> *Ich stehe hier und harre meines Freundes,*
> *Ich harre sein zum letzten Lebewohl . . .*
> Here will I stand and tarry for my friend.
> I wait for him to bid the last farewell . . .

His work seeks to find the 'heavenly bread of self-being', before he dies. And the confirmation sought is that which can affirm the validity of human consciousness—of the life-world in which he has existed. Buber again contrasts the 'unsteady conglomeration' of animal existence, with the transcendent life-world of a man:

> It is only man who replaces this unsteady conglomeration whose constitution is suited to the lifetime of the individual organism, by a unity which can be imagined or thought by him as existing for itself. With soaring power he reaches out beyond what is given him, flies beyond the horizon and the familiar stars, and grasps a totality. The meeting of natural being with the living creature produces those more or less changing masses of usable sense data which constitute the animal's realm of life. But only from the meeting of natural being with man does the new and enduring arise, that which comprehends and infinitely transcends the realm. An animal in the realm of its perceptions is like a fruit in its skin; man is, or can be, in the world as a dweller in an enormous building which is always being added to, and to whose limits he can never penetrate, but which he can nevertheless know as one does know a house in which one lives—for he is capable of grasping the wholeness of the building as such . . . Only when a structure of being is

independently over against a living being (*Seiende*), an independent opposite, does a world exist . . .

The Knowledge of Man, p. 61

It is this world, created by the 'I-Thou', soaring beyond the horizon, created by the meeting of natural being with man, that Mahler's late music celebrates, for its enduring significance.

To invoke such philosophical anthropology in discussing Mahler's music is not an attempt to apply some fashionable new theory. Mahler clearly *knew* he was writing what today we would call 'existentialist' music. For instance, in the 'Programme' of the *Second Symphony* he wrote:

We are standing beside the coffin of a man beloved. For the last time his life, his battles, his sufferings and his purpose pass before the mind's eye. And now, at this solemn and deeply stirring moment, when we are released from the paltry distractions of everyday life, our hearts are gripped by a voice of awe-inspiring solemnity, which we seldom or never hear above the deafening traffic of mundane affairs. What next? it says. What is life—and what is death?

Have we any continuing existence?

Is it all an empty dream, or has this life of ours, and our death, a meaning?

If we are to go on living, we must answer this question.

Gustav Mahler, p. 213

This, as we shall see, is again the theme of the *Ninth*.

Listening for the first time to the *Ninth*, I 'knew' at once that it was about love, exerted against hate and nothingness. This, again, was quite evident to Mahler when composing his *Second Symphony*:

Second Movement

The spirit of unbelief and negation has taken possession of him. Looking into the turmoil of appearances, he loses altogether with the clear eyes of childhood the sure foothold *which love alone gives*, he despairs of himself and of God. The world and life become a witch's brew; disgust of existence in every form strikes him with iron fist and drives him to an outburst of despair.

ibid., p. 213 (my italics)

My exploration of the meaning of the *Ninth* is based on the emphasis placed, by object-relations psychoanalysis and by existentialism, on the primary need in human beings for significant relationship, for love, and for a sense of meaning in their lives—which can enable them to feel that their consciousness manifests an authenticity of existence that can triumph over 'absurdity' ('man is a useless passion'), over death, and nothingness. Mahler knew this, explicitly, too:

Introduction: What is the Point of Life?

Fifth Movement
We are confronted once more by terrifying questions . . .
. . . Our senses desert us, consciousness dies . . .

ibid.

In penetrating to the central human need to feel one has meaningfully existed is to penetrate to the primal problems of *being*: one moves beyond morality, and beyond manic-depressive problems, to the realm of being, and knowing in this realm. *Mahler knew this too*—and expresses it creatively as no-one else in this century has done:

And behold—it is no judgement—there are no sinners, no just. None is great, none is small. There is no punishment and no reward.
An overwhelming love lightens our being. We know and are.

ibid., p. 213

—in the quest for being, there are no 'wicked': all human manifestations are attempts to find meaning, so even hate, in oneself and others, can be loved.

This is the message of the music. Of course, we must avoid coarsening the music by analysis—a problem of which Mahler was also aware, as he shows in a letter to Alma, 20 December 1901:

I only drew up the programme as a crutch for a cripple (you know whom I mean). It only gives a superficial indication, all that any programme can do for a musical work, let alone this one (the *Second*) which is so much all of a piece that it can no more be explained than the world itself. I'm quite sure that if God were asked to draw up a programme of the world he had created he could never do it. At best it would say as little about the nature of God and life as my analysis says about my *C Minor Symphony*. In fact, as all religious dogmas do, it leads directly to misunderstanding, to a flattening and coarsening, and in the long run to such distortion that the work, and still more its creator, is utterly unrecognizable . . .

ibid., p. 217–18

But today, when so much that is inauthentic is being poured out in our culture, while some art has taken such false and anti-human paths, we are forced to be explicit, and to openly declare our allegiance, to the kind of art which belongs to love. To Mahler—to say no more—the debasements of art in our time would have been recognized as insults to the mystery of life, and creativity itself.

The dress rehearsal of the *Tales of Hoffman* . . . went without a hitch. The performance was only broken off once and this was when Gutheil-Schoder came on as Julietta. Mahler ordered her off in a fury. Her dress was slit up each side to the waist and had to be stitched up instantly on account of

15

the gross indecency. As soon as the poor lady had vanished he continued to rail for some time over the heads of the orchestra at Schoder's shamelessness in coming on to the stage in such a state of undress. If he had dreamed that ten years later whole rows of more or less naked women would crowd the stages of the 'straightest' theatres (to mention only *Franziska*, or *The Legend of Joseph* at the Opera) *he would have lost faith in the drama. To him it was sacred* ...

Alma Mahler, Gustav Mahler, p. 15 (my italics)

It is this sense of the sacredness of art as a source of meaning that we have to assert today against a new barbarism, and hatred of the creativity Mahler represents.

*

Psychoanalysis, by penetrating to the schizoid problem, has found our most fundamental problem of existence to be that of feeling real in a real world, able to exert our autonomy in an environment perceived as real. This confirms the emphases of existentialism, that man's primary need is a sense of meaning, and that our capacity to exercise our freedom in an authentic way depends upon our discovery of the true self—that which we have in us to become.

I have tried to employ these insights from various subjective disciplines to the study of poetry and symbolism. This study in the field of music has developed in an almost uncanny way—and has certainly taken me into regions which have startled me—not least because so much in art confirms so strikingly the theories of psychoanalysts like Winnicott and existentialists like May and Frankl. For instance, all through Mahler's work there is an agonized preoccupation with eyes, as the focus of a sense of meaning threatened by love and death, so that perception and encounter are linked.

In the above sketch for a poem, for instance, Mahler is expressing his need, which was for him a life-or-death matter, to find a sense of confirmation of identity. He is 'striving to be seen' by the eyes of the Sphinx: if only those eyes would relent, and reflect him, he would know the secret of life. If he cannot find this he is doomed.

The theme of mutual reflection is, of course, a preoccupation of mine, as I have come to realize, over the years. The way we see the world depends upon our capacity for *liebende Wirheit*: loving communion. Rollo May says, in his *Love and Will*, that the discovery of our need for the 'significant other' constitutes an ethical principle:

Decision, in our sense, creates out of the two previous dimensions a pattern of acting and living which is empowered and enriched by wishes, asserted by will, and is responsive to and responsible for the significant other— persons who are important to oneself in the realizing of long-term goals. If the point were not self-evident it could be demonstrated along the lines of Sullivan's interpersonal theory of psychiatry, Buber's philosophy, and other viewpoints. They all point out that wish, will and decision occur within a nexus of relationships upon which the individual depends not only for his fulfilment but for his very existence.

This sounds like an ethical statement and *is*.

Love and Will, p. 268

What we have learnt, from Husserl, to call 'intentionality'—our capacity to see, and create in the seeing, a meaningful world—depends upon our capacity for love, and our experience of love, in infancy. This is borne out by an increasing number of observers. Besides Sullivan and Buber there is the late work of Winnicott, who saw 'creative reflection' as the origins of the 'I am' capacity. There is the work of the existentialist philosophical biologist F. J. J. Buytendijk on the meaning of babies' smiles, and Helmuth Plessner on laughter and tears. There is Lacan on the Mirror Role of the Mother, and Bowlby on the child's need for interpersonal love, as the basis of mental health.

In existentialism, the stream of thought from Husserl to Binswanger has emphasized that the origins of our capacity to exercise our freedom are in love. Love, as the key to life, is Mahler's theme. The theme of today's culture, alas, has become hate, not least in Sartrean areas of existentialism. To the philosophers of the New Existentialism, however, the 'other' is not, as to Sartre, inevitably a limit on my freedom. On the contrary, they emphasize that in intercourse with others we find our capacity to find ourselves, and to discover our freedom, as in service to our life tasks. This, in turn, would confirm Melanie Klein's theory, that we find our deepest creative satisfactions in reparation, the giving to another in love, and in 'finding' and 'meeting' others, in their own right, for themselves—a process which begins with infant recognition of the mother as a 'not-me' who can be affected by his own impulses, as when he hates.

I have dealt with these theories from philosophical anthropology in detail elsewhere. Here we find yet another manifestation of the quest such as we encounter over the poetess Sylvia Plath: the need for an individual who has not experienced 'creative reflection' sufficiently to feel that she has become herself. With Sylvia Plath, in order to complete this process, she went through life gazing into the face of the Moon, or

17

into pools, or mirrors, to find her self, in terms of what is seen there. This, in its widest implications, was a search for the meaning of life— since the Moon, or the pool, it was hoped, could become prophetic—the ocular become oracular. Sylvia Plath says to the Mother, 'Yours is the one mouth I would be tongue to'—and she gazes into the Mother's face, to find herself 'spoken' by her, in being seen. The same theme is visible in Mahler's poem: 'Her stony, blank gray eyes tell, nothing, nothing.' The Sphinx will not yield the meaning sought in her eyes.

The problem is also one which occurs in the literature of childhood. One of the problems that arises, as we shall see, is that, once the reflecting face has been found, how shall we know it is not malevolent, rather than benign? The child's primitive logic tells him that his need for benign reflection is so powerful that its voracity (if he remains hungry for love) can exert a sucking impulse on the world, which can become immensely destructive hate. Thus, in retribution for this impulse to empty, the world (or the 'other') could well turn out to be malevolent in return. A child with schizoid problems, suffering from a failure of humanization, does not have enough close experience of the other human being, to be confident that what is encountered in the urgently desired encounter will be human, kind and tender. Here we have the origins of infantile feelings of paranoia, and primitive aggression to counteract it.

As the verses composed by Mahler above and chosen elsewhere by him often reveal, this need for creative reflection was a deep hunger in him, and is often associated with urgent problems of the meaning of life and of death. *Seeing* and *being seen* are of great significance to him (and so are *hearing* and *being heard*). At the same time he can be deeply distrustful of any security, or even of the promise of it, such as he does find. This is understandable, for as Mahler knew, no sooner does one find love, than Death menaces it. This he knew, for example, from his experience of a loved brother's death: despite all the love and play he could bestow on Ernst, Death inexorably swept the child away. The memory of those lost eyes haunted him and was exacerbated by his troubled experience of all eyes into which he subsequently gazed. In the *Kindertotenlieder* he sets poems by Friedrich Ruckert which are all about light, seeing, and eye-beams, around the subject of death:

> *Du musst nicht die Nacht in dir verschränken,*
> *Musst sie ins ew'ge Licht versenken!*
> *Ein Lämplein verslosch in meinem Zelt!*
> *Heil sei dem Freudenlicht der Welt ...*

Introduction: What is the Point of Life?

You must not enclose the night within you;
You must drown it in eternal light.
A little lamp went out in my tent.
Hail to the gladdening light of the world!

Nun seh' ich wol, warum so dunkle Flammen
Ihr sprühet mir in manchem Augenblicke.
O Augen! O Augen!

Now I understand why you sprayed such dark
flames at me in many a look, O eyes! O eyes!

Wenn dein Mütterlein tritt zur Tür herein,
Und den Kopf ich drehe, ihr entgegen sehe,
Fällt auf ihr Gesicht erst der Blick mir nicht,
Sondern auf die Stelle, näher nach der Schwelle,
Dort, wo würde dein lieb Gesichten sein . . .

When your dear mother comes in at the door,
and I turn my head to look at her, my gaze
falls first, not on her face, but on that
spot, closer, closer, to the threshold, yes
there where your dear little face would be if
you were entering with her . . .

The almost unbearable tragic sadness of these songs would seem
obviously to spring from the experiences of death in Mahler's family
life, and from his yearning for the ghosts of siblings. To one who
experienced so much loss of the visible, such yearning for what disap-
peared, the already weak experience of 'being seen' must have been
intolerable.

Deryck Cooke writes of 'the intensely unhappy family background
of his childhood. The brutal father ill-treated the delicate mother,
creating a father-hatred and mother-fixation in Mahler himself; despite
the family's poverty, the mother bore twelve children; five died in
infancy, three of them when Mahler was a growing boy. When he was
fourteen, his favourite brother Ernst, one year younger than himself,
died after a long illness: and Mahler saw it through to the end, sitting
for hours by his bed, telling him stories. Of those who survived, Alois
grew up to be a crazy character, wildly parading delusions of grandeur;
Otto, musically gifted, shot himself at the age of twenty-two.' Mahler
himself identified intensely with his sister, and in his blackest moods,
contemplated suicide. The whole family seems to have suffered deep
schizoid problems, and Mahler's choice to live, to be, was itself an act of

great courage. (See *Mahler 1860–1911*, Deryck Cooke, B.B.C., 1960, p. 9, and, of course, the early chapters of Henry de la Grange's official biography.)

We may experience the dreadful pangs of death of brother in the Third Movement of the *First Symphony*. As Cooke says, 'Mahler makes a sinister funeral march out of a children's nursery tune, the German version of "Frère Jacques"—"Brother Martin, are you sleeping?" (Brother Ernst would it be?)' We experience the futility of trying, by jaunty nursery-tale noises, by the cheap band music, by the toy-like 'Last Post', to overcome the relentless march of Nothingness, that swallows the child. In the *A minor Trio* we hear the pluck of the harp like a heart-beat, foreshadowing this underlying motive as it is to be used, to speak of the pulse of the inner self, in *Das Leid* and the *Ninth*. The 'cry of the wounded heart' in the last movement is a record of Mahler's struggle against nihilism—to find a hold on life. (In the *Sixth*, under the smashing blows of fate, he gives way to nihilism.)

But these conflicts arise from the deeper schizoid problem—that (which must be postulated) of his own ontological insecurity, rooted in his lack of sufficient experience of the mother's face, and a consequent inability to find the 'significant other' and to see the world in a benign and meaningful way. It was to recreate this security in himself that he laboured as an artist, and as a man, as we shall see: his work was in a sense a re-mothering, in the attempt to overcome these deep schizoid problems.

In *Das Lied von der Erde*, the theme is more universal, and widens into a problem of relating to the whole world. Life is only twilight: so is death. The protagonist is wandering: wandering is a pervasive theme of Mahler's. In *Autumn Loneliness*, part 2, the world seems as it does in Coleridge's *Ode to Dejection* a place over which he can throw no meaning, and in which one can find no joy: 'O love's warm sunshine, have you gone for ever?'

In the third piece, *Youth*:

> In the tiny, tiny pattern's
> Quiet, quiet pool of water
> See the world reflected lies
> In mirror marvellous . . .

'There was a time, when meadow, grove and stream . . .' Mahler is remembering a time when the world did seem meaningful, as he does in the next section:

20

> See the sunshine weave a web around them.
> Mirrors all their laughing grace in water.
> Sunshine mirrors all their slender beauty,
> Mirrors their sweet eyes in water,
> And the wind of spring with soft caresses . . .

In 5 the moon lights up the darkling firmament, but by this time the sense of not belonging to the world in spring has impelled the poet to drown his sorrows in drink and cynical laughter.

Where, then, is resolution of this existential anguish to be found? The answer is always *in some form of drawing upon the benignity of the Natural World*. It can be Mother Earth: it can be the Moon—as Sylvia Plath said, 'The moon is my mother'. (In such symbolism the moon may be the female light of the world because she is paler than the bold sun, and changes her moods to a monthly pattern.) The moon is a symbol of a redeeming love: her light is reflected light; it is pure white; it reflects our moods.[2] In 6, the Moon-mother sails into the world as she does in Coleridge's *Ancient Mariner*, casting the mother's benignity over it, so that 'the earth breathes gently, full of peace and sleep', and the poet can recapture forgotten joy and youth, and his own sense of benignity. The 'significant other' is encountered, and the suffering is shared, in resignation:

> I no longer seek the far horizon
> My heart is still and waits for its deliverance . . .

'The kingdom of God is an inward condition'. The sense of at-one-ness with the earth brings a benificence:

> The lovely earth, all everywhere,
> Revives in spring and blooms anew,
> All, everywhere and ever, ever
> Shines the blue horizon . . .

This piece of music thus ends in an ecstasy of union with the whole earth as Mother, as universal creativity, continuing for ever—of which eternity the individual soul has been part, even though 'my lot was hard'. *The Song of the Earth* is about 'creative reflection' in its fullest and most universal sense, a drawing upon the dynamics of love in the universe. As Buber said, 'Man . . . wishes to have a presence in the being of the other'.

But this oceanic feeling, and the achievement of the capacity to feel 'I am', such as Mahler achieves in his last works, was won through many

---

[2] See the chapter 'Moony' in *Women in Love* by D. H. Lawrence.

spiritual struggles. Moreover, in one who had suffered so much there is a pervading distrust so that no resolution can be attained without a continual testing of what seems to be authentic. So, there must be continual searching out of anything that smacks of inauthenticity. Thus, in the poem quoted at the beginning, the 'voices versed in soft deceit' are the voices of false solutions to existence problems. They seek to lure him, by manic denial, into the self-deception of (for example) pretending that he need *not* confront despair. But to Mahler despair was necessary, for unless he takes his lonely path of 'abandonment' or 'throwness', he cannot begin to discover his reality. To him the quest for the 'I AM' feeling was the most important thing of all, and he needed to test it against the most dreadful recognition of his ultimate nothingness, and the possibilities of it being impossible to answer those questions in which we may find a firm sense of having been firmly 'there' and 'now'—the *Dasein* questions.

In this quest, despair is necessary, for unless a man takes this lonely, 'abandoned', path of existence-anxiety, in full recognition of his predicament, he cannot begin to feel that he is real, or assert his 'being there'.

But the dreadful catastrophies of his life made Mahler cautious of accepting any comfort or assurances. Nothing would ever satisfy him unless it was tested and tested against despair, irony and the deepest sense of futility—to see if it survived to offer some hope of meaning.[3] Such a quest leads to two fundamental questions. One is, how can we know the difference between True and False Solutions to the problem of existence? How do we tell True from False? And, secondly, what happens to our need for confirmation when we are faced with real death that *is* the end of 'meeting'?

How an artist deals with such problems obviously depends upon his resources. These will include his early environment. As Winnicott says:

> Failure of dependability or loss of object means to the child a loss of the play area, the loss of meaningful symbol. In favourable circumstances the potential space [between self and the world: D.H.] becomes filled with the products of the baby's own creative imagination. In unfavourable circumstances the creative use of objects is missing or relatively uncertain.[4]

Our capacity to be creative and to engage in a creative relationship with the real world emerges in our earliest environment and through

[3] As we shall see, this determined the *structure* of his music.

[4] See Martin Buber on 'making present' . . . 'It rests on a capacity . . . which may be described as "imagining the real" . . . At such a moment something can come into being which cannot be built up in any other way.'

Distance and Relation, op. cit., p. 70

our first relationship—and this problem will be explored around Mahler's life and work below. The attribution of Mahler's torment to a difficult infancy is by no means a reductionist deterministic approach. I am rather seeking to show his immense courage—when (because of 'unfavourable circumstances') his continual fear was the 'loss of meaningful symbols'.

The work of an artist may often be seen to arise out of an urgent need to solve fundamental life-problems, because of early environmental failure. He may be tormented by problems which most of us give up thinking about, except when we are faced with a major crisis. To such artists, the questions are such as will not let them rest. They cannot go on living unless they find a meaning in existence. But it may be that what they seek can only be achieved *in the culture* itself: they may never be able to find peace in themselves. It seems unlikely that Mahler achieved mastery over his deepest psychic and spiritual disorders, despite all his creative efforts. As Jack Diether says of him:

> Mahler, like Beethoven, could only go forward, becoming more and more himself *in music*, and only in music.

The advances made in the art are not always equalled by increased security in the life of the individual artist. Changes here come haltingly afterwards, and much more slowly (but can come in the end, as they came to Dostoevsky). In the end Mahler obviously at least came both to 'know who to love' and 'how to suffer': he came to recognize the existence of his wife as a separate being, in recognizing his own separate existence, and by suffering he became more integrated in his own identity. He achieved meaning in his life. It is this that the great sigh at the end of the *Tenth Symphony* 'means'. Yet he still died tearing pages out of philosophy books and holding them before his eyes.

The artist is not concerned with mortal survival, about which we can do nothing—but with psychic survival. The artist capable of tragedy is capable of looking at the worst that can happen to us—which, indeed is going to happen to us, and in that we are mortal, *has already happened*, since we are doomed—and yet he is able to discover a certain kind of vulnerability of identity, a meaning that transcends nothingness. All he can ever find, I argue here, is a joy in *having existed*: having exerted a *Dasein* quality, here and now, that, since it has existed as a claim for meaningfulness, can never be expunged. That is, he can discover that, fundamentally, he is invulnerable, since the fact of his sometime human conscious existence can never be eradicated even when he dies: his gesture as a manipulation of the forces of life and love is eternal. So he can discover that *gratitude* which belongs to an appreciation of *continuity*—my italicized words being concepts from Melanie Klein which we shall examine later. And with the achievement of a sense of continuity, he achieves transcendence: it is there in his art.

To achieve this 'tragic' sense of invulnerability of being, however, requires a long painful progress of exposing oneself to the processes of integration and self-discovery, the continual peeling away of self-deceptions, and the increasing recognition and acceptance of the nature of being human, and recognition of the ultimate 'nothingness' itself. This is the explanation of the paradoxical maxim, 'Sorrow is my only consolation' (de la Grange, p. 59).

Those individuals who are driven to make this agonized search for a sense of 'the point of life' are often individuals who cannot rest quietly on confident assumptions about their own identity, whose substantiality in a real world they can rely upon. And here we may establish links between psycho-analysis, existentialism and the criticism of art. There are some people who, because of their own problems, can never let the problem of existence rest. Those life-problems which are experienced by infants at the most dreadful episodes of early consciousness (as we can sometimes hear in their inconsolable and agonized crying) are continually experienced by these individuals as adults. They are incapable of facile comfort, and self-deception: they live daily with tragedy and the threat of nothingness, against which they must get what they can from the joys and sorrows of the world. Yet such people can find immense joy, in the discovery of tragic truth: as Alma Mahler wrote:

> It was only in the last year of his life, when excess of suffering had taught him the meaning of joy, that his natural gaiety broke through the clouds . . .
>
> *Gustav Mahler*, p. 120

So, Mahler was that kind of person, who never lost sight of 'the human problematic'. Jack Diether quotes Bruno Walter:

> 'How dark is the foundation upon which our life rests,' he once said to me with deep emotion, while his troubled look gave evidence of the convulsion of his soul from which he had just freed himself. And, haltingly, he continued, speaking of the problems of human existence: 'Whence do we come? Whither does our road take us? Have I really willed this life, as Schopenhauer thinks, before I ever was conceived? Why am I made to feel I am free, while yet I am constrained within my character, as in a prison? What is the object of toil and sorrow? How am I to understand the cruelty and malice in the creations of a kind God? Will the meaning of life be

24

finally revealed by death?' In such and similar words, laments, astonishment and horror would pour from him as from a gushing spring. Fundamentally, there never was relief for him from the sorrowful struggle to fathom the meaning of human existence.

Bruno Walter, *Gustav Mahler*, p. 128

Below I try to explore Gustav Mahler's *Ninth Symphony* as a great tragic work, which explores the regions of love, hate and death. This great work, perhaps the most significant musical work of the century, presses the problem of existence to the ultimate. All the agonizing horrors of inner weakness, of the hate, guilt, and fear associated with it, of ambivalence, of schizoid despair, of accompanying forms of madness are encountered, including even a hideous sense of the possible absurdity and pointlessness of life, and art no less. This is expressed in 'hebephrenic giggles', nihilistic 'disdain', of the kind of which we have clinical accounts in psychotic individuals who can find no point in existence. These voices of nothingness Mahler heard within himself at times. And against them he continued to exert his technical powers as an artist, and to assert his belief in love and meaning. In this he is utterly different from many artists of this century who, in the face of the cynicism and nihilism welling up inside themselves, have 'given themselves up to the joys of hatred' and to 'radical dissolution'.

Only in a very few artists have we any kind of achievement to set effectively against the deepening nihilism of the modern era—in Dostoevsky, perhaps, and Solzhenitsyn. Both of these, like Mahler, pursue the quest for love and meaning, and find these in the humblest human encounters and assertions of freedom. Elsewhere, the existential problem is hidden by the desperate postures of those whose nihilism never encounters true dread, because it is based on false solutions and the denial of humanness.

Winnicott says that, faced with the psychotic, the therapist must help him to seek answers to two questions: 'What is it to be human?' and 'What is the point of life?' Admitting mortality, and the tormented ambivalence of love and hate, it is these questions which Mahler pursues with great courage in his *Ninth Symphony*—ultimately, 'What is it TO BE?'

2

The Problem of Death in Art

Because it was written under the shadow of death, the *Ninth Symphony* is, of course, full of sepulchral moments, and references to death, some explicitly marked (*'Wie ein schwerer Kondukt'*). Yet in this study I explore it in terms of love and hate, while on Mahler's score he wrote 'O scattered loves . . .' What are the connections between death, love and hate?

Both love and hate are manifestations of the urge to survive, and of the urgent and hungry urge in us to find our existence confirmed. Death is the ultimate challenge to survival, and all our psychic effort from birth is devoted to survival. Death really extinguishes one's existence and wipes out the existence problem. While we are alive our deepest anxieties about the meaning of our lives thus focuses on the mystery of death. As a threat, and as a final truth, in the face of which we can only make a subjective adjustment (since we cannot decide not to die) death obliges us to drive ourselves to the extremest efforts in the quest for meaning, to establish our sense of valid being as against 'existence anxiety'. It brings the ultimate threat of a schizoid sense of futility and ultimate nothingness. By contrast, love seems the greatest assertion of being alive.

Death is the end of all relationship. The separation we feared as infants—the separation that would mean our extinction—actually comes about in death, when we are separated from 'the significant other' finally, and from 'Mother Earth'. But this gives a clue to the only possible way of overcoming death—by love. For while in superficial relationship the other may be replaceable, one only has to fall in love once to know that in this we discover what 'irreplaceableness' is. No other will do for the loved one, and this unique mystery of the loved object exhibits a meaning that triumphs over death, since death cannot extinguish it. For to discover the unique irreplaceableness of the 'other' is to find the uniqueness of oneself.

The Problem of Death in Art

In a work of art, obviously, no one can give a first-hand account of the experience of death, though this experience continually preoccupies us, as we ponder 'What must it be like to die?' (meaning, 'What will it be like?'). But in thus pondering death we are not concentrating on the physical event. We are making a poetic-philosophical exploration: we are, as we say, 'seeking to come to terms with mortality'. So the problem of death is a problem of attitudes to life, while we are still alive. This problem is at root a subjective dynamic, involving inward creative symbolism. To accept that we 'owe God a death', to seek to become 'absolute for death', is a problem of maturity: it is a problem of maintaining a subjective wholeness which can endure under the greatest threats of dissolution inherent in the destructiveness we know to be within and without—of which Death is the ultimate symbol. There is a close relation in our minds between Death and Hate, since both stand for the dynamics of annihilation, and we know this from infancy, when we wished people out of the way.

Thus it would be more accurate to say that when we talk about death in art we are talking about phenomena of consciousness, about symbols with subjective referents rather than 'objective' death 'out there'. The dynamics of symbolic engagement here belong to the need to preserve a sense of integration of identity. Death thrusts before us our ultimate ego-weakness, our deepest existence-anxiety: to contemplate Death forces on us the question of 'the point of life'.[1] Maintaining a sense of what Melanie Klein called 'continuity' in the face of this threat requires an intensity of creative effort that is seldom achieved, and which can never be held off securely for very long. Only in a very few works of art is a real triumph over death gained and then only for an instant— even in the greatest works.[2]

[1] This is magnificently conveyed in the traditional Burial Service, which begins with the dramatic ambivalence—as the corpse is brought in—'I am the resurrection and the life'. See a valuable discussion of this (and how it has been ruined by revisions) in *The Survival of English*, Ian Robinson, C.U.P., 1973.

[2] But perhaps here we must accept the continually recurring triumphs of Bach, who creates a relationship with God that shows no faltering when the individual mortal identity is dissolved. Even with Mozart, Beethoven, Chaucer and Shakespeare this confidence in immortality is never so continually sustained. But I would argue that even in Bach the ecstatic joy in death is a symbol of rebirth—which belongs, as I see it, to the element of schizoid suicide in Christianity and its symbolism: as Bruno Walter says, 'Death is our door' to the Christian. To the humanist this is a false belief, for death is the end of identity, not the beginning, and he requires a new concept of Time, in which his meaningful life 'can have existed', and is therefore eternal, in that its sometime existence can never be denied. In a sense this requires a new perspective in Time, perhaps as expressed in Eliot's lines, 'All time is eternally present . . .' and 'only through Time is Time conquered'—by significant choice and action.

When we talk about death in art, then, we are essentially talking about subjective existence problems—*in relation to death*, or under the *duress of death*. Death threatens the total loss of confirmation: it is the ultimate impingement. Death as a symbol in art impels the creative quest for solutions to the problem of existence which are so strong that they can survive mortality and ultimate object-less-ness.

Thus tragedy is not so much a form of drama 'in which the protagonist dies', as a form of drama in which the inescapable and undeniable fact of death enforces the necessity to explore to the ultimate the possibilities of discovering means to preserve the sense of *having meaningfully existed*. Why then do we feel 'strong' after watching a tragedy? Surely because we have experienced the worst that is possible to imagine, of our ego-weakness of being menaced by annihilation, and yet finding a kind of invulnerability. We may come to feel invulnerable, because whatever has perished, whoever has died, it has not been the *meaning* of human existence. The creatures in tragedy have lived: we saw them *act* and *choose* before they died, and the validity of their struggles remains as a meaning in our minds and feelings, together with the values by which they acted. So, even in the lower depths (as in, say, Solzhenitsyn) meaning and authenticity triumph over degradation—as they do not, say, in Beckett, or the sentimental 'black' drama of our time, whose nihilism is an insult to meaning and values.

Death is the ultimate paranoid-schizoid symbol of those forces which threaten to 'eat us up', or otherwise bring about our annihilation. Thus it is an objective correlative of our inward hate, which we fear may do the same—either by its fantasy attacks (such as we have known in infancy) on the object on whom we depend (about which we feel guilt) or by destroying us from within, from the sheer voraciousness of our need to survive by mouth-hunger. All external manifestations of destructiveness (such as war) act as such symbols on us, and threaten our each inward creative struggle with his inner weakness and fear. They are symbols of the intense hunger of the regressed libidinal ego, the unborn, unsatisfied self that is voraciously hungry in proportion to our ego-weakness. In this sense it is true that 'each man's death diminishes me'.

The problem of 'death' about which we can do nothing in reality, nevertheless becomes a perennial subject of art because it impels our attempts to deal with hate and nothingness, and to find a structure of meaning,[3] to set against these. Hate, in the sense I am using the word,

---

[3] By contrast, another (but false) way of dealing with this threat of nothingness is by 'giving way to the joys of hating'. This plunge into nihilism in today's culture, arises

arises out of fear of going out of existence. So dreadful is the menace of such existential despair that we resort to many defences against it—themselves all forms of hate: paranoia, splitting and projection, manic denial, magic. But no mastery of the existence problem can be achieved except by working through these, exhausting them and discarding them, in pursuit of true creative reparation—which means accepting and coming to terms with the worst death can do, which is, in reality, in the end, to take us all out of existence.

In the end, even the creative achievements of Shakespeare and Bach must be eradicated by death and nothingness, when the earth is burnt up in the sun. But the temporality of human existence and meaning does not invalidate the quest for meaning—for even that future universe, dead as it must be, will have some meaning, in that it contains the artefacts, even in ashes, of the sometime existence of human life and consciousness. We HAVE BEEN. It was towards this vision that Mahler strove.

Long after the present work was finished I came across a statement which illuminates what Mahler achieved, not in a critical work, but in a book by an existentialist psychoanalyst, Viktor Frankl, *Psychotherapy and Existentialism*. Speaking of the dangers of the reductionism implicit in the interpretation of religious feelings in terms of mere unconscious motivation, he says:

> What threatens man is his guilt in the past and his death in the future. Both are inescapable, both must be accepted. Thus man is confronted with the human condition in terms of fallibility and mortality. Properly understood, it is, however, precisely the acceptance of this two-fold human finiteness which adds to life's worthwhileness, since only in the face of guilt does it make sense to improve, and only in the face of death it is meaningful to act.

Psychotherapy and Existentialism, p. 30

Das Lied von der Erde and the *Ninth Symphony* are wrung from the threats of guilt and death—and they are themselves forms of creative action, groping towards meaning. The creative work which Mahler does

from the 'longing for non-being', a painful failure of confidence in any possible mode of being. Behind it there is a lack of confidence in ever putting the existential problems to rest, and thus it may be associated with the taboo on weakness in our time, and the taboo on death, which reminds us of the existence problem. Pornography is one aspect of this nihilism: it is a special way of denying love, creativity and time. By its insult to spontaneity and to surrender to life, it offers a manic denial of death, and reduces existence to schizoid de-moralization: but because no sense of meaning can be gained in such ways its inevitable path becomes that of increasing hate, desperation, and destructiveness. Alas, pornography is directed against Mahler himself, in a recent film.

on time and structure, by way of escaping from the limitations of Western modes, is a means of acting in this way:

> It is the very transitoriness of human existence which constitutes man's responsibleness—the essence of existence. If man were immortal, he would be justified in delaying everything: there would be no need to do anything right now. Only under the urge and pressure of life's transitoriness does it make sense to use the passing time. Actually, the only transitory aspects of life are the potentialities; as soon as we have succeeded in actualizing a potentiality, we have transmuted it into an actuality and, thus, salvaged and rescued it from the past. Once an actuality, it is one . . . forever . . .
>
> *ibid*, p. 30

It is from his awareness of this that Mahler distils his '*ewig . . .*' and saves the meaning in his life from being swallowed by the twisting jaws of meaninglessness, associated with hate, guilt and death.

> Everything in the past is saved from being transitory. Therein is it irrevocably stored rather than irrevocally lost. *Having been is still a form of being, perhaps in its most secure form.*
>
> *ibid.*, p. 30

In the rapturous, rising, paeans of gratitude at the climaxes of his later works, Mahler states this last sentence, in music, with a triumph that transcends mortality.

3

'Was war Wirklich im All?'[1]

By accident, during an illness, I listened to Mahler's *Ninth Symphony*. It was my first experience of his work, and I felt I knew at once what Mahler was saying. It was for me one of those major experiences of a cultural artefact such as one experiences when one first comes across a great work such as *Crime and Punishment*, or *Oedipus Rex*.

I felt at once intuitively that the Symphony enacted a conflict between love and hate, under a threat of annihilation. When the horns spoke harshly in the first movement I said to myself, 'That is hate'. And in listening I felt, at times, threatened, in the deepest sense, by a horror of loss and emptiness. For weeks afterwards I listened to the work frequently and began to study Mahler's other music, and his life. As I went on I found my first reaction confirmed: and so I ventured, despite my lack of qualifications, to write this book.

I was delighted to hear Bruno Walter's own testament in the recorded interview accompanying the 1962 recording in which he says 'Bruckner and Mahler are my whole life. I cannot conceive of my life without them'. Mahler was becoming part of mine. I felt that the *Ninth Symphony* was as great a work of art as *King Lear*, and of as great importance in exploring 'the point of life'.

Explicit analysis of Mahler's work has confirmed at every step my original impression. I was also greatly excited, because I was studying psychoanalytical theory, to find that Mahler once sought treatment from Freud for a personal crisis just as the *Ninth Symphony* was being scored. I was delighted to find in American publications the recognition that Mahler was an existentialist composer, as in the work of Jack Diether, whose writings I have since made use of extensively. It was also clear that, while we can barely yet understand what Mahler was doing, his achievement points a way out of the anarchy and nihilism associated with the break-down of idioms in modern art. Mahler is a great positive voice by which we may find new bearings not only in music, but in all

[1] 'What was real in the world?'

31

the arts. He discovered that positive existentialist perspective which recognizes the power of love—and in this, I believe, lies our hope, to escape from barbarism and spiritual death.

I wrote this book because, despite this positive direction, so many commentators describing his later work as *'world-weary'* or *'valedictory'*. They seemed to see Mahler as one who 'withdrew' into the inner life, as if he sought merely to solve his own private problems and was prepared to let the world go hang. They supposed he spoke nostalgically of the past. To me his music seemed triumphantly positive, and offered in its effect on one's sensibility a profound sense of meaningful existence, without God. I was also surprised to find that his work was taken to be 'about death' as if it were an acceptance of some death-wish or some world-relinquishing 'submission' to death. I came to Mahler just as I had tried to demolish the concept of a 'death-instinct' in Freud's work and influence. I had come to believe that the origins of such destructive impulses in man could be adequately explained as distorted manifestations of the urge to survive when love is frustrated and meaning is menaced. I came to accept the point of view that hate and destructiveness (which traditional psychoanalysis had explained as the consequences of an organic death instinct) are rather false solutions to a sense of emptiness and meaninglessness. I believed that Mahler, in his *Ninth Symphony*, was making a true engagement with these fears in himself, and his work seemed to me an embodiment of the real battle that needs to be fought, in the quest for our humanness. The symphony was, I knew, written under the shadow of death. This eventually led me to see, as I have tried to say in the preceding chapter, that the effect of death as a symbol in art is to force upon us the problem of how we can overcome hate. Death urges upon us the need to engage with that hate which psychoanalysis attributed in a natural scientistic way to a 'death instinct', until more psychodynamic theories interpreted it as a distorted claim for love and meaning, by phenomenological investigation. The collapse of religious faith and the death of God (in Nietzsche's sense) have exacerbated this need to confront our ultimate nothingness, and find how meaning is still possible.

As I went on I found a further reason for wishing to explore Mahler's achievement in a positive vein. Mahler is sometimes taken to have led on to Schoenberg and atonalism, as Dostoevsky is taken to lead on to Sartre, Genet, Beckett and Artaud. Goncharev's Oblomov is not far away—with his sense of futility and his 'world-weary' withdrawal; but there is something more sinister—a closed-circuit nihilism that plunges on into futility and moral inversion, in hopeless despair of ever finding meaning. The slogan has become 'if God does not exist, everything is possible'—and what is thought to be most possible is not so much moral anarchy, from which a new morality might begin, but egoistical nihilism. This, in its abandonment of the very quest for meaning itself, could spell the end of art and civilization.[2]

It is true that Mahler does enter this bleak poetic-philosophical territory—as the contemporary artist who has no faith cannot but. So he inevitably came to feel, in some sense, to use Sartre's term, 'abandonné'. Mahler could not at the end of his life accept traditional assurances, and orthodox religious sources of strength for the identity. But he did not give himself over to schizoid futility, nihilism, spiritual suicide, madness, or the anti-human.

I have heard Professor Wilfrid Mellers lecture on the history and development of contemporary music, and speak of Wagner 'destroying the self and obliterating time', the 'collapse of consciousness' and 'submission to the death instinct.' Music, Professor Mellers declared, is regressing toward magic and primitivism *(Pierrot Lunaire)*. Communication is exhausted: and since the ego is a 'failure', man is finding his way back to archetypal primitive existence, so that, in Stockhausen's *Stimmung* and 'pop', audiences are seeking 'trance-inducing abnegations' of Europe's magnificent achievements in music and the other arts. In the face of the 'appalling cruelty of life' man was seeking a release from Being. The individual was becoming a part of the cosmos, not, however by sharpening his consciousness, but by regression. The musician could become a kind of scientist priest, promoting a new integration with the body—but by a retreat in music (in *Stimmung* as in Beckett's *Breath*). I hoped that Professor Mellers would turn to Mahler, to discuss other streams of creativity. But he seemed to be fascinated by the retreat to the 'baby's cry' which, he believed had been 'obliterated by consciousness'.

Isn't there a danger here of endorsing the 'longing for non-being itself', and even accepting the end of musical creativity? Mahler, however much he was aware of the possibilities of chaos, achieves and expresses a hope for man, and a profound acceptance of being human. His confidence in consciousness and being is there, in the lucid and utterly coherent structure of his music. I believe we need to possess this acceptance of human nature, and recapture our belief in it. Of course,

[2] See Masud Khan on Albert Camus in *The Black Rainbow*, ed. Peter Abbs, Heinemann, 1974.

consciousness is a burden, and of course (as we shall see) there is a necessary kind of regression. But there is also a lapse into sensualism which is nihilistic. Saul Bellow, in *Mr Sammler's Planet*, associates the radical dissolutions of American 'protest' culture with a rejection of all possible modes of existence, all ways of being human—and this he sees too terribly similar to Germany in the Thirties:

> As long as there is no ethical life and everything is poured so barbarously and recklessly into personal gesture this must be endured . . . there is a particular longing for non-being . . . Why should they be human? . . . The individual . . . seems to want a divorce from all the states he knows . . .
>
> *Mr Sammler's Planet*, Penguin Edition, p. 164

I was very conscious while listening to Dr Walter's first recording of Mahler's *Ninth* that it was made in Vienna in 1935, and that the audience which stirred and applauded in the background was perhaps to suffer more than any community of human beings has ever suffered from the tide of hate in ensuing years. In his vision Mahler not only foresaw possibilities of such schizoid manifestations of collective psychopathology which have swept the world in our century. (For what else do his horrific outbursts of insane military music, and foreboding drum-thuds presage?) He saw beyond them, towards possibilities of integration, and sources of a sense of meaning in existence which we desperately need to explore and use, albeit expressed with poignancy and tenderness: 'Yes, we should be human, still.'

So I do not propose to discuss Mahler's symphony in the customary terms of the search for 'God', nor of his 'world weariness' when he turned away from God. Nor do I propose to discuss it in terms of nostalgia for a social or historical world which was 'doomed', or even in terms of its place in the musical tradition. As Donald Mitchell says, 'too much in Mahler has too often been conjured up or explained away by seemingly convincing analogies drawn between his music and the collapsing Austrian Empire'.[3] I wish to discuss it in terms of the creative quest for inner spiritual strength, and its indication of the need, if we are to escape from our predicament, to attend to subjective disciplines, to problems of being and existence, and to exert our authenticity and freedom. For Mahler's work, I believe, enables us to resolve inner perplexities of very great depth so that we may be free—acting in full possession of our humanness, and fully aware of our fate. It is in this that it contributes to the 'outer world'. Such art does not merely 'reflect society'—but helps create a new consciousness.

[3] *Gustav Mahler, The Early Years*, Rockcliff, 1958.

4

Nostalgia—or Potentia?

What is Mahler's *Ninth Symphony* 'about'? I believe it to be about the problem of finding strength of identity, and 'ontological security', which could endure, even though, to use a phrase from Schweitzer, 'the world ends tomorrow'.

Of course, for Mahler, the world was likely to end at any moment. We may perhaps begin our examination of his symphony with a note by Henry Boys:

> Mahler gives us no hints as to what the First Movement of the *Ninth* expresses, but most will agree with Bruno Walter, who says, 'The title of the last canto of *Das Lied von der Erde, Der Abschied*—farewell—might have been used as a heading for the *Ninth*'. It was written in 1905, the year after *Das Lied*, and in the knowledge that he had not long to live. Like *Das Lied*, its predominant mood is one of consuming nostalgia and world-weariness; and its drama might be thought of as expressing the conflict and final resolution of Mahler's personal world with some more peaceful world towards which he had always aspired.

As Dr Hans Redlich notes there is a definite reference to farewell:

> Messages of farewell are scattered all over both works, sometimes couched in seemingly enigmatic symbols to be grasped only by a penetrating and thoroughly sympathetic mind. Most significant in this connection is the evidently deliberate allusion to Beethoven's *Sonata*, Opus 81a (*Les Adieux*), at the point where its *Leitmotiv*, '*Lebe wohl*,' becomes so strangely blurred in dissonant canon, fading off in the increasing distance of the final bars of the first movement. To quote the motif used by Mahler:

EXAMPLE 1

35

is to show that he made this allusion quite deliberately and was fully conscious of its implications. Similarly at the parallel passage ('*Sehr zögernd,*' p. 59, pocket score) shortly before the end of the movement, where two canonic strands of this 'Farewell' motif are interlocked in a last romantic echo of Beethoven's *Sonata.*

Bruckner and Mahler, p. 220

The words 'nostalgia' and 'world-weariness' are repeated by Wilfrid Mellers in *Man and His Music*, who reminds us that Mahler regarded his nine symphonies as 'experiments in spiritual autobiography'. He sees Mahler as one without a 'spiritual home', a 'poor boy made good', a Jew who embraced Catholicism as 'part of his life-long struggle for peace'. He was a spare-time composer, whose composing 'was yet in the deepest sense the meaning of his life'.

Unlike Beethoven, the revolutionary elements in whose music are only 'fully intelligible in reference to a norm', Mahler's personality is a 'world itself that seems to be in a flux,' says Mellers:

Nostalgia for past splendour may at any moment become at once an elegy, and a dark prophecy of chaos. The dissolution of the Austrian Empire was indeed to release horrors dreamt of only in the imaginations of artists of Mahler's neurotic sensitivity.

Mellers, *The Sonata Principle*, p. 127

This makes, according to Mellers, for an equivocalness in Mahler. His fanfares and marches seem both a delight in imperial splendour, yet 'nightmarish'. He seems to utter both a yearning for simple-minded vulgarity, and yet a perception of the corruption in popular music itself. Here Mellers quotes a phrase from the *First Symphony*:

EXAMPLE 2

Ziemlich langsam
Mit Parodie

Of this Professor Hans Redlich says

It was Schubert who first made such deliberately 'popular' tunes eligible for serious symphonic treatment, chiefly because of the psychologically complex constructions aroused . . . Just as Schubert's theme is a relaxation from the symphonic rigours . . . it becomes the subtle purpose of Mahler's to act as a weary foil for its parodistic afterthought. Here in a flash all its features are turned into a frightening grimace. The guitar accompaniment of the strings is changed into the spectral crackling of the wooden *col legno* effect; the rhythmic background of the *pizzicato* is savagely underlined by the vulgar 'oompa' rhythm and bassdrum, served by a single player in a manner reminiscent of the booths at a fair, and the melody itself is deliberately vulgarized by alcoholic slaps, culminating in a vile *glissando* slide (Z). The whole intentional vulgarization and the psychological subtlety in utilizing trivial tones of the fair-ground type for the purposes of an escapist anticlimax . . .

Bruckner and Mahler, Dent, 1955

(We shall see later the psychological significance of the 'fairground' vulgarity: far from being escapist, it is rather the expression of a bitter irony about attempts to cheat death.)

Mahler's essence is an 'inextricable medley', says Wilfrid Mellers, of 'positive and negative responses'. He did not 'belong' to an Austrian peasant community—yet the 'contours of his melodies are permeated with the inflexions of Austrian song'. Yet even here 'the sense of estrangement is stronger': while the melodies represent an ideal of innocence, 'Mahler's nostalgia expands the folk-like phrases into periods that become yearnfully emotive, while he subjects them to enharmonic treatment even more extreme than that favoured by Bruckner'.

According to Mellers, Mahler never experienced the serenity of revealed faith: but 'the faith implicit in Catholic dogma became a symbol of the Grail he was seeking', and so his music related to certain 'aspects of Catholic polyphony'. As in the *Second Symphony*, the lyrical solo song of the Fourth Movement manifests a simplicity of being which is the only way to the 'resurrection' of the last choral movement.

Sometimes, as in the *Fourth Symphony*, there is a deliberate evocation of the past, which ends, 'with the appearance of the human voice, in the dream-world of a child's heaven', and in 'naive candour'. But the true implications of Mahler's creative direction are not found in the *Fourth Symphony*. They are found 'most consummately' in the *Ninth*.

Here, Mellers says, we have in the 'dreamfully singing melody in D major' a 'nostalgic vision of "Viennese" serenity', upon which other 'wild and striving elements' make their impact, and modify it. They even carry song melody 'far from the stable props of diatonic tonality into a spare, widely spaced, glassily scored linear counterpoint'.

Yet the whole of this vast movement is enclosed within a dominant-tonic progression. The symbol of the stability of the classical world is strained to breaking point; it hangs on the single thread of the final high D on piccolo and cello harmonic.

Man and His Music, The Sonata Principle, p. 130

Mellers sees the *Ländler* of the Second Movement as a spectral ghost of the past, and the *Rondo-Burleske* of the Third as a wild parody of folksong and monumental polyphony—simplicity and solemnity became savagely grotesque.

> This seems to suggest that for Mahler neither folksong nor dogmatic polyphony could offer salvation; such peace as he can find must be in the meditations of his own spirit.
>
> *ibid.*, p. 130

So the last movement is a 'passionately subjective *Adagio* . . . carrying . . . the enharmonic transitions to so extreme a point that the music literally breaks with its *world weariness*'.

> First harmony *disintegrates* into linear counterpoint, in the chamber-music scoring which anticipates so many developments in twentieth-century music. Then melody itself *disintegrates* into piteous chromatic fragmentariness; with the *fading* of the melodic strands there *vanishes* too a world and a mode of belief. Even the basic tonality has *sunk* from the first movement's D to D flat.
>
> *ibid.*, p. 131 (my italics)

This development, Mellers says, was foreshadowed in *Das Lied von der Erde*; the music, 'without superficial orientalisms', yet takes on characteristics of Eastern music:

> strange linear arabesque—sometimes pentatonic sometimes in chromatically inflected modes, sometimes almost as non-tonal and inhuman as bird-calls: while in the ineffably protracted suspensions on the word *'ewig'* music strains to release itself from harmony and metre.

As with Beethoven, Mahler seems to be striving to 'preserve his sanity' by freeing himself from Time and Will.

> He found his salvation, if Europe did not. In the dying fall of Mahler's last music the madness of a world burns itself out: the obsession with Time, which has dominated Europe with the Renaissance, begins to dissolve with Asiatic immobility; and the process is a laceration of the spirit. Mahler lingers on those suspended dissonances, his last hold on the life he loved with all his richly attuned senses; while the hollow reverberations of percussion sound like falling masonry, thudding through an eternity of years. The chord on which the 'Farewell' finally fades to nothingness is a 'verticalization' of the pentatonic scale; and of all melodic formulae the pentatonic is most void of harmonic implications. Yet out of harmonic integration grows a new seed. The linear principle of twelve-note music is inherent in the texture of the music of Mahler's last years.
>
> *ibid.*, p. 131

Here we may notice that Mellers sees Mahler's development in defensive terms, as if he were *only* trying to preserve sanity against a collapsing structure of civilization. But this is surely to confuse the apprehension of nothingness with the awareness of the collapse of a civilization. These are related, but surely not quite as Mellers expresses it. Professor Redlich also says of the end of *Das Lied* that it represents a disintegration:

> The presentiment of the movement's ultimate end and the disintegration of its music, as indeed of all human flesh, in the infinity of the blue horizon are wonderfully expressed through the subtle introduction of new musical elements: the whole-tone scale . . . the silvery ripple of the celesta . . . (the repetition of the word '*ewig*') . . . no less than nine times in a soft downgrade curve of three notes of the pentatonic scale while the remaining two are supplied by flute and cello. This represents . . . a rounding off of the whole work with an indescribable feeling of final completion, and, at the same time, heart-searing and unconquerable longing for the unattainable— the romantic union of Life and Death.
>
> *op. cit.*, p. 226

From this, Professor Redlich sees the *Ninth Symphony* follow *Das Lied* as 'expressing the premonition of approaching death' and as being concerned with 'mourning and foreboding', and 'approaching dissolution'.

I quote these two authorities at length because they seem to me such sensitive and penetrating analyses, but completely wrong about the essence of Mahler's work. I want my readers to be with me as far as I go with them. I intend to disagree with them, but only insofar as I want to try, if I can, to go beyond them, to try to speak of Mahler's achievement as a much more *positive* one.

Of course, Mahler's music is nostalgic. Of course, he wrote over the orchestra song of the First Movement 'O vanished days of youth! O scattered love!' Of course, the last movement of *Das Lied von der Erde* explores dissolution, and the *Tenth* contains some of the most terrifying portrayals of disintegration ever expressed in music. And yet *is it disintegration and morbid valediction one is left with?* Of course there is a relationship between the break-down of structure in Mahler's later music, and the horrors of European history in this century. As Donald Mitchell says Mahler suffered 'double alienation'.[1] *But there is also wrung from these surely a determined impulse towards resolution and integration?* Is it really 'civilization' as a structure that supports us? Or a sense of *meaning* established by the work we do between our inward dynamics and the symbols *with which civilisation provides us*?

---

[1] *Gustav Mahler*, p. 4—i.e. as an 'Austrian among Germans and as a Jew throughout the world'.

So I want to begin by asking, in what sense do we speak (as Mellers does) of how 'a world seems to be in dissolution'? What is the 'disintegration' that is expressed? Or rather—*where* is this dissolution and disintegration? How, following Mahler, does Schoenberg emerge: how is his work related to Mahler's music? ...

Verklärte Nacht is *Tristan* in a still riper stage of disintegration ...
Romanticism and the 20th Century, p. 185

—how can disintegration 'ripen'? Charles Ives, in isolation from European music, was also going the same way—without reference to the decline of the Viennese Empire. Of his *The Hausatonic at Stockbridge*, Mellers says,

> The sinuous horn melody, with its rich, almost Mahlerian harmonization, is absorbed into a haze of floating strings ...

He says that Ives belongs to the generation of Schoenberg and Mahler, and 'recreates something of their sensuous richness'. Besides the tendency to linear polyphony, there is the same interest in fresh sounds, as of the *bruitistes ('wie ein naturlaut')* and of Ives himself . . .' Elsewhere Mellers speaks of 'the last twitter of Western consciousness' in Mahler's work. But the 'fresh sounds' which lead on to Messaien surely also lead on to a new quest for relationship with the world? Have we yet understood what Shostakovitch tells us, in his *Fourth Symphony* —where he employs a Mahlerian idiom, to express the sorrow and tragedy of life, which no new form of social organization can assuage?

A world is 'dissolving': yet out of it 'grows a new seed'. We are, after all, talking about music which 'leaves us with a feeling of final completion': it is achieved art. Yet this completeness is wrung from 'nostalgia', and from an 'unconquerable longing for the unattainable— the romantic vision of Life and Death'. What can this seed growing out of dissolution be? It is surely not the dissociation and disintegration of schizoid art—self-enclosed, reductive of symbolism, non-communicative, nihilistic? Schizoid art since has moved away from the human, and even at times seeks to dissolve symbolism and creativity itself.[2] Some art even moves towards a schizophrenic incapacity to symbolize, into chance, noise, and the abrogation of creative responsibility, even in music. Mahler's work is magnificently feeling, richly symbolic, and relational. In it we hear human hearts singing and beating 'each to each'. We ex-

---

[2] Masud Khan speaks of 'the corrosive malady of the industrial European cultures: an egoistical alienation that is as lethal . . . to the future of the individual as it is nihilistic of the traditions of the cultures he is reared in'. *The Black Rainbow*, ed. Peter Abbs, Heinemann, 1974.

perience a tremendous degree of *creative reflection* and *resolution of identity*: it is this I want to insist upon, as Diether insists that the word for Mahler *is* 'integration'—as we shall see.

What I am trying to lead towards is the rejection of an oddly negative interpretation of what Mahler was doing, implicit in Mellers' terms, and in the generally accepted cliché about Mahler's 'world-weariness'. I am also trying to reject the way these critics *externalize* the problem, by referring to European events, social change, external culture. It is as if these commentators were clinging to the belief that there can be solutions to our problems of identity in the external sphere. Or perhaps they feel confident that if we change society, we can change the individual: conversely if 'society' collapses, so does the individual. Of course, neither is true, directly. But what we are concerned with is the life or death of consciousness. And in failing to see this these critics seem to be failing to see that in Mahler's acceptance of subjective reality as the only real basis of growth and strength of identity we have something of great significance for the future. For the implications of his work would seem to require a quite different view of society and the individual in it to explain them. His critics' thinking about man in society tends to be essentially 'sociological'—and thus fundamentally nihilistic (man is a 'product' of 'society'). Their psychology is dominated by Freud—perhaps Freud modified by Fromm and Karen Horney. The concept of man in this is too deterministic, too much 'imprisoned in physicalism': it lacks the 'I can' of intentionality. This kind of view suffers from a failure to take account of 'inner reality' and the world of 'internalized objects'—the whole problem of man's relationship with himself which object-relations psychology has obliged us to consider in thinking about the basis of social life and individual identity. So, too, we must take account of the problem of meaning as explored by existentialist psychoanalysis, with its emphasis on Man's anguish about the point of life, and which argues that this is not 'sick', but is what makes him Man. Mahler knew that his only hope in finding a sense of meaning in his threatened life was in the re-discovery of the capacity to be through the inner strength of subjective disciplines. It is not that we begin from Mahler's 'neurotic sensitivity' and follow him *in self-defence* against collapsing social orders, in 'retreat into one's self' as Mellers implies when he says 'Such peace as he could find . . .'—as if existential security *could be found anywhere else other than in the self*. Of course, without it (as we are finding) civilization cannot continue, while in the work of Frankl, Gabriel Marcel, and Maslow it is becoming

41

clear that if civilization is menaced, it is because men cannot find a sense of meaning in their lives—meaning that can transcend the death and mortality, which the 'bustle' of today's way of life simply denies.

Underlying the negative approach I believe we may find vestiges of the influence of Freud's point of view, in which culture is but a sublimation of more 'real' primary drives, while all human activity represents some form of defence reaction against the impingement of a hostile environment. So, Freud's view of man's predicament is itself paranoid-schizoid. Mahler's music is seen in its light as a defence impelled by 'neurotic sensitivity'. A world was tottering: we hear the thudding masonry, as if imperial Vienna were actually crumbling. Faith, too, crumbles: and so all one is left with is 'symbols' of 'the Grail', and the innocence of folksong while 'Mahler makes a symphonic battle out of Catholic polyphony'. What is won is but a self-saving withdrawal from Time, into 'Asiatic immobility' . . . 'in the meditations of his own spirit'.

We may agree that 'the process is a laceration of the spirit', and there is an anguish in Mahler's music, of a last hold on life, loved with 'richly attuned senses'. But what I cannot accept is Mellers' implication that somehow Mahler's music manifests 'the madness of a world' that 'burns itself out', and that there is a *withdrawal* marked by a *retreat* to the 'meditations of his own spirit': itself like so much in modern music, as Mellers sees it—a 'giving up the Self', a view which seems to have led some to become willing to accept the forfeiture of consciousness and civilization. In his *Power and Innocence*, Rollo May sees the attack on the mind made by the drug cult as a form of desperate violence, and this, I believe, is true of some forms of contemporary music, from 'pop' to some of the *avant-garde*. But this is not Mahler's path.

A kind of denial of the primacy of consciousness seems to have crept into some 'social' criticism of music, and the other arts. Where else, other than in one's own consciousness, can 'such peace as we can find' be? Of course, one can see what Mellers means, and in a sense he is right: there was a time when a poet could say *in la sua voluntade e nostra pace*. Order in the world, order in the structure of belief, and order in the soul, were once in harmony to a degree that the quest for peace was a matter (as with Dante) of exploring possibilities inherent in an existing structure, of religion and Christian community. The identity could rely upon external support, and the confirmation of a spiritual world, felt to be 'out there', in what we today would call an 'objective' sense.

Nostalgia—or Potentia?

But there is an implication in Mellers' criticism, associated with his most profitable attempts to link the meaning of music with social and philosophical trends, to imply that music is *about* the collapse of the Austrian empire, the urbanization of the folk, or a composer's relationship with the Catholic faith, his racial background. It is *about* imperial splendour, peasant communities, the urban environment, or Time and Will in the European predicament. Or it is *about* Mahler's 'double alienation'. That is, there is in Mellers something of a deterministic view of music, by which Mahler is approached as if he were recording external events, albeit internalized.

This view has its value, since music obviously 'reflects' its 'time', and is not simply 'pure sound'. But we can, I believe, take matters further and see the composer's use of external experience—the sounds and meanings of his time—as themselves 'objective correlatives', and so symbols of unconscious dynamics which belong to universal and eternal perplexities of existence.[3] Psychodynamic conflict inevitably internalizes social structure and change; but the essential problem of human nature is to achieve a sense of an integrated identity which feels real enough to feel a sense of the point of life. The music, in this view, is a dramatization of endopsychic structures and meanings, in the quest for a secure sense of meaningful existence, from which freedom and authenticity may be exercised in the face of our essential nothingness.

Of course, Mellers sees there is an inward conflict between 'folk' innocence and a sophistication which can no longer rely on its civilized referents: but what is there universal about this conflict? For what Mahler was concerned with were universal aspects of human identity and the problem of what transcends mortality—subjective problems which obtain *at any stage of history*, whatever the 'condition' of man. They are universal tragic problems: problems of being and despair, enacted admittedly, as they can only be enacted, in the one personal and historical setting. Of course, Mellers is also right, if we accept that Mahler is taking us to the heart of the problem of civilization: it cannot go on if there is no confidence in being—and this confidence did collapse during the last century.[4]

There is a more satisfactory earlier essay by Wilfrid Mellers on

[3] Obvious examples of how this could happen are recorded in de la Grange's *Biography*: Mahler, as a child, followed a military band and got lost; on another occasion, fascinated by such a band he failed to answer the call of nature and soiled himself. Such music thus comes to mean anxiety and shame.

[4] See the remarkable historical survey in the first chapter of *Existence: A New Dimension in Psychiatry*, ed. Rollo May and others, Basic Books, 1958.

Mahler, in *Scrutiny* (Volume IX, No. 4, March, 1941, p. 343) in which he recognizes Mahler as a key-figure in the twentieth century. Yet even here I find Mellers' position equivocal. He says:

> The end of a world: and yet, it may also be, the birth-pangs of a new. For just as the chromatic-harmonic and orchestral-exotic elements of Mahler's work look forward to these elements in the work of Schoenberg, Berg and Webern, which are the last nocturnal glimmer of romanticism, so the fragmentary polyphony of his final compositions look forward to those elements in the music of the atonalists which are expressive of a strange realm of feeling, a newly awakened sense, which may yet play an important evolutionary part in music's future . . . the precise degree of this evolutionary significance is difficult to estimate, since we cannot speculate with conviction upon the direction which the formulation of musical language will take . . .

> p. 349

The discussion which follows, about whether traditionalism or the new radical modes, were likely to become most appropriate for the future, is one which Mellers has pursued in his writing ever since, for thirty years. But there is a somewhat chilling implication in one phrase used here: 'the culture of the future, *if there is any* . . .' (my italics). Today, in the seventies, the decline of culture seems not to trouble Professor Mellers as much as it should—he seems to see the 'newly awakened sense' in areas which are as far from Mahler's achievement as one could get, such as the manipulated pseudo-rituals of 'pop'.

But in the *Scrutiny* Essay, he pays an impressive tribute to Mahler:

> We can see, in this *Ninth Symphony* of Mahler, the main problems of European music—the polyphonic principle of the sixteenth century, the symphonic ideal of the Classical tradition, the nineteenth-century cult of the personal and dramatic, the baroque notion of rhetoric, the twentieth-century explorations into an 'unterrestrial' linear counterpart—all touched upon and synthesized. I doubt if there is any single work that can shed more light upon the difficulties of the composer in relation to the contemporary world. And it contains music wild and passionate and painfully beautiful which only those whose response has been atrophied by our sophisticated refusal to feel anything without the 'ironic' protection of intellectual canniness can fail to recognize as the expression of a spirit at once noble and incisive, of an age which, if in some respects outmoded, has much to teach us if ever the 'new world' so frequently discussed, is to be, in reality, born.

> *op. cit.*, p. 351

What I mean by equivocal is that Mellers still seems reluctant to see music of such traditionalism and passion as being seminal in the 'new world' of music. Yet, in the tribute he so generously pays, it seems obvious that Mahler's *Ninth* remains the key work of this century—and that the nobility and incisiveness in an engagement with the difficulties both of technique and of meaning, are yet to be understood and 'taken' by modern music. Since this essay was written, Mahler has 'come into his own', because he has something to say, as so much that is 'ironic' has not: his passion has made its way in the face of the predominant intellectual canniness of our culture.

What can have happened, that Mahler no longer seems to occupy pride of place in Mellers' account of the development of contemporary music. Is this because Mahler's 'message' had not yet been made explicitly clear? Is it that philosophy lags behind—for Professor Mellers' 'model' of man seems out-of-date—belonging to those tendencies today in which man's primary reality is his instinctual life, to which civilization and consciousness are 'burdens'. The New Existentialism, fortunately, is restoring the balance, emphasizing that man's primary need is for meaning—an emphasis so clear to Mahler, and so important, if we are to have any culture at all.

Does Professor Redlich's final comment on *Das Lied* take us further? In what sense can a piece of music represent a longing for an unattainable 'romantic union of Life and Death'? What exactly is meant by the last two terms? A man cannot be alive and dead at the same time. It is not even possible to express the experience of death. Music can only express the anxiety, or the mourning, of the living in the face of death. It is possible to say 'farewell to life': but what is the motive of so doing, that leaves us 'with an indescribable feeling of final completion'? If the romantic 'union' is 'unattainable'—how is it that we feel a sense of completion—as though the unattainable had been attained? Mahler was, after all, still alive when he wrote the piece, though he never heard it performed.

So the achievement must be in the *readiness to die* and the sense that there is a triumph over death. 'He has found his solution, if Europe did not': in saying this Mellers seems to imply that Mahler draws aside from European disintegration, to save himself. (Or does he mean that if Europe had been able to hear Mahler she might have avoided her disaster?) But it sounds rather as if, with Redlich, Mellers implies that Mahler was intent on merely saving himself: if this is all, what value is his work to us? The growing interest in Mahler seems to suggest that he has something important to offer us: can it be that this is only the readiness to die?

45

Gustav Mahler and The Courage To Be

There is, I think, something of a truth in Mellers' attitude; but we need to re-examine it in a different perspective. Can we not see that disintegration in Europe had to do with the same kind of problems of *identity* with which Mahler is grappling (which is what Mellers is really noting)? Most of Europe in 1914 and again after 1930 took to schizoid false-solutions of hate (some, indeed, took to 'the final solution'). These false solutions were based on splitting, projection, and the violent incorporation or destruction of others.[5] Discussing the disintegration in his historical survey in *Existence*, Dr May says that the compartmentalization of Victorian culture had its 'psychological parallel in radical repression within the individual personality' (p. 22). Freud's best work was in seeking to cure this fragmented individual personality. He quotes Tillich on what shows still today, in the 'souls of many Americans as disruptiveness, existential doubt, emptiness and meaninglessness.' The existential movement arose as a spontaneous answer to this disintegration—and moved towards a heightened self-consciousness. Mahler belongs to this spontaneous movement, seeking integration. But, though his solutions may be possessed directly into the soul on hearing his music, its explicit implications are only now being made articulate. But his time *has* come at last. For Mahler offers us solutions by which we (and Europe—and the world) *can* save ourselves if we choose. What he offers us is a concern with *being* and *love* instead of false doing and hate: in this his preoccupation with Eastern modes may be seen as parallel to the gaining interest in Eastern poetry, philosophy, and modes of 'being', in the West today.

The earlier critical approaches of the kind suggested by the phrase 'world weariness' may indicate something of a resistance to what Mahler is really saying. Bruno Walter, devoting his great musical talent to human good, was a devout Catholic: and a devotee of both Bruckner and Mahler. To him both speak God's Word. To Walter, Mahler's music was a searching for God even though Mahler had lost his faith: and to him (as appears in a recorded interview) death is 'our door'. To him, obviously, world-weariness would be a commendable attribute: yet, I think, to attribute it to Mahler is to put a wrong interpretation on his music. *The Song of Suffering of the Earth* is a richly compassionate humanistic work; a going out to man in his struggle. Mahler's

[5] Combined with 'a militant negation of all intellectual and moral values': the phrase is from Masud Khan, *op. cit.*, and used of the hippies and others 'imprisoned in their immediate subjectivity and corporeality'. See for a historical study, Michael Polanyi in *Knowing and Being, Beyond Nihilism*. See also Clifford Adelman in *Generations: A Collage on Youthcult*, on Nihilism and Solipsism, p. 308, Pelican 1973.

attachment to the joy and beauty of the earth is intense ('O wild delirious world'). It is stoical. It recognizes no Heaven or transcendental realm to which death is our 'door'. Even though Mahler's quest is intensely religious and philosophical, it does not in the end reject this world: this is all we have.

It may be this that Professor Redlich means when he writes about 'the union of Life and Death': the achievement of a state in which death ceases to matter. This attitude Mahler does attain in his music, if only from moment to moment. The structure 'strained to breaking point' which Mellers notes is not a symbol of an attenuated 'stability of the classical world', but of a triumphant sense of 'at-one-ness', held for a moment only, as a glimpse of heaven. By 'heaven' I mean here that which establishes a transcendence such as to make death no longer of any account. But this (to Mahler) was not a glimpse of another world or after-life: it is a glimpse of meaning in the face of a recognition of mortality and temporality.

Only if we understand the kind of creative achievement we have in Mahler can we begin to solve the artistic and philosophical problems of the contemporary world. For we urgently need, in the arts, a viable philosophical anthropology. In music the creative problems tend to take the form of asking—what have the new non-diatonic idioms been forged for? To express *what*? In other arts besides music the contemporary problem presents itself in terms of what may now be said, in the new idioms (if indeed that is what we have) that is not savagery devoted to expressing a false attitude to man which travesties and vitiates the truth about us. For today, the Arts, largely fleeing from life problems, or taking refuge in black or barbarous lies, are left with nothing to say and seek only futile 'technique' in a schizoid breakdown of communication. Some painters are left with only paint,[6] composers dwell on the possibilities of new sounds, to no purpose than to exploit aural potentialities—but not, apparently, human ones.

In some directions there is even a withdrawal from symbolism itself and a regression to the pre-symbolic modes of the paranoid-schizoid stage in infancy—that is to 'equation' symbolism, in which instead of creative satisfaction there is the satisfaction of feeling real by coming up in an aggressive way against others who stand for the object of relationship which needs to be hated (and bludgeoning by sound is thus 'event'

---

[6] In a recent newspaper report it was said that a Jackson Pollock, for which a museum paid a huge sum, was painted by the artist and a sculptor colleague, by paddling about on the paint on the canvas on the floor, in bare feet, while drunk.

not art).[7] In this, as I have tried to say elsewhere (e.g. in *The Masks of Hate*) there is a forfeiture of human creative power, a narrowing of interests in art. These are false ('acting out') strengths: the real strength is in accepting one's weakness and vulnerability, through *symbolism*.

Mahler's sinking or rising key relationship, his uncanny sounds from the heavenly celeste to the cow-bells and *col legno* playing, his 'grisly' use of percussion, his escape from tonality, his 'unfolding' structure, all had the function of *extending* symbolic creative perception, in order to arrive at 'unity'. His simple tender and poignant melodies in his later work are no manifestation of sentimentality, but a way of baring his humanness to ultimate questions, in recognition of human weakness and the anguish of the regressed ego—akin to King Lear's confession, 'I am a foolish fond old man . . .' Our problem now is how to make use of such extended ranges of symbolism for creative purposes in music and the other arts.

Erwin Stein indicates some of the problems of contemporary idioms in music in *Orpheus in New Guises*. After pointing out that the new freedom means 'an immense enrichment' he says:

> The disintegration of tonality has shaken all the formative principles of music . . . we are returning to a polyphonic style . . . (but) the situation is more difficult (than it was at the time of the crisis of transition after Bach from polyphony to the harmonic style of the classics). Tonality was one of the strongest means of formal organization. An equivalent substitute has not yet been found. The new combination of notes have not yet stood the test of new, extended forms . . . their functional possibilities have not yet been ascertained.
>
> *Orpheus in New Guises*, p. 59

Through Mahler and Schoenberg these changes perhaps had to come: '*Kunst kommt nicht von karnen, sondern von müssen*'—as Schoenberg himself put it ('Art is not a faculty, but a compulsion'.) But a compulsive activity may be no more than a schizoid need to utter or 'act out', without symbolic achievement. True symbolic gain needs a different kind of compulsion—the impulse to find meaning. The problem would seem to be that we do not yet understand what direction might be taken by the impulse towards 'dissolution', as exemplified by departures from classical tonality and homophony. The preoccupation of the schizoid individual with the human identity and the meaning of existence has been confused with the schizoid (or schizophrenic) erosion of symbolism by 'acting

---

[7] In the world of 'pop' young people are inducing dangerous states in themselves by psychedelic lighting and drugs, so as to actually damage or destroy their hearing by too-loud sound. See also, on 'events' in 'serious' music, *Cross-Currents with Expressionism* in Donald Mitchell's *The Language of Modern Music*.

out'. 'Freedom' has become freedom from artistic responsibility, and 'radical dissolutions' have supplanted 'radical solutions'. Yet it is by creative symbolism alone that confirmation of being can be achieved. Thus to such a figure as John Cage, his obsession with mushrooms seems more important as symbolism than his 'random' composing, which (in the way he describes it) seems to manifest a terror of emotional commitment, even if his music does not. The effect could be to trivialize art, emotion and human being itself. (That his music is not like that *in effect* perhaps indicates that there is an unrecognized organizational creative dynamic at work—which Cage is simply not willing to admit explicitly.) In theory, such composing, even the choice of notes and time, must be left to chance, as if Cage feels that to make one's own significant choices would be likely to be too dangerous. If in a composer's work the audience must be 'alienated' and the performers left to their own inventions, surely we may suspect a schizoid fear of losing one's identity by communicating?

Perhaps we should examine the phenomenology of John Cage's fascination with mushrooms? He shares this with Sylvia Plath, who shows a schizoid fascination with the strange, magic, non-human emergence of these growths:

> Nobody sees us,
> Stops us, betrays us . . .
> Perfectly voiceless . . .
> >   we
> Diet on water,
> On crumbs of shadow . . .
> >   . . . asking
> Little or nothing . . .
> We shall by morning
> Inherit the earth . . .
>
> 'Mushrooms', *The Colossus*, p. 34

To her, mushrooms seem admirable for being non-human, because they are without any of the dangers of being human, and of relationship ('Nobody . . . betrays us'). But yet they are also terrible because they threaten to take over the whole world, ruthlessly. To John Cage, too, as a representative figure concerned with creativity in the modern world, parallel fears of being human seem to make him feel that the best thing of all would be to be 'perfectly voiceless': his book, after all, is called *Silence*. Such music, like Beckett's *Breath*, moves in the opposite direction from Mahler, towards the silence of ultimate withdrawal, while

Mahler moved towards being—and towards life, even when he was dying.

As I have tried to demonstrate elsewhere, 'schizoid' is the diagnostic word not only for our society, but also for much of its fashionable and *avant-garde* culture. Its impulse is to give way to moral inversion and a desperate nihilism. Mahler, despite agonized schizoid problems, strove to *complete* 'the schizoid position', as did Dostoevsky—and to move beyond it, to become capable of love and being: for the schizoid condition is a state of being arrested in development, before becoming capable of love and creative perception. His regression had a positive goal.

From Laing's studies of how schizoid individuals fear human contact, because it can bring loss of self, can we not understand the pathology of a great deal in modern 'experimental' art that simply avoids human 'meeting' and so can offer nothing essentially creative? Because of this, it cannot enrich the lives of others, as Mahler's music enriches us. To enrich the lives of others is an act of love. By contrast, the avant-gardist shrinks from anything so human: often (as with the painting that stuns us, sadistic pornography, and theatre that makes people vomit) we merely *suffer*, from the impact of hate.

Donald Mitchell quotes from a pompous chronicle about *avant-garde* music: 'of new works of more "human" character heard during the festival . . .' —and comments, 'I wish I could assume that those quotation marks round "human" were ironic.'

> Is it meaningful, in short, to attempt to convey to us the experience of Mumma's *Megaton for William Burroughs* in the same terms that we would normally reserve for, say, Beethoven's *Ninth*—'a work of prophetic vision and artistic grandeur'?
>
> *The Language of Modern Music*, p. 157

Where an individual is so unwilling to speak clearly as a man speaking to men, we may doubt whether he has made any genuinely creative progress in getting in touch with himself: as Bachelard said, to speak one must be able to listen first. And we shall see what Mahler meant by listening. It is nothing less than enquiring into one's place in the scheme of things.

5

Envy, Gratitude, and the Problem of Existence

Jack Diether speaks of Mahler's 'almost schizoid' inner tensions and strivings. I propose to discuss Mahler's search in his music, for integration, and for a wholeness which he could assert against meaninglessness. But I want to discuss some of the dynamics of the personality in psychoanalytical terms, such as *ambivalence*—the mixture of love and hate in us; *reparation*—the need to give, benignly, to others to atone for one's guilt in having hated them; and *gratitude*, the benign feeling which is released insofar as one can accept one's ambivalence, come to terms with one's hate and guilt, and feel capable of reparation, leading to the capacity to believe in *continuity*.

We may find our first clues to Mahler's personality problems in Henry Boys's remarkable notes to the first recording. He observes that Mahler's compulsion was to find in music a 'temporary solution' to his subjective problems:

All his life was spent in frantic attempts to escape from . . . contradictions in his nature . . . in the immense *Third Symphony* to become one with nature, in the idyllic *Fourth* to find consolation in a childhood heaven . . . each represents a fresh attempt to achieve equilibrium, and may be regarded as a temporary solution.

Boys here quotes Mahler himself:

Strange! When I hear music . . . even while I conduct—I can hear quite definite answers to my questions and feel entirely clear and sure. Or rather, I feel quite clearly that they are no questions at all.

We may interpret this as indicating that Mahler sought to find in music a relationship between the self and the real world which he found it difficult to find outside music. His true identity was realised in his music. He sought to repair and keep whole in music a sense of *being real* that he could not sustain in ordinary existence. While music is an echo in the mind, and a transient phenomenon of fantasy, nervous condition, and intellectual apprehension, nonetheless to create a musical structure is in

51

a sense to objectify the subjective world, to *create a world*, and so to make whole and to preserve what cannot be preserved whole in living.

Music, however, does not exist except as it is played, and heard, and re-created in the minds of those who listen.[1] So, to achieve wholeness of being in music requires that the work of art can be possessed as the artist meant it to be possessed. This accounts for Mahler's intense pre-occupation with exactitude—his orchestration of clarity, of 'remarkable originality and purity', his thoroughness of orchestration and revision, and his meticulous indications as to how his music should be played:

> Mahler's music often gives the impression that he is compelling the listener to feel things to the same intense degree as Mahler felt them himself . . .
> 'All music since Beethoven', said Mahler, 'has been programme music.' On the other hand, he was equally emphatic that, though the composer might use as a sort of scaffolding for working out his structure a scheme of ideas and concepts, generally a very simple one, the music should be constructed in such a way that what may have been necessary to the composer should not be so to the listener, *whose job it was to listen and not to ruminate.*

This explains why Mahler even went so far as to rescore Beethoven and Schubert. His own creative effort and its possession by us was to him a matter of life and death of his identity, and this perhaps explains also the care with which he cut himself off from contact, in order to listen to his inward voices and rhythms.[2] The exactness of his self-exploration was a guarantee of being able to hold his world together by creative effort: to hear and be heard was a form of creative reflection.

Yet despite this self-exploration and the accuracy with which he sought to make his inner world objective, Mahler could not convince himself that he was making touch with human beings (and as we shall see, in his life he often could not).

> He certainly felt (says Boys) most acutely his own essential loneliness; and that, in spite of his fervent desire to communicate, a desire which is exemplified in the extreme pains he took to make every element in his music as clear as possible, real communication was impossible; so that in his own eyes he was separated from the world.

The 'unity' is thus only accomplished in terms of 'temporary solutions' to chaos or disintegration. This music is thus quite different from (say)

---

[1] That Mahler never heard his *Ninth* is a dreadful fact which has haunted me all through writing this book.

[2] 'Mahler got up at six or six-thirty every day. As soon as he was awake, he rang for the cook, who promptly prepared his breakfast and carried it up a steep, slippery trail to his forest study, 200 feet above the house. (She was forbidden to use the regular road, lest he meet her on his way up; before work, he could not stand seeing anyone.)'
And the Bridge is Love, Alma Mahler, p. 30

Beethoven's heroic, more classical, conflict between the composer and 'the world'. It is music of a progressive attempt to create and sustain a 'structure of being'.

So, as Boys says, the First Movement must not be approached according to Classical models: 'it does not solve anything, it presents an emotional situation, and the whole symphony must be heard before its full significance can be grasped.' But this is not quite true, either. Something *is* solved even in the First Movement (as the coda eminently conveys) and at least the composer has defined the area in which the creative work needs to be completed. What is achieved in the First Movement, however, needs yet to be tested, and depends upon the rest of the symphony for its final resolution. It is thus true to say of the First Movement (as Boys does):

> · The Second and Third Movements emotionally depend upon it; they are written under its shadow; and the symphony works towards the great *Adagio*, which is an attempt to alleviate, tranquillize and complete what has preceded it.

Jack Diether says of *Das Lied von der Erde* and the *Ninth*:

> the resolution seems to be found not in personal salvation and immortality as in II and VIII, but in the great 'collective unconscious':
>
> > *Die Liebe Erde allüberall*
> > *Blüht auf im Lenz und grünt aufs neu!*
> > *Allüberall und ewig blauen licht die Fernen!*
> > *Ewig . . . Ewig . . .*

The term 'collective unconscious' however, does not seem quite right— for what exactly can it mean? There can only be the collocation of individual consciousnesses—and perhaps of individual engagements with the problem of existence. How can we experience the 'collective' *unconscious*? In art we can only experience through symbolism in what one soul (Mahler's) came to discover and achieve. If we possess this we may be stimulated to seek integration and meaning, employing the content and structure offered us by the artist, from his own struggles.

But certainly, what we may agree about is that Mahler's in the *Ninth Symphony* is not seeking to escape into a better world, but rather to be glad of his existence in this. Diether discusses this thus:

> We see that in these last works of Mahler, Catholicism is completely replaced by Pantheism. That is the final paradox of Mahler's paradoxical life: that, faced with actual death, he no longer strove for reconciliation with eternity, but with *this* world . . . Mahler's final rejection of the orthodox theologies which so troubled him seems implemented by his

53

instruction that during his funeral not a word should be spoken nor a note sung . . . The dissolving into *nirvana* at the end of the *Ninth* even hearkens somewhat back to the oblivion of the end of the *Lieder eines fahrenden Gesellen*, under the snowfall of blossoms from the lime tree of childhood where 'all was good again: love and grief and world and dream'. But this in the *Ninth* is the reconciliation of childhood through the mind and heart of a man . . .

Chord and Discord, 1963, p. 107

This account, however, does not yet seem adequate: Pantheism again seems hardly the adequate word to describe Mahler's joy in the continuity of growth and life in the real world, nor does *nirvana* seem the right term to describe his achievement of transcendence.

We may begin with these elements in Mahler—preoccupations with childhood; with the resolution of grief, and making the world 'good again'. Here I believe certain key concepts of Melanie Klein's are relevant—*Envy, Reparation*, and *Gratitude*. Let us begin with *gratitude*. It is plainly this that bursts forth in Mahler—in *The Song of the Earth*, for instance. He can express a grateful sense of having belonged to 'the continuity of life'. The capacity for this benign gratitude seemed to Melanie Klein to be connected with the degree to which the individual had experienced satisfactory (psychic) nurture at the mother's breast— and without this, gratitude has to be bitterly striven for. The alternative to gratitude is *envy*, the impulse to 'empty' others, and take what is due to one from them by force. It is not difficult to see how, in tragic art, one expects a struggle between envy and gratitude. The weak hunger-to-survive, which manifests itself in hate, hungers for sustenance. It seeks to empty others or to rob them of their happiness. Beneath envy there is an underlying impulse to annihilate others. A character in Tolstoy sees in his dying brother's eyes 'the envy of the dying for the living'. Thus the threat of death exacerbates the problem of envy. To overcome envy requires sufficient reparative achievement to find gratitude—a gratitude which can enable feelings of love to flow out to others, to fresh generations, and to the world:

Oh life of endless loving!

A creative contest with such problems requires, as I believe, the re-experiencing of primal being. Where envy is a problem, the individual has not had enough of the 'maturational processes and the facilitating environment'. He needs creative encounter. Only in this way, he feels— by adequate mothering—can he begin to be. Unless he can 'be', he cannot become, or be effective in autonomous freedom. '*Being* comes first, *doing* later' is Winnicott's emphasis in his most important paper on the origins of identity.[3] *Being* belongs to 'the female element' and *doing* to the 'male element' in the personality.

Now it seems possible that there are different kinds of music, in this sense, too. While all music may spring from the creative female element in both men and women there are obviously some forms of music which go out aggressively male into the world. The music of conflict, and revolution, of dealing with the world 'out there' seems to belong to this male element (Beethoven's *Eroica*, for instance). In turning away from music of such structures, of statement, counter statement and resolution —to the music of linear development and the escape from tonality and time into suspended time and cadence-less transcendence, Mahler was perhaps concerned with the problem of what Winnicott calls *female element being*, with the earliest experience in the formation of the identity, and also with what it is to be. The *Ninth Symphony*, as I shall try to suggest, is a massive piece of regression to the stage of primary identification with the mother, and a rediscovery of this realm of 'female element being', in order to achieve a new sense of human capacities in this dimension. Mahler goes back to the very start of the self, in pursuit of 'togetherness' in primary confirmation. The rediscovery of this realm is of course, one which is being made by modern psychology and philosophy as will be clear from the Bibliography to this study: many of these works are about the origins of being. From this area Mahler exerts what I have called 'the courage to be'.

Mahler was thus investigating a problem which is today pressing itself on us from many directions. The symphony both begins and ends with the *'ewig'* theme, with the most primaeval sound of the gently beating heart, both as at the beginning and ending of life. So, he enacts the truth which psychology is now beginning to recognize—that 'in our end is our beginning'. This is, the sense of transcendence in which we may find our most complete authenticity and assert it against our eventual nothingness is to be found if we search for the kind of 'at-one-ness' we once knew, at the beginning of our lives, in the first encounter of *liebende Wirheit*. In our beginning we existed in union with the object. In the womb and in the mother's arms we identified with her (as subjective object). Later we emerged as a self over against her, seeing her as 'objective' object. Only by 'being for us' does the mother enable us to be,

---

[3] *Male and Female Element*: see *Playing and Reality*. The phrase above, 'maturational processes and the facilitating environment', is the title of an earlier book by Winnicott: see Bibliography.

whole. But the fragmentations we have suffered in our consciousness have arisen because in many ways we have lost the capacity to be (while the East seems less to have lost touch with Being). To recover this, and the deep sense of meaning in the universe it can bring, we need to re-explore the experience of at-one-ness, in terms of at-one-ness with the universe, and Mother Earth. By the musical experiences of the *Ninth Symphony* and *Das Lied* Mahler relates being and eternity—the ring of the blue horizon symbolizing a perfect sense of reconciliation and integration in the self, and of the meaning of our existence in its eternal processes of becoming.

If this can be achieved, we may feel that gratitude which 'finds the end of life to accord with the beginning'. Melanie Klein says:

> Those who feel that they have had a share in the experience and pleasure of life are much more able to believe in the continuity of life. Such capacity for resignation without undue bitterness and yet keeping the power of enjoyment alive has roots in infancy and depends on how far the baby has been able to enjoy the breast without excessively envying the mother for its possession. I suggest that the happiness experienced in infancy and the love for the good object which enriches the personality underlie the capacity for enjoyment and sublimation, and still make themselves felt in old age. When Goethe said, 'He is the happiest of men who can make the end of his life agree closely with the beginning', I would interpret 'the beginning' as the early happy relationship to the mother which throughout life mitigates hate and anxiety and still gives the old person support and contentment.
>
> *Envy and Gratitude*, p. 42

Mahler, I believe, was not one who had a 'happy relationship to the mother' in infancy—as his own relational difficulties seem to indicate. He was not convinced of a rich core of being: so, he has to seek to re-enact and rediscover this first source of being, as from the female element in himself. He has to father and mother himself.

As he does so, he reaches out, and then out of the experience of love at once emerges the threat of envy—that consuming hunger for the richness in the object, which, unsatisfied, seems to be likely to destroy the world. To find mitigation of this envy, and to discover the 'belief in continuity', is Mahler's creative task here: to express 'the sorrow of the earth itself' is a step towards recognition of that continuing life which must needs to endure suffering as a condition of continuing. (When Mahler's wife suffered in labour he said, 'How can men bear the guilt of such suffering and go on begetting children?'[4])

[4] Compare the attitude of a child quoted on the same page as the quotation from Melanie Klein: a boy of five expressed hope that his mother's unborn child should be

Mahler's *Ninth Symphony* is thus virtually 'about' Melanie Klein's paragraph above. The 'fate' theme (as Diether calls it) of the chromatic 'ape' turn, is hate and envy. It emerges out of rising passion—because love inevitably brings the problems of ambivalence. Love is threatened by the life-hunger of the regressed libidinal ego—which Mahler knew only too well from the appalling experiences of his childhood—and this life-hunger too often meets the nothingness it dreads.

As Guntrip says, the 'regressed ego' that hungers for being is experienced not only as a threat to existence: 'I feel like a big hungry mouth wanting to eat everyone and everything.' It can also be 'very clearly experienced as a fear of dying', which may at times lead a schizoid person to seek death as rebirth. To engage with the problem requires a going back to the earliest need to be given a sense of being, and this, I believe is what Mahler does. He does not try to find strength in the voices of hate—but by continuing to explore the anguish hidden behind it, discovers the pitiful plight of the weak unborn True Self behind them, the potentialities for being, never realised.

Had Mahler not been able to accomplish this inward quest he could never have finished his symphony, and there might have been consequent risks for his personality. But having done so, his enriched capacity to mitigate and to find gratitude for having existed, since he communicates it so exactly, can enrich and strengthen our own sense of meaning in existence. In this he makes profound contribution to the future of culture and man's capacity to be 'at home' in his world. For this kind of inner enrichment is possessed by us inexplicitly and intuitively, and fosters the inward struggle to modify envy and hate by love. This kind of nourishment for *being* is exactly what our starving world yearns for. Mahler achieved these spiritual gains without need to accept that dependency which religion traditionally manifests: he accepts the independence of man alone in a godless universe but still able to discover reconciliation—the path to which was his discovery of (stoical) Chinese poetry.

a girl: 'then she will have babies and her babies will have babies, and then it goes on forever . . .' *Ewig! (Op. cit.,* p. 42).

As will appear, I believe the death of his brother Ernst also brought him a deep inability to feel confidence in a sense of continuity, for here was a promising encounter that was swept into oblivion—a recurrent theme in his music.

6

The Anguished Life

Before we examine the music further in the light of insights from psycho-analytical theory it may help to link his existence problems with aspects of the life of this composer, to show that I am not merely inventing a psychology for him. Mahler had a severe problem of envy, in Melanie Klein's sense. He admitted, for one thing, that he could not tolerate youth and beauty. An envy of the young comes out in *Das Lied*—we might call it a deep sad feeling that others are enjoying a richness in life and love one has never known. The kind of feeling in its turn may be linked with a fear of humanness—which must then be *controlled* (by what in psycho-analytical language is called *controlling hate*). Mahler sought to control his wife and his environment with the same compulsive exertion he employed as a discipline for his creativity. If anyone inter-rupted his concentration on creativity, he would collapse, and feel 'as if he had been thrown down from a church tower' Tormented as he was by manic-depressed mood swings, his world seemed likely to collapse at any moment, and joy seemed to him a threat and doom. From his under-lying schizoid weakness he felt a continual threat to his sense of a point in life.

Mahler's whole life was an attempt to hold some sense of structure together by his music against the blows of the world. And, as so often with those who suffer a sense of being pursued by a malignant fate, his paranoia seemed to receive an astonishing amount of confirmation. There was his heart disease. There was the obligation to do his creative work (which was the point of his life) in vacation times only. There was the loss of loved members of his family. There was the tension of his authoritarian directorship of the opera conflicting with all the scheming and virulent opposition he suffered there. And there was his marriage to the formidable Alma which was threatened at one time by impotence, and occasionally by the possibility of infidelity.

On a now notorious occasion he consulted Freud about his sexual life. Freud elicited two relevant aspects of Mahler's make-up: Mahler felt about his wife as if to a mother (Freud drew from Mahler that he called her 'Marie' which was his mother's name.)[1] Moreover, Freud found that he attributed his failure to achieve music of the highest order to an incident in his childhood in which his mother was attacked by his father.[2] As we shall see this early experience of hate—or rather the fact that Mahler remembered so vividly—has immense musical significance.

According to Freud's biographer, the effects of Freud's discussion with Mahler were successful: Mahler (it is claimed) regained his potency and the marriage was improved until his death: yet by Alma's account it seems rather that the truth had to be kept from him, while in fact the relationship did not become a fully rich one. But in one respect it did become radically different—by the new sense of responsibility Mahler came to feel for another life, and in his own increased *recognition* of Alma as an individual. Freud's (typical) exclusive preoccupation with Mahler's sexual life rather than his whole problem of identity seems itself to be a preoccupation with a form of 'secondary elaboration' hiding the deeper problems of object-relations and identity underlying it. Of the Summer of 1910, after the declaration of love by Gropius, Alma writes:

> I was able to tell him all. I told him I had longed for his love year after year and that he, in his fanatical concentration on his own life, had simply overlooked me. As I spoke, he felt for the first time that something is owed to the person with whom one's life has once been linked. He suddenly felt a sense of guilt . . .
>
> *Gustav Mahler*, p. 173

Such deeper problems may be glimpsed from Alma Mahler's account of her relationship with the sensitive, domineering, neurotic man: her honest explicit account of her own relational shortcomings enhance our understanding. Beneath these relational problems again, we may glimpse a schizoid fear of love, both physical and as an emotion:

> In Dresden, one sleepless night soon after our engagement, a thought had flashed through Gustav Mahler's mind: 'What if I am too old, after all?' He had lived a life of austerity; with the possible exception of a few seductions by experienced women, he remained as virginal at forty as I was at twenty . . . we were baffled and sad and tormented, not by love but *by the fear of love* . . .
>
> *And the Bridge is Love*, p. 26

It would seem from Alma's accounts that Mahler was essentially in many ways a child, and could (apart from his music) in many ways only

---

[1] See Appendix on the 'Holy Mary' Syndrome.
[2] Ernest Jones, *Sigmund Freud*, Life and Work, Volume II, p. 89.

meet the world as a child. He had an aversion to insects. He was in great fear of the sea journey on the *Amerika*

> Mahler had difficulty in concealing his fear of the sea voyage . . . Soon I felt with joy that we were moving. Mahler scowled when I mentioned it . . .

He lay on his bed motionless through the stormy trip, in a kind of trance of sea-sick withdrawal. He was superstitious: he would not go to events without Alma. He resorted to a kind of magic, as a child does, as by trying to make out that his *Ninth Symphony* wasn't his ninth, in order to cheat the gods, who allowed composers only nine symphonies before their death:

> he was afraid to call it a symphony. It would have been his ninth—and neither Beethoven nor Bruckner had lived beyond their respective *Ninths*.
> Later, when he wrote his *Ninth Symphony*, Mahler said to me: 'It's really the *Tenth*; my *Ninth* is the *Song of the Earth*.' He thought he had out-smarted Our Lord . . .
> All his suffering, all of his fears went into this work. As *The Song of the Earth* it would be known the world over. But his working title for it was 'The Song of Sorrow on Earth'.
>
> p. 45

Normal reality, to Mahler, often seemed a threatening and terrible thing. The origins of this fear were obviously in his dreadful experiences as a child brought up in poverty and distress, while within him he could find insufficient ego-strength, by which to endure adverse circumstances. In many terrible ways the circumstances of his life seemed to confirm his superstitious sense of needing to outwit a predatory reality, as if, like a child, one could do so by tricks, like not stepping on the lines in the pavement.

Mahler's face bore the marks of great psychic strain. He looked old and feeble in middle age. On one occasion Alma at a concert in Philadelphia suddenly saw

> unveiled in Mahler's face such horrible new lines of suffering that in my mortal dread of losing him I fainted.

In all their life in later years they had to avoid all undue strain on Mahler's heart: he was now continually in danger of extinction:

> Once we knew he had valvular disease of the heart we were afraid of everything. He was always stopping on a walk to feel his own pulse; and he often asked me during the day to listen to his heart and see whether the beat was clear, or rapid, or calm. I had been alarmed for years by the creaking sound his heart made—it was particularly loud on the second beat—and I had

always known that it must be diseased . . . he had a pedometer in his
pocket. His steps and pulse-beats were numbered and his life a torment.

Gustav Mahler, p. 122

He carried a stop-watch to count his steps and his pulse, and kept asking
me to listen to his heart sounds. His life was torment . . .

p. 45

The focus of Mahler's sensibility and all its forebodings is thus the
heart: and here lies the crux of his psychic problem—and the source of
some of his musical symbolism, from the opening rhythms of the *Ninth*
to the cataclysmic drum-strokes of the *Tenth*.[3] For the heart is at once
the symbolic focus and the physical actuality of vitality—in its lift at
joy, its increase in pace in love-making, its surges of passion, its vigorous
delight in action and fresh air. Mahler had earlier exerted his vitality in
extreme forms (bicycling, mountain climbing and swimming under
water) with great joy in physical earthly being. Now he had to stop,
cultivate the tranquil heart, and seek the 'quiet object': even vitality
in passion became a threat. Yet obviously such a situation must undermine a man's capacities for object-relations: the failure of physical love,
which is so great an assurance of one's existence, would bring a fear
of loss of identity (cf. Lawrence's *Song of a Man who is Not Loved*).
But impotence also threatens the capacity to feel real by 'meeting',
and to leave one exposed by a kind of object-loss, to predatory fears.
We have a glimpse of these relational problems from Alma:

> In our first years together I had felt very insecure by his side. Having
> unwittingly won him by my impudence I had lost all physical aplomb by
> my premature pregnancy. And Mahler, from the moment of his triumph
> on, ignored me and did not begin to love me again until I was free from
> his despotic spell.

In both there seems to have been a need for an overdependent
relationship in which there was an excess of identification, and something of a schizoid substitution of 'achievement' (showing) and 'inner
contents' for living. The fear of emotional commitment in life generated
in Mahler an intense puritanism that manifested the severity of his anti-

[3] Cf. The musical phrase, ubiquitous in Mahler's
work, a falling tonic-triad (*Sixth Symphony*, etc.) which
'was said by his friends to mirror uncannily the
sudden clouding over of his features after he had
made a cheerful remark'. (Diether.) A similar look on
Dylan Thomas's face is recorded by observers at the
end of his life, when his alcoholic self-cure defences began to fail and death began to
overtake him. See *Dylan Thomas in America*, ed. M. Brinnin.

libidinal ego in its denunciation of joy—though no doubt it contributed to his creative disciplines:

> he played the part of a teacher, relentlessly strict and unjust. He made the world appear unpalatable, a kind of horror.
> That is to say, he tried to. Money—vain! Clothes—vain! Looks—vain! Travel—vain! Nothing counted but the spirit. I know today that he was really afraid of youth and beauty. 'If only you were disfigured,' he used to tell me; 'if you were suddenly pock-marked and no one else could like you any more—*then* I'd be able to show how much I love you!'
> To render me harmless, he simply took away what living things he did not know how to handle. I was the little girl he had desired and who was now going to educate.
> One day I told him that what I really loved in a man was his achievement. 'The greater the achievement, the more I must love him.'
> 'Sounds dangerous', said Mahler. 'What if one should come along who tops me?'
> 'I'd have to love him', I said.

For her part, Alma could not either give Mahler all of her love. Both seemed afraid of giving and unable to accept their dependence or to meet, wholly, a whole independent person. She said of him, 'I felt I was nothing but his shadow'; 'his genius ate me up although he meant no murder.' Whole experience was split away from abstract mind-existence. ('I lived his life, I had none of my own. I separated myself from him . . . and waited for a miracle . . . the miracle was there beside me—in the shape, at least, of pure abstraction . . .') The problem is startlingly symbolized by one incident. When Alma was having her pains in labour with their first child:

> trying to relieve my pains by suggestion, he had the crazy idea of reading Kant to me. I sat at his desk, writhing in pain; the monotonous sound of a voice reading things entirely beyond my comprehension at this moment was maddening. It was too much! I rebelled . . . today I know that he was perfectly right: the only way to conquer pain is by mental concentration. But the object he chose was far too difficult to grasp.
>
> p. 32

Mahler was not right. Though inevitably it is special pleading for a man to say so, it would seem that the way to lessen the pangs of childbirth is to practise acceptance of them—what was needed was love and the physical comfort of touch—or even of the soothing lilting voice we know so well from Mahler's lyricism. But not—surely not—Kant? The choice itself seems to imply the denial of human experience,[4] by

---

[4] Jack Diether says that Mahler's 'final agony of self-recrimination was that "my life has been all—paper" '.

intellectual hate, and a flight from life.[5] During his wife's first delivery Mahler

> ran through the streets like a madman. A friend who asked about me was yelled at: 'You ass, I forbid you to ask!'

While their child was being operated on for diphtheric scarlet fever Alma

> ran screaming along the lake shore . . .

To such schizoid individuals life is full of terrors they can neither accept nor overcome; life often seems to present to their paranoia more than their fair share of torment. Their anguish is that of being able only to meet such crises in an intellectual way, or by flight—or to be tormented by their own hate. When his younger child was one year old Mahler (who had 'an intimate, oddly individual relationship' with his children, which helped to make him 'more human, more communicative') had gone back to his *Kindertotenlieder*. Alma says:

> To my mind there was something eerie about it; in the garden, these two wonderfully gifted children were squealing with joy, and in his study Mahler could sing of their death.
>
> p. 34

But Mahler's essential preoccupation here was not with real children, but with the repressed libidinal ego—the unborn infant self, the dark hunger-to-exist within, that any actual child evokes in us. He was preoccupied with the threat to the meaning of life experienced when his brother died, or when love went out of his life—under the influence of predatory demons. But then another child actually died: Mahler's elder daughter died of diphtheria and he hid in his room when she was mortally ill, as if hiding from the demons of fate. Two days later Alma suffered a temporary cardiac weakness: Mahler said jokingly, 'Look, Doctor, why don't you take a look at me? My wife is always worried about my heart: she needs some good news today.'

The doctor's reply, after examination, was, 'I shouldn't be too proud of that heart if I were you!' A specialist in Vienna confirmed that Mahler had a heart disease: Mahler was henceforward virtually condemned to death. The gibbering monkey that mocks our life *('hinausgellt in den sussen Duft des Lebens')* had shrieked again. Can one not under-

---

[5] I don't mean to imply that Kant is in any sense a flight-from-life philosopher. Indeed, in his emphasis on how we make the world in perceiving it, he helped begin the overcoming of dualism, while his pursuit of the question, 'What is Man?' brought philosophy to work on philosophical anthropology. But such philosophical writing belongs to male capacities at the other extreme from an appropriate 'being' response to an accouchement!

stand, from this, how a man, already inclined to paranoia, could write the Third Movement of the *Ninth Symphony*, with its grisly atmosphere of sardonic, Satanic and cruel mocking 'humour'? Mahler must have felt—as a child feels—that life was full of malignant predators. The only defence one could have was to resort to magic or to hide in the cupboard—to switch the numbers of one's symphonies, to cheat paranoid demon-creatures by legerdemain, or to withdraw from life altogether. Though it is too easy to say so, for us who are not faced with such dire coincidences, the truth is that the events simply happened by chance. The paranoid 'explanation' is merely a defence mechanism, and arises from splitting—which in its turn is a way of avoiding the feeling that it was one's *own* hate that caused the outward events, like the brother's death. Insofar as Mahler was paranoid about hate in the world he had not yet learned to accept his own: in striving to accept it he had to suffer a dreadful burden of guilt.

Here we came closer to the connections between sex, violence, hate, guilt and death. The child whose hunger for love is unappeased feels that his hunger-to-be may eat up his whole world, his mother, everyone and everything about him. Thus, sexual relations between his parents as he becomes aware of them, or as he fantasies them between the imago parents, will seem full of the same hunger, and thus terribly destructive. Where the parents quarrel fiercely, this fear is deepened.

It is interesting to note that from the intervention of Freud, Mahler came to see as one of his problems the intrusion of the commonplace and of the manic idiom of 'light entertainment' into his highest moments. As Ernest Jones says,

> In the course of the talk Mahler suddenly said that he now understood why his music had always been prevented from achieving the highest rank, through the noblest passages, those inspired by the most profound emotions being spoiled by the intrusion of some commonplace melody. His father, apparently a brutal person, treated his wife very badly, and when Mahler was a young boy there was a specially painful scene between them. It became quite unbearable to the boy, who rushed away from the house. At that moment, however, a hurdy-gurdy in the street was grinding out the popular Viennese air, '*O Du liebe Augustin*'. In Mahler's opinion the conjunction of high tragedy and light amusement was from then on inextricably fixed in his mind, and the one mood inevitably brought the other on.
> *The Life and Work of Sigmund Freud* by Ernest Jones, Vol. 2

Whether or not any such actual incident was the traumatic origin of Mahler's problems as explored in his music, for him to relate it to Freud indicates that it had great symbolic importance for him.

It perhaps indicates that for Mahler such forms of grotesque manic sound were associated with the loss of all objects, and all existence security. This hate-filled, threatening and mocking moment attached itself to the ontological insecurities he was left with from childhood. 'Creative reflection' as the source of a strong identity, seems likely to have been deficient in the Mahler household. One child committed suicide, and others such as Justine and Gustav were strangely out of touch with reality and needed to sustain themselves by intense forms of identification. Gustav identified in an extreme way with his sister Justine. The father was brutal and sensual, while Gustav's problems of relationship were also much affected by witnessing in childhood a brutal love scene between a youth and a maid-servant.

> While yet a boy, he was sent to work in Prague for a time, and here occurred what he related to Alma as his worst experience. While sitting in a dark room he was made involuntary witness of a brutal love scene between servant and son of the house[6] . . . He jumped up to go to the girl's help, but she did not thank him for his pains. Instead he was soundly abused by both and sworn to secrecy. This little episode left a deep mark on his mind. Thus was further confirmed what must have been a strong unconscious identification of *pain with sex*, as exemplified in the relationship of his mother with his father. The close interaction of erotic and painful stimuli, amounting almost to inseparability, may be seen throughout the texture of his musical work.

Moreover, his mother was a cripple, and was married to a man she did not love. He was also unfaithful.

In such a situation a child would have tremendous inner conflict, certainly if his identity were as insecure as Mahler's, from infancy. Such scenes would seem like grotesque sadistic fantasies of the Primal Scene and seem to confirm a child's primitive talion fears, of the castrating mother and father, turning against him because of the menace of his curiosity.

Infant fantasies of *desired* sadistic intercourse between the parents would also seem to be confirmed by actual events. The horrible imago of the combined parents which to a child in fantasy seem to threaten annihilation by incorporation (according to Melanie Klein) would lurk under the surface of such memories, and they would seem to confirm his dread of malignancies in the world.

The vulgar tune would therefore seem to say to the child: 'You wanted this to happen. You have a libidinal attachment to this sadistic

[6] De la Grange suggests it was simply a sexual encounter in which the girl's reactions were interpreted wrongly by young Mahler.

sensuality. Be gay, for *you wanted this hate to threaten your existence.* You enjoy ugliness and hate. You gloat on destruction.' And so would rise the spectre of the horrible satisfaction of the envy of sibling-rivalry, when the brother died, combined with a deep sense of loss. Around such feelings the guilt would be bitter, and the depression accompanying it could feel like madness. It is all this that the monkey stands for, whether or not (as a matter of historic fact) there was a monkey on the hurdy-gurdy. The monkey and the commonplace tunes are continually saying to Mahler, 'man can seek to feel alive by hate and sadistic cruelty, and so threaten your existence. He can coarsely mock with manic derision your whole existence'. And what is being threatened is the idealism—that is, the child's need to preserve a good image of his parents, because his existence and his identity depend upon internalizing them as good objects. Mahler had to 'make' a good mother who was not a cripple, and who was capable of love: he had to 'make' a father who was not merely cruel, sensual, indifferent and tyrannical. He had to do this in order to make good the male and female elements of his own make-up, formed by identifying with his parents. He had to make his world perfect (the rim of the blue horizon)—and death urged this urgently on him. He had to find himself good, beneath his guilt.

As Freud discovered, Mahler was much affected by the episodes of aggression between his parents and the subsequent anxieties lay behind his impotence. Here we may link them further with his existence dread —and the way for him threats of annihilation seemed to emerge out of joy.

Since a child conceives of sex as a form of eating, and its fantasies arising from curiosity about parental sex are in consequence sadistic, it tends to fear destructive threats to be inherent in passion, in libido, in joy, itself. Hence, love and delight, because they are expressions of the needs of the hungry soul, seem to the schizoid individual threatening and dangerous: the libidinal must be renounced, and split off from the ideal. Thus, to delight in love, in one's children, even in life itself, brings the threat of destructive envy from the paranoid imagos over which the split-off hate has been projected. In these mechanisms we may see Mahler's plight. Libidinal pleasure is best avoided: it is not for him. It would be better if the love-object were not libidinally inviting. Since she is, it is safer (the individual 'unconsciously' concludes at the levels of psychosomatic meaning), to be impotent.

These mechanisms in Mahler involved splitting the libidinal from the ideal, the pure innocence of child feeling from the grossness of mature emotion (as in the *Eighth Symphony*). It involved separating music and its highest and purest standards from contact with living persons and their imperfections, and intellectual systems (Kant) from living experience (birth). Yet in the symbolism of the *Ninth* hate breaks through into the rising passion, and so has to be symbolically dealt with, in a creative way, to make survival possible—reassurance of continuing existence *in the music*.

Such terrible suffering as Mahler's, and the strain of the obsessional countermeasures he felt to be necessary against paranoid fear—the despotic tyranny at home and at work—obviously disrupted Mahler's relationship with all around him, not least with his wife. Since Mahler so feared giving in joyful love, he felt that he could only have loved his wife had she been 'ugly'. These feelings of fear and envy of the human and libidinal on the one hand were combined on the other with ruthless idealism, an idealism which sought perfection in music, and attachment to the perfect 'earth mother' of the blue horizon, detached from any real woman. Inward frozenness, deepened by the compulsive overdependence of the relationship, tended to go with split-object-relations behaviour. Alma records in her diary.

> I have such a horror of him, I'm afraid to see him come home. He fawns on Mme X., dances round Miss Y.—and here he is quite detached, the tired husband I have to care for. If he just didn't come home any more, ever! . . . We had a bitter squabble. He said he could feel that I don't love him . . . The last scene has frozen everything inside me . . . Mahler did not feel me beside him as a living being. He had his peace, his carefully prepared meals, his warm home, and an opportunity to discuss art at any time, day and night. This was all he needed, all he wanted . . .
>
> p. 35

Mahler's anguish was that he came so short of loving, in life, in terms of 'finding the other person'. This seems to have been associated, too, with a fear of relaxing standards: Mahler and Alma went to *The Merry Widow* and enjoyed it so much that 'we danced at home afterwards.' However,

> There was one passage in it that we could not remember, however hard we tried, but both of us were then too 'highbrow' to consider buying such music
>
> p. 35

—So Mahler talked to the assistant about sales of his own music, while Alma thumbed through the stacks of *Widow* potpourris until she found the passage she wanted, sang it to Mahler in the street, so he could remember it for them!

Treated so coldly, and unsatisfied by her life, confined to aridity and intellectual sternness, however, Alma obviously responded to other men —to Ossip Gabrilowitsch, *an ugly young man* (his very ugliness, Alma suggests, attracted Mahler, who 'kept telling me that there were not enough lines of suffering on my face'). Ossip declared his love to Alma:

> so I was loveable, after all . . . In the darkness Gabrilowitsch groped for my hand . . . Then the light flashed on, Mahler stood in the room, full of kindness and love, and the spook vanished . . .
>
> p. 38

But the spook of dissociated object-relations continually reappears in their lives and one can see how it is associated with Mahler's need to keep his objects 'split' so that the bad libidinal object should not 'spoil' the ideal. Meanwhile beneath everything lay the unconscious blame Mahler apportioned to Alma, for allowing their child to die. This was surely a way of denying the unbearable reality of death and escaping the problem of guilt within: Alma, too, becomes in her husband's unconscious the paranoid agent over whom he had to project his own hungry hate, because it was too threatening within:

> life . . . Ours could have been beautiful if we had not been undone by our child's death. Unconsciously he blamed me for it, and for a time we became strangers to one another, estranged by grief.

Even at times when things seemed to heal, and they could temporarily forget Mahler's heart disease, the doom would break through. They had sleepless nights, and the most harrowing time was Christmas Eve—the first without the children and in a strange country.

> Mahler did not wish to be reminded of Christmas, and I, alone and lonely, cried all day long . . .

A caller took them to a Christmas-tree party:

> The sight delivered us from ourselves. But after dinner a group of actors and actresses came and we left when one of the women, a deformed wretch, was called 'Putsi'. It had been our pet name for the dead child . . .
>
> p. 42

No wonder the *Ländler* of the Second Movement ends in sepulchral inanition! Whenever suffering seems to fade in a moment of social jollity, some menace recalls the problems of guilt and hate. The menace of split-object-relations returns: Gabrilowitsch comes to America and threatens Mahler's marriage.

Alma too had her emotional problems: she had a noble painter father *(Maler)* and an inept and nagging mother who did not understand him, and whom Alma seems to despise. So, she will take her mother's place—and tries to perform the part of good mother in Mahler's life. Both sets of parents fought terribly: the urgent desire to avoid any repetition of any such situation leads both out of the frying pan of passionate engagement into the fires of over-dependence and over-idealizing. Alma loves only 'achievement': Mahler wants an 'ideal little girl' dominated by himself, and he wants to control her as mother-as-ideal-object. The basis of this controlling idealism is in primitive fear of ambivalence and of the dangers that lurk in adult sexual love. Alma could perhaps only identify with her ('noble') father, and not with her mother: so, she loves only 'achievement', and art: the real physical living man however, despite his inadequacy, she serves as a daughter to a father. Her libidinal drives she can, however, release on an ugly man (whom her husband admires).

> Each time we met, the struggle in us was rekindled . . . but Mahler had been listening and the upshot was a big discussion . . . Having just only won over all my instincts and desires, I defended myself with spirit and conviction; soon my husband went back to bed with his faith in me restored, and I stood all night by the open window, praying for the strength to end my miserable life.   p. 46

Thus, division in the capacity of both partners for object-constancy threatens Mahler's marriage, and with this came threats to his identity and to Alma's: neither felt they could live without the other. Yet Alma yearned to love her husband, while Mahler yearned to be whole to Alma, for the 'primary goal of the libido is the object'.

Unless they could find love for one another, and in that love confirmation of identity, they probably felt unconsciously that they each would lose their identities and die, especially since they identified so closely. Yet even the love they sought was also feared, because it seemed so likely to bring deadly dangers from within, and predators from without, full of death and hate, of the kind which Mahler would associate with a brutal father attacking his mother, and with the raucous hurdy-gurdy and the ape squatting mockingly on it. The vulgar noise which he experienced so vividly and brutally during a parental quarrel became associated with his own unconscious fears of 'damaging the object', and his despair of ever 'repairing' it. No wonder Mahler set out, in recording his own inward suffering, to sing the whole earth to peace and wholeness against the raucous and vulgar noises of the gutter! Meanwhile, both he and Alma yearned for a love they did not know: and knew that to this the external world was savagely indifferent in its hate.

> Friends took me to the house of the . . . illustrator who gave the world the
> 'Gibson girl' . . . his wife, a beautiful but vacuous socialite . . . (asked me)
> in her quaint, sumptuous automobile: 'How can a beautiful woman like
> you marry an old, ugly impossible man like Mahler?'

—the world of *Vogue*—of meretricious journalism—was no less destructive and evil in 1910 than it is now![7]

> Nothing I could say of Mahler's genius, fame and triumphs brought more
> than a disdainful smile to her lips. I wanted to mention love—but broke off,
> embarrassed by the realization that he ignored me daily in the transcendent
> sense of his mission . . . It would have been quite senseless to tell Mrs
> Gibson that I was yearning in vain for my husband's love.

>> pp. 49–50

Alma was sent to a sanatorium because of exhaustion: a German
doctor prescribed dancing. There Alma met Walter Gropius, and he fell
in love with her. She left Toblach and found Mahler more amorous than
ever. But because Gropius addressed an envelope to 'Herr Direktor
Mahler' her husband received a passionate letter to Alma, 'to ask me
for your hand' as he put it. Alma and her husband then poured their
hearts out, to one another and Mahler

> for the first time in his life, felt that there was such a thing as an inner
> obligation toward the person with whom one has, after all, been joined
> together. He suddenly felt guilty.
>> p. 53

But Alma is wrong: Mahler had already discovered the capacity for
'inner obligation' in his *Ninth* and *Tenth Symphonies*: he needed only
to come back to living reality with the knowledge. In the crisis Alma
came to feel 'I had the elemental feeling that I could never leave Mahler.
When I told him so, his face became transfigured and he clung to me
every second of the day and night, ecstatic with love'.

His letter, which she quotes, is significant: it speaks of things enacted
in the *Ninth Symphony*:

> My breath of life! . . . You took pity on me, glorious one, but the demons
> have punished me again, for thinking of myself and not of you . . . I can't
> move from your door; I'd like to stand there until I've heard the sweet
> sound of your living and breathing . . . Every beat of my heart is *for you* . . .
>> p. 53

They slept in adjoining rooms, but the doors had to be left open; 'he
had to hear me breathe'

---

[7] Cf. How it destroyed Scott-Fitzgerald. Of course the latter 'used' the *Vogue*-world
for his own self-destruction.

in his excessive dread of losing me—of having already lost me, perhaps, he often lay on the floor of the hut and wept. For thus, he said, he was nearer to the Earth.

p. 53

Yet Alma knows, inwardly, that her marriage was 'no marriage': that 'my own life was utterly unfulfilled'. 'He knew it as well as I . . . To spare him, we both played the comedy to the end.' The robust wooing of Gropius had taught her what love could have been.[8]

Yet Mahler remained the pivot of her existence!

The ironic comedy is echoed by both the sublimity, and the bitter sardonic elements, of the *Ninth Symphony*, at this time complete in draft form, and being scored.

It was at this point Mahler consulted Freud, who said to him sternly 'How can a man in your condition tie a young woman to him?'

> I know your wife . . . She loved her father and can seek and love only his type. Your age, which you are afraid of, is just what attracts your wife. Don't worry about it. And you yourself loved your mother and are looking for her type in every woman. Your mother was careworn and ailing—and that, unconsciously, is how you want your wife.

For a time Mahler's potency, it is claimed, was restored: but he was never to know a full love relationship, for soon afterwards he sickened and died: the heart of which we are so conscious in his music became still.

In truth it might have taken many years of therapy for Mahler to have become fully capable of relationship. But doesn't Freud's attitude, based on his sense of the primary importance of the sexual element, not seem today crude and even destructive? From Alma's account there were great satisfactions in her life with Mahler, of a kind Freud did not, however, value. Yet, it seems, something positive came from Freud's intervention—at least Mahler began to accept his responsibilities in love ('every beat of my heart is for you') and he overcame the strange barrier between his inward creative disciplines and his real living enough to dedicate his *Eighth Symphony* to Alma. In this he began to accept 'the object' as a real woman—not the earth, or the mother, or Holy Mary, merely projected over Alma, but a real living partner to whom one has responsibilities. From this inward achievement we—his listeners—can draw psychic sustenance for it is in part the suffering this exacted, and the courage by which the growth of the reality sense was accepted, that makes Mahler's later music of such overwhelming beauty.

[8] She records a night when Gropius was waiting under a bridge near their home. She told Mahler, who brought him in, and ordered her to choose. Gropius was put on a train in the morning—and sent her a telegram from every station down the line!

However, in order to find the 'other' as we have seen, one must find oneself—and accept both one's ego-weakness, and the envy and hate in oneself that arise from this.

To a Mahler this problem is bedevilled by the inability to tolerate hate in himself because he could not tolerate the hate in his brutal and vulgar father, while he lacks an adequate conviction of 'being' from the mother.[9] As I have said, he virtually had to mother and father himself, and to re-create his own male and female elements. At first dissociated— tenuous and idealized on the one hand, or raucous and disruptive on the other, these gradually become humanized.

A relevant discussion of Mahler's parental problems, in relation to his development of the capacity to love, is to be found in an article by Robert Still on 'Gustav Mahler and Psychoanalysis' (*The American Imago*, Vol. 17, 1960, pp. 217–40). Still points out that psychoanalytical interest in Mahler arose because of his meeting with Freud, and has been centred round his Oedipal problems and his 'Holy Mary complex'. It was too early, says Still, for Freud to explore the deeper problem of Mahler's identification with the mother. Still uses in his discussion some remarks of Winnicott in *Psychoanalysis and Contempory Thought*:

> whereas the earlier work of psychoanalysts dwelt on the conflict between love and hate, especially in the three-body or triangular situation, Melanie Klein more especially has developed the idea of conflict in the simple two-body relationship of the infant to the mother, conflict arising out of the destructive ideas that accompany the love-impulse . . . destructive ideas unaffected by concern . . .

Still tries to relate Mahler's development to his discovery of concern, and the development of a person's sense of 'value' in complex with the capacity for guilt-feeling. Still believes that

> Analytically, at the time of the *Eighth Symphony* he was just beginning to move out of the 'paranoid' stage into that of the 'depressive'.

Up to the *Eighth Symphony*, Still suggests, 'Mahler's life had been held together by an obsessional system which controlled persecutory fantasies'.

> But from the *Eighth Symphony* onward the position began to change. Henceforward there is less aggression, less sadism, and more idealism . . . the collapse (of his obsessional system) heralded the appearance of massive guilt. 'I have lived wrongly' was his repeated cry at this time.

[9] See my *Sylvia Plath and the Problem of Existence* in which I discuss how she set out to mother herself.

This sense of guilt was certainly linked with his deepened sense of the 'otherness' of Alma, as we have seen from her comments on the scene over Gropius.

Still feels, from Winnicott's remarks, that Mahler's problem was less to be explained in terms of the triangular (Oedipus) problem, but as one of identity.

> Why for instance did Mahler forbid his wife to compose, and make it a condition of his marriage that she gave it up, even though she was an accomplished musician and had written more than 100 songs?

She was in many ways obliterated by her husband. After Gropius courted her

> We spoke to each other as we had never spoken before. But the whole truth could not be spoken. My boundless love had lost by degrees some of its strength and warmth; and now that my eyes had been opened by the impetuous assaults of a youthful lover . . . I knew that my marriage was no marriage and that my own life was utterly unfulfilled. I concealed all this from him, and although he knew it as well as I did, we played out the comedy to the end to spare his feelings . . . I could have found in my music a complete cure for this state of things, but he had forbidden it, and now I dragged my hundred Songs with me wherever I went—*like a coffin in which I dared not look.*
>
> (my italics)

The remark 'we played out the comedy' surely makes nonsense of Reik's confident report on Freud's contributions: 'They removed his doubts and inhibitions, restored his capability for love and strengthened his self-confidence.' Yet in a sense Mahler did become increasingly aware that his wife was a separate person:

> whereas Mahler had ignored his wife before, he now heaped her with presents and became extremely angry if he thought she was being ill-treated or insulted in any way.
>
> Still, p. 237

—and in the coma before his death he repeated her name hundreds of times (as well as Mozart's).

But the truth seems to be that Mahler's was a deeper problem of identity and existence than Freud could at the time comprehend, because it belonged to the schizoid problem, into which we have only gained insights since his time. For instance, Mahler so identified with his sister that it was to him virtually as if he *was* her or 'was actually part of his sister'. Still suggests that for him the discovery of his separate identity was 'shattering' at the very beginning of his life:

73

The wounding blow which must have contributed so much to the disturbance of Mahler's psyche was that his mother gave birth to another son soon after his own birth. Mahler was born in July 1860 and his brother who died at age 12 was born sometime in 1861 . . . but even if we leave out of account the probability of his sudden weaning at a very early stage, it is safe to assume that another pregnancy so soon, with Mahler's consequent neglect by his mother in a poor home, would have aroused the most negative feelings at a very much earlier date than children are usually called upon to face these things . . .

Still goes on to ponder whether his confusion with his sister,

reflects the dismay at the discovery that he was a separate entity from his mother, that instinctual disaster from the shattering of 'primary identification', whether this disaster was not sufficiently compensated for and lived through the oral stage, because of the infant brother . . . are matters for conjecture.

Still, p. 239

I would perhaps say that I began my exploration of Mahler's existence problems before I knew that he had been treated by Freud, and long before I came across Robert Still's paper. It was both astonishing and gratifying to find the latter thinking so much in the same way about the origins of the meaning of Mahler's music, in terms of the psychodynamics of schizoid states. Still's exploration of the problems of identity, I believe, confirm our first impressions that in his music Mahler was seeking *to preserve an identity against forces which threatened to disrupt it, or annihilate it*.

But Still does not quite pursue the psychodynamic approach far enough. He is inclined to explain Mahler's predicament in terms of sibling jealousy and hate directed at the mother ('negative feelings'). The 'shattering' of 'primary identification' is not an 'instinctual disaster': it must, after all, happen to all of us: so here we need further recourse to Winnicott, and object-relations theory.

In Mahler's early life, there would seem to have been a combination of factors which left a sense of the vulnerability of his identity: his mother was quite probably unable to 'go over' to primary maternal preoccupation successfully, so left her infants with a profound sense of weaknesses in the *being*. This threat to existence could have been exacerbated by the arrival of another sibling very soon after the birth of Gustav, and later by the loss of the rival sibling in adolescence, with consequent effects on the mother's capacity to 'confirm' her child at an impressionable age. There would seem also to have been a failure of 'psychic weaning' towards disillusion and the discovery of the reality of the Self and the world.

If we accept Winnicott's theory, this might well leave an individual with a weak female element, and an impulse in consequence to deal with life by 'pseudo male doing', and intellectualization. This perhaps we can see in Mahler's obsessional preoccupation with technical perfection, and even in the meticulousness of his composing and his compulsive disciplines. But, as Winnicott and Guntrip suggest, because of the fear of the weakness in the female element of being, a schizoid individual can tend to project his fear of his own female element over woman and attack it in her. Mahler's attempt to control his sister, to control his wife and to deny her creativity, could be manifestations of this—as perhaps Still recognizes when he talks of Mahler's 'obsessional control of the female factor'. By contrast, in his music, Mahler is seeking the true self, by seeking to put himself in truth with his female element: he had to both mother and wean himself, there, because real woman had proved so unreliable: and he had to come to love the female element as well as the harsh and aggressive male element.

From an analysis of changes made in the story for *Das Klagende Lied* Still concludes that Mahler had some strong unconscious motive to 'mask and control an intense fear and hostility in his mother and sister relationships'. He sees Mahler as intensely hostile to his mother while also seeking to proclaim 'I am the mother'—to 'act for her'.

Hatred of this kind, however, is the manifestation of an excessive need for the object, so we have to try to understand it in terms of Mahler's intrapsychic dynamics and capacities to relate to the object. The fantasy attack on the mother's body seen by Melanie Klein as a predominant element in the infant's inner world is a manifestation of the desire to survive, to empty the mother and become 'full'. It is thus a manifestation of primitive hate. Where the female element is projected and attacked this too is a complexity whose origins are in the fear of inner weakness, so that the attack is really an attempt to control or destroy a weakness that threatens psychic viability from within.

In Mahler's *Klagende Lied* the essential point would seem to be that marriage to the Queen involves a murder: that is, to fulfil love for the object must involve some destruction of an aspect of the self—and that aspect is identified with a male rival. This could possibly symbolize the sibling who arrived too soon after Mahler's birth, and who died, both bringing consequent threats to the identity. Marriage with the object means 'Sorrow and Woe': at the wedding feast it is the King himself who plays on the bone flute and makes it utter its tale of fratricide. Having taken the place of the father, the son bitterly lays the blame for the death of the brother at the door of his own envious need to claim the mother—and to survive himself. The hero become King has also become the scornful and guilty father, whose hate has threatened his own existence. What I believe Mahler was symbolizing in this legend was the disastrous death-circuit of his inward dynamics: he needed to embrace the female element, but felt that this could only bring threats to the identity, since it seemed to involve treachery to his own false self, and to involve him in a whole tradition of rivalries, with his brother who died, and with his father, in return for which he expected talion revenge. So in the end all is death and chaos: 'The Queen collapses . . . the castle walls begin to crumble.'

The identity was threatened with collapse because to find and relate to the object could not be achieved without disastrous consequences to the 'male element doing', with all its obsessional compulsions, which held the identity together. This was prophetic, in that as Mahler discovered his own reality, and that of his wife, he began to collapse, and then died.

One can agree with much in Robert Still, about the way Mahler projected the image of his split-off ideal mother over his wife, but I find it difficult to follow his apparent belief in Mahler's 'mother hostility', and 'negative feelings' as a mainspring of his psychodynamic life and his creativity. Mahler seems to be doing something much more positive. Still says,

> The only way a child of this age can deal with the wish to destroy his mother and her children is to identify himself with her in giving birth . . .

I think there is no justification for this in Kleinian theory, while it also seems to me to fall short of an adequate explanation of Mahler's existence problems. We are not, after all, trying to diagnose Mahler's problem for therapeutic purposes, a point with which it is perhaps worth dealing. Jack Diether, in an article also called 'Mahler and Psychoanalysis' seems to find it likely to offend some to call such a genius 'neurotic'. He discusses Freud's phrase:

> '. . . the symptomatic façade of his obsessional neurosis'? Can that be compatible, some may ask, with '. . . this man of genius'? Anyone perceptively acquainted with the psychological studies of such undisputed men of genius as Leonardo da Vinci and Ludwig von Beethoven can answer that in the affirmative.
>
> p. 4

Diether's view of psychological states and of psychoanalysis, however, is traditionally American. Mahler was 'one of modern life's most notable victims', 'a man of tremendous intellect crushed by the weight of our modern conflicts'. When he met Freud he met one who was bringing the world

the new scientific weapon of psychoanalysis, with which (mankind) might in due time complete its rapidly accelerating conquest . . . even of its own primitive irrational foundation.

The effect of the work of Klein, Winnicott and Fairbairn has, I believe, been to penetrate beneath this somewhat deterministic view of the psychology of culture. Today it is possible to see geniuses such as those whom Diether mentions as having existence problems *such as we all have*, though they have them in more urgent life-or-death forms. In this they are not 'victims of modern life' but rather individuals who have not been able to complete processes of psychic growth in infancy in a facilitating environment: the original weakness almost certainly being in the processes of primary identification by which one becomes a human being at all. They are thus forced to ask, with all the energy of adult intelligence and sensibility, *What is the point of life?* They may not be able to cope with normal everyday reality, and relationship, because they have not yet solved this problem, which is integral with the question 'What am I?' But this, as Winnicott, belongs to those questions which are every man's.[10]

Psychoanalysis in the face of this is by no means such a 'scientific instrument' as Diether suggests. As Winnicott indicates, even though it cures patients insofar as it removes barriers to their psychosomatic functioning by the re-experience of togetherness in therapy, it may not even have begun to answer the question *What is the point of life?*

Thus it is no use saying, as Still says:

There is no doubt that Mahler lived over again in his symphonies (particularly numbers 5 and 6) the infantile fury against his mother, and that he used his father, an uninhibited and brutal man, as sanction and culprit for his functional and intellectual brilliance in these monumental works . . .

p. 229

This is to 'explain away' in a reductive way the pursuit of fundamental problems of existence as though they were merely infantile problems which one could solve for ever, once one 'grew up'. Still is using the Kleinian concept of the fantasy assault on the mother far too crudely, and explaining creativity away in terms of earlier and more primary impulses.

[10] Viktor Frankl also insists, in *Psychotherapy and Existentialism*, that it is not 'sick' to have existence problems, but it is this that makes us human.

Later Still says 'Mahler sometimes gives a horrifying sense of ultimate emptiness . . . which makes him peculiarly significant to us'—a much more profound observation, which draws our attention to the essential *schizoid* problem—and our universal existence problem of nothingness which Mahler explores.

The fantasy attack on the mother by an infant, after all, is a desperate manifestation of the urge to survive—that is, it is a manifestation of the hunger of primitive hate, expressing needs to be. Where the mother has failed to provide a sense of being, as when perhaps a rival sibling takes away her 'preoccupation', or where she recovers her self-interest too rapidly (as when grieving for a dead child, or turning to a new baby) then the child suffers a threat to his existence which impels him to employ fantasy, omnipotence and magic, as manifestations of hate. But at first he only wants to 'empty' her by taking her into himself through love, to fill himself and find confirmation of his existence: her withdrawal, interpreted as rejection, may be interpreted as meaning that love is harmful. Here we have the root of the schizoid problem, associated with the roots of envy. The basic schizoid fear is that love will empty and bring loss of existence, at a time of close identification with the mother.

Later the problem becomes one of *filling in* the emptiness caused in the mother by the fantasies of incorporation: and this is the root of concern. Depression is the effect of unconscious guilt over the fear that our hate may have emptied the object. And since we depend on the object, we fear that this emptying by hate may bring our own annihilation: so out of this ruth is born, and the impulse towards reparation that is the spring of all morality.

As I hope to show, Mahler's *Ninth Symphony* enacts and works on the schizoid fear that out of love comes the threat of loss of existence. At first this threat seems from without—one is being punished for loving: as Still implies, this belongs to the paranoid-schizoid position. Later Mahler discovers how it is possible to find this threat as hate which is within oneself: the First Movement is a coming to terms with the urge to survive become hate, which is gradually found to be *weakness*: it is found to be the *female element*, or that unborn part of oneself *which belongs to being that the mother should have given but did not*. It is not that he identifies with the mother in birth, but re-discovers primal togetherness.

This explains the marvellous tenderness which Mahler achieves, even at the heart of the feeling of cosmic emptiness, even through the transformation of hate. As Boys says of the 'hate' theme at the end of the first movement:

> it is as if its significance had utterly changed and what had appeared as terrifying is in reality, or when seen in another light, a comforter . . .

What Mahler makes in fact is a 'schizoid diagnosis' of his own problem: the violent hunger of hate, when looked at as an existence problem, is seen only as a manifestation of a pitiful regressed libidinal ego in need of confirmation: it is really love in need of resolution. It is only the 'female element of being' which yearns *to be*, and its poignancy is of a mouth to mother, with the consequent terror of nothingness. To transmute hate into love is to overcome nothingness.

We can also, of course, reverse this and say that the 'emptying' hunger directed at the mother in envy, threatening to obliterate the whole cosmos as object, can come to be seen as the expression of a desperate need to be confirmed. Once it is known as such, it is also seen to have the latent capacity to make reparation and to find gratitude. Gratitude is achieved by both making good the object and making whole the self, and it goes with the sense of 'having meaningfully been'. It is exactly this that is achieved in Mahler's symphony by the resolution brought about in the 'hate' theme towards the end of the First Movement:

EXAMPLE 3

Ninth Symphony, pp. 58–9

This is not the only problem, however (so the symphony cannot end there). This transformation achieves a degree of inner ontological security, by 'including' destructive aspects of the 'male element'—all the problems associated with the father, which emerge from the development of passion. The male element, largely derived from the father, must be understood, learnt, and integrated as an element of the personality. As we have seen, this creates for Mahler a problem of a feeling of having within him a destructive vulgarity and commonplace raucousness which threatens his higher flights of soul and emotion. The next problem now is to test the inner security found by recognition of one's weakest needs in the wider contest of life's reality. Mahler's early experiences and his feelings about his father are associated with a 'pseudo-male' element, and forms of 'doing' which are a false way of dealing with the world—which in its turn also presents a great deal of hate and 'false male doing' at us, from mocking monkeys to aggressive bugles and drums. As Still says, the father can be experienced in the 'bitter' music:

> The ironic and bitter medium of military music is suffused with cruelty and masochism. How he hates those imaginary soldiers who rape and pillage the earth and how incredible to reflect that these imaginary activities became true only three years after his death! At time irony, banality, and the sinister are so intermingled that the listener can find it hard to get his emotional bearings and perhaps Mahler can be criticized on this account ...

Could we not put it in a different way? Every individual in the modern world finds it so difficult to 'get his bearings', because 'false male doing' in collective schizoid manifestations in man at large, have caused such catastrophic devastation.[11] Mahler in his vision, as one concerned with the deepest possibilities of existence, saw this before the worst consequences came. If we put it this way, we surely need to criticize our civilization rather than Mahler? And to see how penetrating his perception is, of the underlying truth, ('The faults . . . lie . . . in ourselves . . .')

If we find it hard to get our emotional bearings when listening to Mahler, this itself merely registers that ours is a world in which it is almost impossible to organize one's sensibility to reflect or encompass whole human experience, so fragmented has it become. Mahler's creative efforts to overcome this problem by 'male doing' were themselves heroic:

> As musical and artistic director in opera, he had raised the art of operative production to unheard-of standards of integration and perfection, and

---

[11] 'As is the case of the individual neurotic, the compartmentalization [of man] became more and more rigid until it approached the point—1 August 1914—when it was to collapse altogether.' Rollo May in *Existence*, p. 22. Mahler's horrible military noises presage this collapse.

introduced modern principles of staging that are still being developed today. As a composer, he had extended the classical principles of symphonic development in new and unlooked-for directions, and provided aesthetic impulse for the revolutionary new music that succeeded him.

Diether

For this effectiveness he had his father to thank to some degree. Still perhaps tends to have too negative an attitude to the effect of identification with the father—his view seems derived from the Freudian preoccupation with Oedipus problems. Still sees the hurdy-gurdy, which figured so largely in Mahler's afternoon with Freud, as a symbol of the parents in coition. This seems somehow too mechanical.

> The hurdy-gurdy itself symbolizes the mother, albeit sarcastically and ironically, while the man turning the handle is his father . . . Henceforth he would use his father as an agent who would play his fantasies out with him, and in this way he would be protected both against his frightening heterosexual fantasies, and against his homosexual wishes. And his parents should be kept grinding away all day, this should be his defence and the basis of his obsessional system . . . History does not relate whether or not there was a monkey on the top.

Still also tries to link Mahler's tic in his right leg (which Mitchell suggests may have been a sympathetic imitation of his mother's limp) with the castration complex which underlay his impotence. But this is surely to cling to a somewhat reductive mode of Freudian interpretation of symbols? Because he clings too persistently to Freudian theory Still fails to hear the meaning of the music itself. He treats it as if it spoke of primary sexual or Oedipal problems. The biographical facts are only of value if they illuminate the existence problems explored in Mahler's music. Mahler's flight as a child was from a sadistic scene in which his capacity to identify with his father as a positive source of inward strength was threatened. He saw the father doing to his mother what he secretly wished to do (in terms of Oedipal feeling)—that is to 'go for her' sadistically. The fear and excitement are transferred (in his memory) to the barrel organ which symbolizes the father's misuse of the mother —he plays on her, and his contempt, and the sensual coarseness of sexual hunger, are spoken of by the vulgar music. To a child the assault would seem like his Oedipal fantasies of the combined parents in coition. He feels excited by this, but since the activity is so full of threats to his existence, because of incorporated dangers, he is terrified by talion fear. All these feelings attach themselves to crude music.

At such a time, a child may be in what Melanie Klein called 'the homosexual position' of desiring to displace his father with the mother, but the essential problem is that he fears that the aggression aroused in him may annihilate him. Melanie Klein says of her patient Fritz:

> As little Fritz consciously accepted and absorbed the knowledge of the Father's sexual role, his Oedipus complex became fully conscious, bringing out a flood of aggressive fantasies in this hitherto very unaggressive little boy . . . Oral, anal and genital sadism and general aggressiveness were exposed against the father and symbolic father figures in his fantasies, followed by clear primal scene fantasies in which Fritz showed himself to be involved in identifications with and displacings of, both parents . . . in the form of a fear of his father's penis and of castration. It is evident that the child must be a victim, not aggressor, in the face of his own anxiety and guilt. Finally it emerged that it was anxiety over his mother's fate in the sadistic hetero-sexual situation that dictated his flight into the homosexual position. For ultimately the fear of the castrating mother emerged from behind the fear of the punishing father, related to the child's own hate and aggression against his mother which he turned back on himself.
> From the account of Melanie Klein's work by H. Guntrip in *Personality Structure and Human Interaction*, p. 97

Fear of the 'castrating mother' may have been the cause of Mahler's marital failure. But, more significantly for his work, the hurdy-gurdy with its monkey represents the combined parents and all the threat to his existence inherent in their sexual life. The ape that grins and represents animal urges, and the raucous noise of mechanical music, both threaten nothingness and meaninglessness. They menace all that security which belongs to 'female element being' and creativity. Because he witnessed the surprising scene of sex with the servant, Mahler associated sex with dangers to existence in the aggressive assertiveness of the male element; and yet also with the dangers of annihilation through incorporation, in the yearning and emotional vulnerability of the female element: the masochistic desire to be taken.

So, wherever Mahler turns to find confirmation of his existence, whether he turns to the female elements of being, or the male element of doing in its fully libidinal role, to sexual passion, to gaiety, to identifying with mother or father—what mocks him at every turn is the hurdy-gurdy jeer of the combined parents and memories of his infantile involvement in sadistic intercourse that seemed to threaten him with nothingness, by hate.

Since it is intolerable to bear this conflict within, he tends to split off the sadistic and aggressive element—the hungry 'mouth ego'—and to project it over the ape, which seems at times to be a paranoid hallucination (like Mahler's own face which he once saw in the wall menacing him). As we shall see, much in his music is directed at exorcizing this spectre, which is fundamentally the spectre of annihilation.

These insights into how the ape relates to his problems of male and female explain many features to which Still draws attention. For instance, the male element in Gustav came to be attached in childhood to the barracks of Inglau where as a child he used to memorize the bugle calls, 'storing up bad material for a symphonist worried about the universe'. In his fantasies the soldiers came to take their part either in 'brutality' or 'martyrdom', identified with the father or mother respectively. These conflicts were the *Fifth* and *Sixth Symphonies*—and reconciled in the *Ninth*.

If we follow Still's view, however, we are likely to become involved in the kind of psychoanalytical approach which often tends to reduce art to a defensive activity—against primitive or infantile fears. The hurdy-gurdy element for him is a 'defence' and the 'basis of an obsessional system', so that 'the bad parents, associated with the hurdy-gurdy, must be kept grinding away all the time to protect him from his own sexual and hostile fantasies.' It is true that Mahler seems unable to pursue joy or love for very long without encountering the raucous destructiveness of this element, or hate threatening him. But what we become aware of, surely, is the immense positive effort and achievement in his work, of *sweetening* and *transforming* raucousness and hate. Here it helps, I believe, if instead of being transfixed by the sexual problem we examine further the more complex elements of identity, of male and female element. Here we encounter problems of how, in an individual suffering from deep inward insecurity, it is difficult to maintain integration. Since the root of the insecurity is in a deficiency of 'female element being', the female aspects of the personality present the greatest difficulties. These inner problems affect the person's attitude to the external world, and the 'other'. Where the area of inner being is weak an individual often finds it most difficult to reconcile the object in her libidinal capacity, with the object in her ideal aspects. So, we encounter deep splits in an individual's attitude to woman. In Mahler we often encounter the problem of the split-off ideal object. In his music, Mahler strove to overcome what we may call (after Freud) his 'Holy Mary' syndrome. He sought at first to serve the 'eternal feminine' in his music, and yet tended in life to obliterate his real woman. The problem underlying both, surely, was his difficulty in accepting his own vulnerable 'female element'?

Inevitably, his creative struggle, meant that in pursuit of integration, he was bound to suffer because he had to accept that both female element vulnerability, and the 'monkey' savagery of 'false male doing' (in hate), were within himself, while the consequences of their meeting might be disastrous. Yet he sought a true solution, by accepting his weakness, his need for being, the hunger of his regressed ego, his need for mothering, and his need to embrace 'female element being', and include it in his personality.

It is possible for such a truly human solution to be successful, for, as with the child, the discovery of the humanness of the real parents modifies and relieves primitive anxiety, because the real parents are less terrible, than the imago parents, however unreliable they may have been. In coming to terms with the reality of the real parents as they have been internalized an individual is, of course, coming to terms with his own human nature. Mahler's path was the path of finding, in anguish, one's true human qualities.

This is Mahler's progress—and so he comes to be able to relate to a world discovered as more real, from a self felt to be more real. As he 'finds the object' as real he becomes himself more integrated, and his music comes to speak of more universal existence problems, rather than of a world distorted by subjective needs to split and project.

Robert Still sees that a process of this kind takes place in Mahler's music:

> Donald Mitchell has given a searching account in his book on the *Third Symphony*, of how Mahler as a young man distilled his own version of Nietzsche's philosophy into this symphony, his acceptance of the world 'whole' both in its joy and its 'suffering', embracing the concept that if Man wants 'joy' he must accept 'suffering'. In all Mahler's symphonic work which apart from some *lieder* means all his work, we find the mother symbol, usually the 'Earth', but occasionally as in the *Eighth*, the 'creator Spiritus', or as in the *Fourth* 'Vienna' he varies the symbol. Only the unfinished *Tenth* is different, and here probably for the first as well as for the last time the music seems to be written direct to his wife, she is personalized direct and there is no symbolization except in so far as she herself is symbolizing the mother. Here at last we sense a music which links the infantile with the adult, probably a characteristic of all really great music.

I shall try to show how I feel Mahler 'finds the object' and makes reparation in the *Ninth Symphony*. What is involved is a magnificent completion of the 'depressive position' as a stage in the developing sense of being real in a real world. Mahler is able to find true concern for the consequences of one's hate in the world, through re-enacting of 'encounter'.

But, of course, to relinquish splitting, omnipotence, magic and projection can expose an individual to the most appalling threats to his existence and even to his sanity. Still quotes Mitchell,

'The state of mind in which the *Tenth Symphony* was composed must have approximated very closely to a private hell'.[12] And Mahler has left a very convincing confirmation of this in the shape of his scribbled outbursts and exclamations on the manuscript. Third Movement *('Purgatorio')* Compassion! O God! O God, why hast thou forsaken me? Death! Transfiguration! Fourth Movement title page: The devil leads me in a dance . . . Madness seizes me. Accursed! Demolish me that I may forget my being! That I may cease to exist, that I may . . . End of movement (muffled drum): None but you knows what it signifies! Ah! Ah! Ah! Fare thee well, my lyre! Farewell, Farewell, Farewell. Ah well—Ah Ah. Fifth Movement, Finale: To live for thee! to die for thee! Almschi!'

An interesting point here is that this is the kind of material from which significant form in art originally stems. It is the basic emotional content of the work, or rather its scribbled reflection, before it is taken over to be expressed and elaborated in the 'plastique' of sound.

The title *'Purgatorio'* suggests an attempt by Mahler to rid himself of his internalized bad parents who are persecuting him inside, and thus to effect a psychological change. The cry, 'O God! O God, why hast thou forsaken me' preceded by 'Compassion!' and followed by 'Death!' 'Transfiguration!' suggests that life on one psychological level is shattered, that a change is imminent, and that Mahler has projected the 'process of change' on to Death, and its 'result' on to 'transfiguration', a kind of manic state. The demand for 'compassion' conceals the expectation of punishment and thus the confession of guilt, while the feeling of being deserted by God, also suggests a lessening of the persecutory super-ego coupled with a great fear of the sense of internal responsibility which this may bring.

'The devil leads me in a dance', 'madness seizes me', and 'Accursed', are suggestive of conflict between id and super-ego, he is suffering deeply for his attacks on his mother, his appalling guilt at last breaks through in the cry 'demolish me that I may forget my being! that I may cease to exist that I may . . .'

Robert Still

In the *Ninth* we experience thus with Mahler the most extreme sense of guilt and loss, and fear of extinction, in the agonized quest for reparation. In the *Tenth* the experience of the threat of loss of existence is almost unbearable: and in it Mahler combines the recognition of mortality with intense gratitude—the ultimate of which he had seen in

[12] Footnote in original: Some notes on Mahler's *Tenth Symphony* by Donald Mitchell: *The Musical Times*, December 1955, p. 656.

the death of the fireman in New York, who had sought to put out the flames of hate by such selflessness that he had died.

The muffled drum, and the cry to his wife 'None but you knows what it signifies' does in fact refer to an incident in New York when Mahler and his wife watched a funeral procession from the windows of their flat. A fireman had died in an heroic rescue attempt.

Alma writes, 'The scene brought tears to our eyes and I looked anxiously at Mahler's window. But he too was leaning out and his face was streaming with tears. The brief roll of the muffled drums impressed him so deeply that he used it in the *Tenth Symphony*.'

However, in the setting under discussion the muffled drums symbolize Mahler's willingness to sacrifice himself for his mother and wife, to die heroically to save them from himself. Thus are his love, hate and guilt, jointly revealed, and in his concluding outbursts he shows how great is his love and how much the funeral procession of the heroic fireman meant to him. It is likely that the very fact that the hero was a fireman meant much to Mahler, since the aim of firemen is to extinguish the consuming flames and save objects from destruction .

As Melanie Klein says:

In extreme cases, feelings of guilt drive people towards sacrificing themselves completely to a cause, or to their fellow beings, and may lead to fanaticism. We know, however, that some people risk their own lives in order to save others, and this is not necessarily of the same order. It is not so much guilt which might be operative in such cases as the capacity for love, generosity, and *identification with the endangered fellow being . . .*
Our Adult World and its Roots in Infancy, p. 12

Mahler identified with the dead fireman hero, who had taken the ultimate path towards love and generosity, and had purged all his guilt. Through such suffering Mahler 'found the object', as a real person: and found a way to 'die for her' by making reparation through his suffering. In the great sigh at the end of the *Tenth Symphony* we realize that death no longer matters—he has finally solved the problem of establishing an invulnerable sense of having really existed and a gratitude for this which death can no longer threaten to extinguish. In this achievement there was the essence of true tragedy.

Concluding, Mahler gives three sighs of Ah, and then he writes, 'Fare thee well my lyre' ('lyre' was a nickname for his wife) then 'Ah well' then two sighs and for the Fifth Movement he writes, 'To live for thee! to die for thee! Almschi!'

The fact that in this particular jumble he includes his wife's name is significant, the more so because he repeated *her name hundreds of times in coma before* his death: the fact that he called out 'Mozart' twice at the very last, though superficially incongruous, is nevertheless perfectly apt, for Mozart's music is the finest flower of the age of beauty, and beauty is akin to love. The reason why what there is of the *Tenth Symphony* is so good, and close to this, the reason why Mahler, though desperately anxious, preserved his love for his wife to the last, is because through death he atoned for his unconscious hostility against her, through death he saved and restored her, and through death he at last linked his personal with his artistic life since the *Tenth Symphony* is the expression of all this.

His wife, his music, love, beauty and guilt, are all very closely linked in his mind at the last, which clearly shows the integration possible to him, had it not been conditioned on the loss of his own life. But once his dormant guilt had been aroused by various means, culminating in his wife telling him the real state of affairs, a tragedy was inevitable, since all the guilt in respect of the fantasied attacks on his mother's body, which, under his obsessional system had been held at bay for so long, suddenly turned against him when the system was shattered.

While Still is correct here about the tragedy, I cannot help feeling he is wrong about the hate turning on himself. Though this interpretation seems 'realistic' it seems to me something of a false comfort—an attempt to analyse away the truths of bodily existence. Mahler was dying anyway, he was not 'psychologically consumed from within'. He was simply mortal: his music could not save him, nor could Freud then, nor could psychoanalysis now.

As a physical being he was dying anyway: there need be no suggestion that his psychic state killed him, or that, if his psychic state had been amended, he might not have died. All he could do in his memoir was to reach a subjective reconciliation with the fact of imminent death, a universal problem, the tragic problem of finding a meaning that transcends one's nothingness.

Once one has seen this, so many 'psychological' explanations seem merely sentimental. It seems sentimental to imply, as Diether does, that Mahler's heart disease was psychosomatic.

His very heart condition, a functional disease, was possibly psychosomatically induced as a final means of escape from this unbearable biological vs. moral dilemma. At the very least it would excuse him from active coitus; if, even in abstinence, the dilemma were still intolerable, it would kill him. Angina pectoris is described, for instance, as 'a paroxysmal affection characterized by severe pain radiating from the heart'—an almost exact somatic anchoring, perhaps, of the feeling described in his youth, *'Ich hab' ein gluehend Messer in meiner Brust'*. In this disease there is 'a sense of impending death, and frequently there is a fatal termination'.

p. 9

It is sentimental, too, surely, to reduce Mahler's achievements to the expression of 'regret' or 'world-weariness', or to see these as a longing to 'lose consciousness'—as if he sought some form of schizoid suicide:

> In a sense the apparent imminence of death was a further expressive release. The unconscious longing for death expressed in his reality. Death is more omnipresent in these works, and more bitter for its proximity. At the same time life is more actively longed for and less feared, since it is now an impossibility anyway. 'In Mahler's last compositions,' says Reik, 'desperate hunger for life and utter weariness, the wish to lose one's consciousness and the last clarity, fight one another.' 'Regret' is not, as Desmond Shawe-Taylor claims, a special characteristic of the *Tenth Symphony*, but is spread out over the whole period. Adoration seems to disappear altogether, along with the rest of the Catholic symbology.
>
> Diether, p. 8

Mahler may have written on the score of the *Tenth*, 'My God, why hast thou forsaken me?' But his achievement, which we are only beginning to understand, was to find a triumphant and positive gladness to have lived. He accepts that one only has a life ended by death, but sees it lived in the quest of the whole object, whose independent existence can be recognized, as the focus of love. If the 'other' as a real woman, then the creative effects of 'encounter' can generate a deep sense of meaning in life. As Diether says:

> The words *'Fuer dich leben, fuer dich sterben'* accompany in both cases the same melodic phrase near the close of the Fifth Movement *(Adagio)*, to which they would actually be sung . . .
> . . . it is consistent with Mahler's compulsive characteristics that he scribbles in the words on *both* pages. After a few dark echoes of this motif, the symphony ends with a sudden passionate upsurge (probably intended for the violins), under which he wrote the word 'Almschi!', and then a subsiding again into silence.

Mahler's amazing achievement was to 'find the object', even in the heart of dissolution, and with her, find meaning in life, and peace without God.

7

'Love Envieth Not':
Mahler's Struggle Against the Greatest Sin of All

As we have seen, Mahler felt that fate had played some cruel tricks on him, and (rightly) that he had had more than his fair share of suffering. Is this life, then, a cruel joke, merely? A sound and fury, signifying nothing? We hear in the collosal drum-strokes of the *Tenth*, and in the yawing chromaticism and dissonances of the *Ninth*, the possibility of there being no meaning in existence. How does a man whose God has deserted him establish any sense of such meaning?

In the *Tenth Symphony* there are those other, muffled, drum-strokes, and as Robert Still suggests, they have a different meaning: they stand for reparation. They 'remember' the funeral of a fireman who gave his life for others. In Mahler's last work, they stand for his immense capacity for *ruth*, expressed in that work—for it pours out a deep sorrow for all human beings who have ever lived their brief mortal existence. And it expresses in its last hundred bars a love which gives the life meaning: 'to live for thee, to die for thee, Almschi!'

To become capable of such love, an individual must be able to find 'the other', and this cannot be achieved until an individual has found himself. That is, the self must be integrated, before it is capable of loving —and this, for the schizoid individual, is a most difficult achievement. So long as the self feels fragmentary, empty, and dissociated, love is full of terrible dangers—of emptying, or being emptied, of being annihilated, of falling to pieces. The schizoid individual may well suffer from 'diminution of affect' or inadequacy of feeling. He cannot feel, because he dare not, because he is not integrated enough to feel—and so cannot 'find' the other and share his suffering. A great deal of our art today is obsessed with this kind of schizoid condition but plunges into the schizoid mode, with the result that it cannot say anything, between man and man. Only if we become capable of finding the 'other' and going out beyond ourselves can we solve our problems of existence.

89

In Mahler's *Tenth Symphony* he utters perhaps the most tragic and poignant awareness of universal human suffering in music. He has become capable of this by the integration achieved in the *Ninth*. The act of 'finding the other' is an imaginative act, and we may see what is involved in a passage by Martin Buber, in the essay already mentioned, 'Distance and Relation'. Men need, he says, to confirm one another in their individual being by means of genuine meeting. 'But beyond this, they need, and it is granted to them, to see the truth, which the soul gains by its struggle, light up to the others, the brothers, in a different way, and even so be confirmed.'

> The realization of the principle in the sphere between men reaches its height in an event which may be called 'making present' . . . It rests on a capacity possessed to some extent by everyone, which may be described as 'imagining' the real . . . 'imagining' the real means that I imagine to myself what another man is at this very moment wishing, feeling, perceiving, thinking, and not as a detached content, but in his very reality, that is a living process in this man . . . So-called fellow feeling may serve as a familiar illustration of this if we leave vague sympathy out of consideration and limit the concept to that event in which I experience, let us say, the specific pain of another in such a way that I feel what is specific in it, not, therefore, the general discomfort or state of suffering, but this particular pain as the pain of the other. This making present increases until it is a paradox in the soul when I and the other are embraced in a common living situation, and (let us say) the pain which I inflict upon him surges up in myself, revealing the abyss of the contradictoriness of life between man and man.
>
> *The Knowledge of Man*, p. 70

The *Tenth Symphony* is a supreme work of the imagination, in which this kind of 'making present' is achieved. It both gives us a specificity of pain—Mahler's pain, over his impotence, his struggle to 'find' Alma, and to overcome the drum thuds of nothingness—and it gives us a sense of the 'abyss of the contradictoriness of life between man and man'.

But before he could become capable of such an immense work of 'mutuality of acceptance', Mahler had himself to become whole enough to 'make present' in this way—and this he achieves in the *Ninth*. The *Ninth* resolves hatred, and escapes from the deadliest sin of all—Envy—into gratitude. How can we relate these terms to musical art? And what have they to do with Mahler's existential quest?

Here, I believe, we can best explain what happens in the *Ninth Symphony* in terms taken from Melanie Klein. She was a psychotherapist who applied Freudian analysis to children, some of whom were as young as two-and-three-quarters. From her work others, like D. W. Winnicott, have gone on to explore the stages of the very start of the human identity, and the primitive stages of our earliest development[1] It is in these earliest months of life that we encounter the primary problems of being, and it is here that we must be prepared to discover the threat of nothingness. Winnicott, for instance, discusses a baby who looked to see what image of himself his mother had in her mind—and found nothing, a vortex of non-being.[2] The exploration of these areas of psychic parturition takes us back to the 'paranoid-schizoid' stage, as Melanie Klein called it the stage before the infant is integrated enough to feel a whole self, set over against a whole world. At this stage, the infant cannot 'find' the 'other', and so cannot feel 'ruth' or concern—or love. It is to this stage that we must go, in order to understand what immense achievement lies behind Mahler's creative work.

Like Dostoevsky, I believe, Mahler was a schizoid individual, who was not, in many ways, able to relate to 'the significant other' until he had achieved, through his creative effort, a development parallel to what in infants is called the 'depressive position' (by Melanie Klein) or the 'stage of concern' (by D. W. Winnicott). There are those who cannot throw themselves imaginatively, in Buber's way, into the life of another, because they have never been whole enough themselves to perform the act of finding and meeting another being. Mahler, as we have seen, in many ways displays an anguished bewilderment about the status of other persons. This failure surely lay behind the failure to grieve adequately for his brother—so that the ghost of the child swept away by death pursues him all his life, in the *First Symphony*, the *Gesellen* cycle, the *Klagende Lied*—and on to the *Ninth*. I am not, of course, saying that this was a disability, for the incomplete grieving produced marvellous works of art which express profound and tragic sorrow. But these arise out of the essential problem—of not being able to accept a whole self, in a whole world, in which hate and destructiveness, and death, are accepted together with love, joy, and peace. But (as Mahler's anguished music shows) finding a sense of responsibility to the 'other' is a terribly painful process, because the adult pursuing it has to experience, with mature emotions, problems usually solved in infancy.

Until this acceptance is made, the individual may continue to resort to primitive solutions, and it is in understanding these that Melanie Klein's work helps us. For the problem we are faced with, if we lose our faith, and are faced with nothingness, is the kind of problem experienced

---

[1] See my chapter 'The Heart of Being' in *Human Hope and the Death Instinct.*
[2] 'George', in *Therapeutic Consultations in Child Therapy*, Hogarth, 1971, p. 391.

by the infant, before it becomes capable of love and gratitude—that is the paranoid-schizoid problem of feeling nothing in a hostile universe.

If we see the universe as nothing, and our lives as possibly meaningless, we are faced with the possibility that we shall be swallowed up, having no substance to set against malignancy. This may happen either because we have rapacious forces within us, arising from our hunger to survive, or it may happen by forces outside us swallowing us—the forces of death. Although they often have some kind of rational basis, there are many fashionable preoccupations today which have in them elements of unconscious fears of this kind: the growth of ecological concern, for instance, could seem to be an expression of concern that the world, ravaged by our own destructiveness, will destroy us. Certainly, the present alarm about 'black holes' in the universe, despite its 'scientific' guise, seems to be a paranoid-schizoid fantasy, arising from the fears of infancy. The prevalent nihilism and decadence in our culture arises from the general deficiency of any sense of what kind of meaning might be set against nothingness.

The only way to overcome such feelings, of nihilism and paranoid fear of extinction, is by love. Only by a deep feeling that one has had one's share of the joys and satisfactions of existence, can one achieve that gratitude for having existed which alone can triumph over death and nothingness. And these satisfactions are not merely ingestions, and certainly not mere acquisitions. The only thing that can satisfy us in this realm is the achievement of a sense of meaning.

The progress of an individual towards unity may be discussed in terms of struggle between the forces of life and the forces of death. Only here I am in difficulties, because of the concept in psychoanalysis of the 'death instinct'. As I have explained in another work, I do not believe that the concept from Freud of an ineradicable instinctual drive towards inanition in the organism is at all necessary to explain the prevalence in human life of the dynamics of death. As Winnicott, Guntrip, Fairbairn and others have tried to explain, destructiveness and hate in human life can be perfectly well explained, as the dynamics of frustrated love, or of a distorted search for meaning. Yet Kleinian dogma today rests upon the concept of the death instinct. This debate, however, may be left to be pursued elsewhere. Here, however, instead of the phrase 'death instinct' I will substitute the word 'hate'.[3]

[3] For the official view, see under 'Death Instinct' in *The Language of Psychoanalysis*, J. Laplanche and J. B. Pontalis, Hogarth Press, 1973. See Harry Guntrip, *Personality Structure and Human Interaction*, Hogarth, 1961, and *Human Hope and the Death Instinct*.

'Love Envieth Not': Mahler's Struggle Against the Greatest Sin of All

Melanie Klein says that 'envy is an oral-sadistic and anal-sadistic expression of destructive impulses, operative from the beginning of life, and . . . it has a constitutional basis'. What does this mean? From the beginning of an infant's life, he has bodily feelings, and desires at times to use his mouth, and his excretory organs, to express hostile (or loving) feelings towards other people. But we must see this observation in the light of Fairbairn's remark that 'the child's ego is a mouth-ego'—that is, we are talking about the primitive human personality as that of a child who feels about the world in ways very much bound up with bodily feelings and their meaning—as to 'inner' and 'outer'. Thus, if an infant feels hungry, he will feel threatened by death. The breast (meaning the mother's body, her handling, her warmth, and her presence) is what keeps him alive—and so to possess the 'inside' contents of the breast. And when this satisfaction is denied him, he comes to feel that there is something 'bad' and hostile in the breast which is in some way persecuting him. In such feelings, according to Melanie Klein, originate those paranoid-schizoid feelings towards the world which she dealt with in disturbed infants.[4]

Mahler, of course, was not a disturbed infant, but he was evidently a man who had severe paranoid-schizoid anxieties about the world. And the work he had to do, to become capable of solving our own problems of emptiness and destructiveness, runs parallel to the work the infant has to do, to find his wholeness and humanness. The essential problem involved is that of *finding reality* and discovering that the 'bad elements' one projects over reality out of one's own internal 'badness' are not 'out there', but 'within'. Unless this process of accepting ambivalence in oneself is understood, I believe we cannot really understand Mahler's *Ninth Symphony*. The theme of chromatic dissolution which Jack Diether calls the 'fate' theme is not a counteracting theme like the 'fate' theme in Beethoven's *Fifth*. It is, rather, a threat of death and dissolution that seems at first to come from the 'world out there'—but is gradually, and by immense effort of resolution found to be 'within', part of oneself and an ineradicable element of one's humanness. It is, in a sense, one's nothingness. What was at first projected over reality is found to be part of oneself.

[4] And these paranoid-schizoid fantasies and feelings are the basis of a great deal in today's primitive hate culture, such as pornography—see *La Grande Bouffe*, and the anal sadism in films like *Last Tango in Paris*, etc. See also my analysis of the anal-sadistic elements in the typical myth of capitalist society, *Goldfinger*, in *The Masks of Hate*, Pergamon, 1972.

93

Let me quote Melanie Klein on this problem, as the infant experiences it, but substituting the word 'hate' for her 'death instinct':

> The immature ego of the infant is exposed from birth to the anxiety stirred up by . . . the immediate conflict between the life instinct and (hate). It is also immediately exposed to the impact of external reality, both anxiety producing, like the trauma of birth, and life-giving, like the warmth, love, and feeding received from its mother. When faced with the anxiety produced by (hate), the ego deflects it . . . The ego splits itself and projects that part of itself which contains (hate) outwards into the original external object—the breast. Thus, the breast, which is felt to contain a great part of the infant's (hate), is felt to be bad and threatening to the ego, giving rise to a feeling of persecution.
> *Introduction to the Work of Melanie Klein*, Hannah Segal, p. 12. (My term 'hate' substituted throughout for 'death instinct'.)

More recent attention to schizoid problems would, I believe, place more emphasis on ego-weakness as the origin of hate. But certainly, it is true that 'part of the hate' remaining in the self is converted into aggression and 'directed towards the persecutors': that is, the assertiveness aroused by paranoia becomes the source of a *seeming* strength, by the mechanisms of hate themselves. We fear hate 'out there' in the world because we have projected our own hate over those who seem to threaten us.[5]

Projection, however, solves very little, for a complexity of further anxieties arise, to do with the self being 'attacked' or 'invaded'. If the self can project, so (it is felt) the 'enemy' can also resort to magical procedures, too:

> Various mechanisms of defence are used to protect the infant from within, to begin with and from persecutors, external or internal, when (hate) is deflected. They all, however, produce in turn anxieties of their own. For instance, the projection of bad feelings and bad parts of the self outwards produce external persecution. The reintrojection of persecutors gives rise to hypochrondriacal anxiety. The projection of good parts outwards produces the anxiety of being depleted of goodness and of being invaded by persecutors. Projection identification produces a variety of anxieties. The two most important are these: the fear that the attacked object will retaliate equally by projection; and the anxiety of having parts of oneself imprisoned and controlled by the object into which they have been projected. This last anxiety is particularly strong when good parts of the self have been pro-

[5] Of course, at times, there are real forces of hate which *do* threaten us. I am talking of when we *create* the predators we fear. A characteristic feature of youth today who have been conditioned by 'pop' and the media is a new paranoia, expressed as a fear that others are pushing something harmful into their minds, as reported by Cambridge University examiners, 1970.

jected, producing a feeling of having been robbed of these good parts and of being controlled by other objects.

ibid., p. 17

Such insights explain why, if it is true (as I suggest) that Mahler is concerned to overcome the consequences of projecting his hate into the outer world, his contest with that hate is so complex. The hate theme speaks as if 'from another world': yet, while Mahler seeks to embrace it as an aspect of his own self, it yet recurrently threatens to destroy everything that he has achieved in terms of inner organization, even nearly to the end of the First Movement and at times in the Second and Third, until it is finally dispelled on the last page.

It requires only a moment's inattention, or absorption in passion, it seems, for hate to reveal that hate can't be trusted. It snarls and becomes its disruptive self again even in the heart of peace. Thus, whenever the hate theme is 'embraced' it evokes further dangers of 'hypochrondriacal anxiety' in the self, which may feel invaded, or poisoned by the hate which has been taken 'within'. There are moments of diabolical laughter in the First Movement of the *Ninth Symphony*, at which the hate theme, being 'worked on' as Mahler begins to find it 'in the self', seems to threaten to ruin everything from within (e.g. p. 33 pocket score, cue [12] and thereafter.) This hate shows itself as irrepressible (as irrepressible as death), as on p. 55 (bars 2 and 3), and is still 'there' at *Etwas belebter* (horn) on p. 57, even after a moment of gladness (bar 5 in the top line). Yet this comes even just before a glimpse of the possibility of fully 'including' hate, in the last but one bar of that page.

Melanie Klein discusses how this kind of insecurity, inability to trust in benignity, can arise from paranoid feelings, by which even the source of life can seem persecuting—which explains how 'hate' can arise, as it does in the *Ninth*, from the heart of primal togetherness:

> The infant grossly distorts and magnifies every frustration from outer sources, and the mother's breast turns externally and internally pre-dominantly into a persecutory object. Then even actual gratification cannot sufficiently counteract persecutory anxiety.

In Mahler, as we shall see, the tide of gratification often leads again and again to a new threat of persecutory anxiety. This pattern in the music recurs throughout in various forms, to menace any gains, as if from 'without', or from some 'split-off' element. Hate can emerge from all kinds of sources—apparently benign, but really not to be trusted: even towards the end of the *Tenth* the terrible drum-strokes of nihilism fail:

95

but this is (too) how death does behave—being untouched by love itself, or by pleas of pity (as Mahler knew, over Ernst): all that *can* be 'touched' is the sense of that which death cannot destroy. The structure of these late works is that of trying, over and over again, to 'counteract persecutory anxiety'—by a massive attempt to believe in 'gratifications', and to find sufficient gratitude for them, to overcome a 'distorted' sense of a hostile universe and a horror of the possible total triumph of death-as-nothingness.

One source of benignity (as we shall see) is the world of 'natural being', Mother Earth as the 'good breast':

> When there is a predominance of good experience over bad experience, the ego acquires a belief in the prevalence of the ideal object over the persecutory objects, and also of the predominance of its own life instincts over its own (hate). These two beliefs, in the goodness of the object and the goodness of the self, go hand in hand, since the ego continually projects its own instincts outwards, thereby disturbing the objects, and also introjects objects, identifying with them.
>
> *ibid.*, p. 24

From this we can see how the presence of death in the outer world exacerbates the inward conflict between 'life-instinct' and hate. But we can also see how the quest for integration of the self is *at one with attitudes to the whole of the world and of life*: the loveliness of the world and birdsong can be 'introjected' as 'life'. The process of integration and overcoming of envy also go with the discovery of the self as a separate independent creature: this shows how Mahler's search for a degree of resignation which could enable him to feel philosophically strong enough to bear death has much to contribute to the whole schizoid problem of man in the modern world, seeking to find a sense of meaning in his life without God, in terms of an independence of identity which also recognizes our dependence—on the original object, on the Earth, on other human beings, in recognition of our human weakness and need. Accepting, that is, both our need for 'encounter' and our essential nothingness—to which problems the only solution is in 'meeting': this overcomes our dissociation:

> At the same time as splitting lessens and the ego has a greater tolerance in relation to its own aggression, the necessity for projection lessens and the ego is more and more able to tolerate its own aggression, to feel it as part of itself, and is not driven constantly to project it into its objects. In this way the ego is preparing for integrating its objects, integrating itself, and, through lessening of projecting mechanisms, there is a growing differentiation between what is self and what is object.
>
> *ibid.*, p. 24

Mahler's final problem is to see death not as a projection of his own hate, but as a cosmic, biological fact: becoming able to see and accept this fact is at one with accepting his own hate, and 'feeling it' to be part of his ego. This he achieves stage by stage, and it is this that is celebrated finally by the huge sigh of 'great contentment', towards the end of the *Tenth Symphony*, as culmination of the last hundred bars of anguished resignation in that work—a monumental achievement of acceptance, of being human, mortal and temporal—and yet able to love. The problem opened in the First Movement of the *Ninth* is that of an intolerable aggression emerging from love: a projected hate, split off, seems to emerge from the object itself. This, as Melanie Klein suggests above, happens because of a weak self.

Working through these primary *schizoid* problems leads him towards the *depressive position itself*, which is a stage of tormented concern for the effects of one's hate on one's object, and one's world. Mahler's first problems are earlier than this position or 'stage of concern', and so, like Dostoevsky's and Kafka's, schizoid problems. His first problem is to find a self and the 'other' at all. His discovery (that Alma records) of a sense of responsibility for another person marks his growing discovery of the 'other' or object as a separate being. Then, following this discovery goes all the deep anguish recorded in his music—the tender *outflowing* pity which is never self-pity, but a profound recognition of the sorrow of our 'solitary category', our need for confirmation, our weakness and mortality. Through encountering and resolving hate in the *Ninth* Mahler goes on in the *Tenth* to celebrate all that is meant by 'ruth'—to feel concern and to *be* 'for' the other, in love: so, 'To live for thee, to die for thee, Almschi!'

The intensity of this true grieving, true experience of depression, is at one with the 'egosyntonic' effect of the music, its integrative effect enabling the composer to express gratitude:

In more normal development, envy becomes more integrated. The gratification experienced at the breast stimulates admiration, love and gratitude at the same time as envy. These feelings enter into conflict as soon as the ego begins to integrate, and, if envy is not overwhelming, gratitude overcomes and modifies envy. The ideal breast ['O life of endless loving'] introjected with love, gratification and gratitude, becomes part of the ego, the ego is more full of goodness itself. And thus, in a benevolent circle, envy lessens as gratification increases, the diminution of envy allows more gratification, which in turn furthers the lessening of envy.

ibid., p. 39
(My interpolation in brackets)

97

This 'circle' is the circle of the eternal blue horizon in *Das Lied*. That is, once the fear of the inner destructiveness of hate has been overcome, the individual is freed, to emulate the mother, and to pour out in gratitude a universal love from the female elements of being—such as is released in the passages of peace at the close of the *Ninth* and the bittersweet passages in the last bars of the *Tenth*. By such creative, integrative processes, the world comes to be recognized as a whole by a whole person, and ruth generates the capacity to feel joy even in full awareness of one's transience and nothingness:

> object synthesis, and therefore a mitigation of hate by love, come about, and greed and envy, which are corollaries of destructive impulses, lose in power . . . To put in another way, persecutory anxiety and schizoid mechanisms are diminished, and the [subject] can work through the depressive position. When his initial inability to establish a good object is, to some extent, overcome, envy is diminished and his capacity for enjoyment and gratitude increases step by step . . .
>
> p. 91

Such 'steps' in analysis as Melanie Klein describes them thus correspond to the episode progress of Mahler's last works, in their 'linear' pursuit of the capacity for gratitude.

Mahler's *Ninth Symphony* virtually enacts the above paragraph, and in its utterly resigned close we have expressed the deep satisfactions of such achievements of joy and gratitude which have been won 'step by step' out of chaos and destruction, to yield transcendent meaning.

As Melanie Klein points out, her own theories developed from work by Karl Abraham on manic-depressive patients, from which he decided that 'envy is an oral trait'. And while this indicates oral sadism, we need to realize, too, that the overcoming of envy is a positive oral act: and if we contemplate this, we find that all such creative cultural effort, which makes man capable of imagination, love, and meaning, begins in play at the mother's breast. This primal encounter, and the Mother, as the source of goodness, are also present, I believe, in Mahler's *Ninth Symphony*. To solve our life-problems Mahler regressed to our deepest need: togetherness:

> The importance of the infant's first object relation—the relation to the mother's breast and the mother . . . if this primal object, which is introjected, takes root in the ego with relative security the basis for satisfactory development is laid . . . the breast is felt to be a source of nourishment and therefore, in a deeper sense, of life itself . . . This . . . restores the lost pre-natal unity with the mother and the feeling of security that goes with it . . . It may well be that his having formed part of the mother in the

pre-natal state contributes to the infant's innate feeling that there exists outside him something that will give him all he needs and desires. The good breast is taken in and becomes part of the ego, and the infant who was first inside the mother now has the mother inside himself . . .

ibid., p. 3

This feeling of 'security and well-being' is bound up with the feeling of 'ontological security'—our sense of the point of life. As Winnicott argues in his chapter 'The Location of Culture', culture begins in 'transitional object phenomena'—that is, from those play-things to which in a way (for a time) the child 'relates', and which symbolize the internalization of his mother, and thus the degree of independent security of existence as a separate being he has achieved. To this capacity to be separate the particular state of psychic parturition between mother and child observed by Winnicott and called Primary Maternal Preoccupation contributes a great deal.

This origin of our attitudes to the world in our first relationship to the mother can, of course, be put in many different ways, and has been seen by other thinkers before the psychoanalysts. Guntrip quotes Martin Buber:

> The ante-natal life of the child is one of purely natural combination, bodily interaction and flowing from one into the other . . . (There is) a mythical saying of the Jews, 'in the mother's body man knows the universe, in birth he forgets it' . . . It remains indeed in man as a secret image of desire . . . the yearning is for the cosmic connection. Every child that is coming into being rests, like all life that is coming into being, in the womb of the great mother, the undivided primal world that precedes form. From her, too, we are separated, and enter into personal life, slipping free only in the dark hours to be close to her again; night by night this happens to the healthy man. But this separation does not occur catastrophically like the separation from the bodily mother; time is granted to the child to exchange a spiritual connexion, that is, relation, for the natural connexion with the world that he gradually loses.

I and Thou, p. 25

It is this quest for *connection* (or 'encounter') that Mahler's music pursues, from *Das Lied* on. 'Rest for my lonely heart' for him can only come by the achievement of a particular kind of feeling towards the circle of the blue horizon, towards the object of his love, his woman and the whole earth. He was driven to pursue this quest so urgently because his 'knowledge of the universe' did not arise naturally from an adequate experience of togetherness in infancy. Like his siblings, who could not go on living, so committed suicide, he did not feel an existence security built up by the exchange of a 'spiritual connexion' in the experience of confirmation by his mother's capacity to 'be' for him in earlier infancy. This predicament was followed by a disastrous childhood environment, and a tormented adulthood of double alienation. He had, almost, psychically speaking, to begin from the absolute beginning.

Yet, of course, in doing so he engages with problems that are universal. No infant's environment is perfect, and so every individual comes to idealize: he develops a longing for an 'inexhaustible and ever-present breast'—as 'constant evidence of the mother's love'. He tends to respond to painful experiences paranoiacally and to feel them as persecutory: the mother's breast, he wishes to believe, can do away with these paranoid anxieties, and with his own destructive impulses. The conflict between these impulses (both of which originate in the urge to exist)

and the ensuing threat of annihilation of the self and the object by destructive impulses are fundamental factors in the infant's initial relationship to his mother—in every human existence.

Envy and Gratitude, p. 5

Melanie Klein points out that when we use the word 'breast' here we are lending a word from our conscious realm to 'translate the language of the unconscious into consciousness': the feelings involved are 'felt by the infant in much more primitive ways than language can express . . . "memories in feeling" . . . I would call them . . .' (Footnote, p. 5). Such memories in feeling can be expressed in musical symbolism, without seeming explicit.

The word 'breast' is virtually a poetic-philosophical term for Melanie Klein when she says:

the breast in its good aspect is the prototype of maternal goodness, inexhaustible patience and generosity, as well as creativeness. It is these fantasies and instinctual needs that so enrich the primal object that it remains the foundation for hope, trust, and belief in goodness.

ibid., p. 6

Melanie Klein is, I believe, using the word 'breast' to represent the experiences of 'creative reflection' as Winnicott was later to call it—or, as Buytendijk, and Binswanger call it, *liebende Wirheit*, loving encounter, as the origin of the sense of identity and meaning. In his later works Gustav Mahler expresses the very texture of 'encounter' and its feel and rhythms, in the 'language of the unconscious' made music. And he pursues this quest for a foundation of hope, trust and belief in goodness, and of 'inexhaustible patience . . . generosity and creativeness' in the 'connexion' with the 'object' which is both the mother and the whole earth. His quest moves from 'the breast in its good aspect', towards the *experience of benign forces of inexhaustible creativity in the Universe*: it is this that 'O life of endless loving' means: and what, musically, the following 'turn' cadences mean:

EXAMPLE 4

Tranquillo

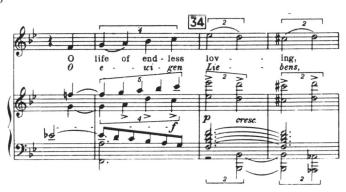

EXAMPLE 5

Äußerst langsam

—in their different ways.[6] In his music 'creative reflection' and love are explored and found as the path to the deepest ontological security. The 'circular' movements in each of these consummating phrases are a kind of musical '*mandala*' of the security to be experienced in *liebende Wirheit*. And this kind of 'secure' turn is a dynamic in music utterly at the other extreme from the collapsing chromatic turn of the 'hate' theme.

It must be understood that hate is a most destructive dynamic. Melanie Klein seeks to distinguish between envy, jealousy, and greed though these are, of course, related. Jealousy is mainly involved with a relationship

---

[6] See also the concluding turn and cadence in the song *Wenn dein Mutterlein*, No. 3, in the *Kindertotenlieder*.

with two people—love that the subject feels is his due is likely to be taken away by his rival. 'Greed' is an impetuous and insatiable craving, 'exceeding what the subject needs and what the object is able and willing to give'.

> At the unconscious level, greed aims primarily at completely scooping out, sucking dry, and devouring the breast: that is to say, its aim is destructive introjection.

Envy is more complex, because it is an angry feeling 'that another person possesses and enjoys something desirable—the envious impulse being to take it away or to spoil it'. So

> Envy seeks not only to rob, but also to put badness . . . into the mother . . . in order to spoil and destroy her. In the deepest sense this means destroying her creativeness . . .

Thus envy is mainly bound up with *projection*: and it is an attempt to attack the breast which, it is felt, keeps its nourishment for its own gratification. This feeling adds to the infant's sense of grief and hate. If envy is excessive, 'paranoid and schizoid features are abnormally strong'.

In Kleinian theory, in later stages, envy is focused on the mother receiving the father's penis, having babies inside her, giving birth to them, and being able to feed them. Melanie Klein says:

> I have often described the sadistic attacks on the mother's breast as determined by destructive impulse . . . envy gives particular impetus to these attacks . . .

This 'envious spoiling of the object' inevitably brings fears of talion retribution, and even of bringing about one's own annihilation.

From these connections made by Melanie Klein we can perhaps see that when, in his brief exchanges with Freud, Mahler mentioned his anguish at the conflict between his mother and father, and elsewhere mentions his observation of a love-scene which seemed cruel to him, he is indicating that his own problems had a good deal to do with 'sadistic attacks on the mother'. Even the normal child experience some sense of unfilfilment, because no mother can be as perfect as the idealized breast of fantasy unlimited by experience of reality. Where there has been severe deprivation of happily-given love, and maternal preoccupation, envy becomes intense. So, in his memory, Mahler's father, in his coarse ill-treatment of the mother, was only doing to her what he himself wished to do: that is to scoop out, eat and take the mother into himself. But in doing so he would be *felt to threaten his own existence and to destroy the creativity in all things.* He was therefore tormented by fear of loss of objects, a problem which imminent death exacerbated: and at a deeper level still, he feared the destruction of creative meaning. The *Song of the Earth* and the *Ninth* were creative attempts to overcome paranoid and schizoid feelings, and to love the Earth as the source of all creativity (the ultimate Mother's breast) and to overcome the envious 'spoiling of the object' which threatened to destroy love and meaning— as his father's destructiveness menaced the child.

Because of the complexities of Mahler's association of love and hate the problem already discussed of finding trust in positive gains is acute in him.

Melanie Klein also makes some philosophical generalizations which help us to relate the problem of envy to male and female elements in the personality, and to the wider problems of relationship with reality, and problems of meaning. As we have seen one of the problems of envy is envy of the mother's female capacities to create. We may link this with Winnicott's distinction between 'female element being' and 'male element doing'. Envy of creativity can mar our capacity to be glad for the creative, feminine aspects of the whole earth, for creative *being*, in ourselves and others. If we attach our sense of identity wholly to 'doing' the male-element posture (which can be a form of defensive 'bustle') it may be that our existential problem may come to seem forfeit to death as the ultimate doer—who 'does us in'. As Sylvia Plath says in *Death & Co.*, 'Somebody's done for'. If we only *do* (and achieve no sense of meaningful BEING) we may feel all is extinguished by our end. Gabriel Marcel says, in our society, in which man is conceived of in terms of his functions, 'death becomes, objectively and functionally, the scrapping of what has ceased to be of use and must be written off as a total loss' (*The Philosophy of Existence*, p. 3). What is there to set against death, in mere manipulations of externals? This male, analytical, 'objectifying' influence is a predominant tendency in our scientific age—and it even plays a large part in Freudian theory and practice. Even 'analysis' (and over-interpretation) can damage our (female) capacities to be; as Winnicott has suggested.

Melanie Klein's influence in psychoanalysis, despite her attachment to the dogma of the death instinct, has been to restore attention to the female role—to creativity, and its contribution to the *Dasein*:

The 'good' breast that feeds and initiates the love relation to the mother is the representative of the life instinct and is also felt as the first manifestation of creativeness. In this fundamental relation the infant receives not only

103

the gratification he desires, but feels that he is being kept alive. For hunger, which arouses the fear of starvation—possibly even all physical and mental pain—is felt as the threat of death.

We can, I believe, add to this that hunger is associated with the need to have our existence confirmed, while that envy which is associated with hunger is, as we have seen, a hunger to be filled with a rich security of feeling alive, and full of significance, become distorted and destructive.

So, when meaning is hard to achieve, and the unborn self in one hungers for it, this hunger arouses a fear of (spiritual) starvation, of emptiness of meaning, while mental pain is felt as a threat of death, and *is* envy and hate. (The terrible dissonant chord in the First Movement of the *Tenth* conveys this mental pain). The threat of actual death exacerbates these problems of death, envy, and hate within. All these problems are associated with the envy of creativity—of life-giving benignity itself. Melanie Klein says

> The capacity to give and to preserve life is felt as the greatest gift and therefore creativeness becomes the deepest cause for envy.

We can turn this round, and say that in seeking a sense of 'ontological security' we need to overcome this deep envy and become able *to cherish the capacity to preserve life*. It is this that Mahler does by his music, not least by his radical transformation of the 'hate' theme, which he transforms into an expression of gratitude and joy in creative existence.

Melanie Klein refers to the attempt to destroy creativity by Satan and the Fallen Angels in *Paradise Lost,* who 'became the destructive force which attempts to destroy what God creates'. She quotes *The Wisdom of Solomon.* 'But by the envy of the devil, death entered into the world, and they that are of his portion make trial thereof.'

> This theological idea seems to come down from St Augustine, who describes life as a creative force opposed to Envy, a destructive force. In this connection the *First Letter to the Corinthians* reads 'Love envieth not'.

'Envy of creativeness', says Melanie Klein, 'is a fundamental element in the disturbance of the creative process.' What Mahler feared was that his own envy was undermining his own creativity—and so the 'hate' theme, not least, threatens the very process by which he could come to feel that his problems could cease to exist (as he did when he heard music). He denied in Alma the very feminine poetic creativity he *feared* in himself because of its vulnerability. Mahler's envy turned to good purpose when he rescored other composers: such musicianship offers a way out:

The person who can ungrudgingly enjoy other people's work and happiness is spared the torments of envy, grievance, and persecution.

But the deeper solution to the problem of envy is a path to a triumphant attitude to the problems of existence:

whereas envy is a source of great unhappiness, a relative freedom from it is felt to underlie contented and peaceful states of mind—ultimately sanity. This is also the basis of inner resources and resilience which can be observed in people who, even after great adversity and mental pain, regain their peace of mind.

ibid.

The anguish recorded in Mahler's last works not only secured some peace of mind for him, but can help us, in possessing them, to preserve sanity in the face of nihilism, and our existential problems today. He offers, in the face of death, serenity:

Such an attitude, which includes gratitude for pleasures of the past and enjoyment of what the present can give, expresses itself in serenity . . .

These attitudes are explored first in *Das Lied von der Erde*, and the greatest achievements of serenity are in the last pages of the *Ninth* and the last hundred bars of the *Tenth*.

Perhaps we need a necessary extension here of the concept of gratitude (one which we can learn from Mahler). While it may be 'pleasant' to revive 'memories of the past' as Melanie Klein puts it, it is also necessary for us to feel that the *life we have had has been significant*. This was Thomas Hardy's predicament, over his first marriage, in the poems *Vestigea Veteris Flammae*, in which he tried to find meaning in a relationship which, over several decades, had been dead. His effort to find such meaning, in the face of a meaningless universe, can be especially seen in the poem 'At Castle Boterel':

> As I drive to the junction of lane and highway,
>   And the drizzle bedrenches the waggonette,
> I look behind at the fading byway,
>   And see on its slope, now glistening wet,
>   Distinctly yet
>
> Myself and a girlish form benighted
>   In dry March weather. We climb the road
> Beside a chaise. We had just alighted
>   To ease the sturdy pony's load
>   When he sighed and slowed.

105

What we did as we climbed, and what we talked of
　　Matters not much, nor to what it led,—
Something that life will not be balked of
　　Without rude reason till hope is dead,
　　　　And feeling fled.

It filled but a minute. But was there ever
　　A time of such quality, since or before,
In that hill's story? To one mind never,
　　Though it has been climbed, foot-swift, foot-sore
　　　　By thousands more.

Primaeval rocks form the road's steep border,
　　And much have they faced there, first and last
Of the transitory in Earth's long order;
　　But what they record in colour and cast
　　　　Is—that we two passed.

And to me, though Time's unflinching rigour,
　　In mindless rote, has ruled from sight
The substance now, one phantom figure
　　Remains on the slope, as when the night
　　　　Saw us alight.

I look and see it here, shrinking, shrinking,
　　I look back at it amid the rain
For the very last time; for my sand is sinking,
　　And I shall traverse old love's domain
　　　　Never again.

This is written not merely 'to revive pleasant memories', but to assert that the relationship was meaningful even though later the marriage lost its meaning, and even now the woman is dead. That

　　　　we two passed . . .

is sufficient justification for the creation of the world, and of his existence. Not to believe this for an atheist is to face effacement in an indifferent universe—the stark nothingness that menaces one who does not believe in any transcendental reality. Mahler's relationship was meaningful, but menaced by his inability to 'find' Alma, and by his impotence: he *had* to find it thus transcendent.

Thus 'gratitude' in Melanie Klein's sense we may extend to mean *the capacity* to be able to recognize the existence of others and of the natural world, and to see a value in one's having existed, with all one's

106

human consciousness, in this living reality. It is necessary to 'listen' to 'natural being'—or the '*nisus*' as F. R. Leavis calls the forward-moving principle of life in the universe (see 'Justifying One's View of Blake', *The Human World*, No. 7, p. 42).

A secondary problem of importance for our consideration of Mahler is indicated here by Melanie Klein. We have seen how difficult it was for him to trust his gains. Even if a sense of meaning is gained in therapy, it is likely to be attacked, Melanie Klein says, and envy even occurs in the transference situation:

> For instance: the analyst has just given an interpretation which brought the patient relief and produced a change of mood from despair to hope and trust.

Let us apply this to Mahler's relationship with himself in the *Ninth Symphony* and say, 'At the end of the First Movement Mahler has worked on the conflict between love and hate (or generosity and envy) until he secured a change of mood from despair to hope and trust'. But what happens then? In the music, exactly the same process takes place as in therapeutic encounter:

> This *helpful interpretation* may soon *become the object of destructive criticism*. It is then no longer felt to be something good he has received and has experienced as a an enrichment.
>
> (my italics)

A patient may devalue the help given, and may also feel

> because of guilt about devaluing the help given, that he is *unworthy to benefit* . . .

This need to devalue constructive achievement is an expression of envy, and marks an attachment to destructiveness

> Destructive criticism is particularly evident in paranoid patients who indulge in the sadistic pleasure of disparaging the analyst's work even though it has given them some relief . . . The slow progress we make in such cases is also connected with envy . . . their doubts and uncertainties about the value of the analysis persist . . .

Defences here involve splitting off the hostile part of oneself, and 'becoming confused'. These manifestations have early origins:

> The infant who, owing to the strength of paranoid and schizoid mechanisms and the impetus of envy, cannot divide and keep apart successfully love and hate, and therefore the good and bad object, is liable to feel confused between what is good and bad in other connections . . .
>
> p. 12–13

In analysis such 'negative therapeutic reactions' play an important part. So, too, do such reactions play an important part in the testing of feelings of existence-security gained in the course of true creative reparation.

Mahler was not working with an analyst: his relationship was between himself as 'separated', and the 'union' which musical culture represents: between his creative genius and the tradition to which he belonged. Music itself represented his transitional object, by play with which he seeks integration. Because of his acute paranoid-schizoid problems of splitting, his envy even interferes with his own achievement of integration, and progress is very slow, moving against desperate self-doubt. This accounts for the form of the *Ninth Symphony*, and its slow episodic progress from point to point. The middle two movements exert 'destructive criticism', from all the doubt and confusion of the envious dynamics in Mahler, on any security gained by the music of the First Movement. Hence the ironic—and essentially destructive and sadistic—dedication 'To my brothers in Apollo'. This is surely almost a rejection of the possibilities of gaining ground by creativity altogether—implying 'And as far as we shall get in combating our existential despair by anything as ephemeral and manic as mere music! (Especially the inadequate music which I inherit from you!)'

The hebephrenic laughter in the *Rondo-Burleske* is thus an expression of doubt as to the value of the quest for integration, and so an attack on creativity itself—such as a patient may experience, in Melanie Klein's view. Yet out of the very 'negative reaction' itself the lineaments of gratitude themselves develop. Envy arises out of hungry love and the desire TO BE—so, even the worst moments of paranoia and destructive doubt are themselves the pathway to greater existential security. The squeaking mad irony expressed by the clarinet just previous to cue [39] (pocket score p. 141) becomes the great theme of the last movement: it even becomes the theme which is to reverse the threat of chromatic dissolution and turn it into an outflowing of gladness-to-have-lived. Similarly the grotesque carnival dance of the *Ländler*, in the Second Movement, dissolves into confusion and inanition, from doubt: the spectral gaiety of the manic vitality of dance becomes the butt of feelings of doubt, of 'envious criticism'. But even there we can see themes being transmuted, towards the final resolution. In the *Tenth* the conflict is no longer with hate and envy, but rather with nothingness itself: yet again we experience 'doubt' and even 'destructive criticism' from time to time.

As I have suggested, Mahler's predicament was that a threat of annihilation seemed to develop out of the very source of confirmation of existence, out of passion and vitality themselves. Melanie Klein suggests how this can be, in introducing her concept of gratitude. What I have called the 'hate' theme suddenly arises (after a cry of alarm) from a rising passion, which in turn emerges from the very sounds of primal encounter—the original quietness and togetherness, mothering, albeit with ominous undertones as of 'a soft drum' and the '*ewig*' evocation of ends even in beginnings.

In these opening bars, I feel, we have a re-experiencing of the 'early bond' from which all object-relations derive. But, as Mrs Klein said,

> destructive impulses, especially strong envy, may at an early stage disturb this particular bond with the mother . . .

This is what Example 33 below virtually tells us. Gratitude is bound up with generosity and the capacity to give and love. 'Belief in the good breast' is derived from 'the infant's capacity to find and invest the first external object with libido'.

> In this way a good object is established, which loves and protects the self and is loved and protected by the self. This is the basis for trust in one's own goodness.
>
> p. 19

It is this 'trust in one's own goodness' which Mahler seeks, by continually subjecting his positive gains to testing, against those chromaticisms and drum-strokes that might be expected to destroy them. What survives is the quiet voice of love, trust and goodness—positive qualities of being.

This essential problem of life affects our whole perception, and so our sense of the meaning of existence. In the end, as we experience in the *Ninth* and *Tenth*, to solve it demands that 'condition of complete simplicity / Costing not less than everything': total resignation. Here, significantly, Melanie Klein has a footnote referring to an essay by D. W. Winnicott, who begins in this essay to explore the nature of perception ('Psychoses and Child Care', *Collected Papers*, p. 219). He emphasizes that at first our perception of the world is a fantasy of our own spinning: *we make our world*, and only by degrees what we make is found to correspond to reality. The individual at the beginning is only one of a 'nursing couple':

> At first the individual is not the unit. As perceived from the outside the unit is an environmental-individual set-up. The outsider knows that the individual psyche can only start in a certain setting. In this setting the

individual can gradually come to create a personal environment. If all goes well the environment created by the individual becomes something that is 'ike enough to the environment that can be generally perceived, and in such a case there arrives a stage in the process of development through which the individual passes from dependence into independence.

The origins of a satisfactory perception of reality are in the capacity of the mother to be so aware of her infant's needs that 'she provides something more or less in the right place and the right time'.

This, much repeated, starts off the infant's ability to use *illusion*, without which no contact is possible between the psyche and the environment.

Later, this area of interchange becomes that of the transitional object, and then the possession of the culture between the psyche and the environment, and without 'a greeting of the spirit'[7] the real world cannot be found.

In Winnicott's theory there comes a moment at which the infant emerges from the situation of being 'devotedly held'; he cites Humpty-Dumpty:

> He has just achieved integration into one whole thing, and has emerged from the environment-individual set-up so that he is perched on a wall, no longer devotedly held. He is notoriously in a precarious position in his emotional development, especially liable to irreversible disintegration.
>
> *Collected Papers*, p. 226

At the moment when the self begins to emerge there is a severe threat of persecution and disintegration:

> integration activity produces an individual in a raw state, a potential paranoiac. The persecutors in the new phenomenon, the outside, become neutralized in ordinary healthy development by the fact of the mother's loving care, which physically (as in holding) and psychologically (as in understanding or empathy, enabling sensitive adaptation), makes the individual's primary isolation a fact. Environmental failure just here starts the individual off with a paranoid potential . . . In defence against the terrible anxieties of the paranoid state in very early life there is not infrequently organized a state which has been given various names (defensive pathological introversion, etc.). The infant lives permanently in his or her own inner world which is not, however, firmly organized. The external persecution complication is kept at bay by non-achievement of unit-status. In a relation with this kind of child one floats in and out of the inner world in which the child lives, and while one is in it one is subjected to more or less omnipotent control, but not control from a strong central point. It is a world of magic and one feels mad in it. All of us who have treated psychotic

[7] This phrase is from Keats' *Life and Letters*, Everyman Edition, p. 132.

110

children of this kind know how mad we have to be to inhabit this world . . .

p. 227

I have quoted Winnicott at some length here because he communicates what it is like to be involved in the experience of a failure of integration and perception, in those who resist integration, who have not achieved the capacity to perceive, through using illusion, who are paranoid, and threatened like Humpty-Dumpty with irreversible disintegration. Any sense of meaning which man can achieve today must be exerted against a break-down of consciousness and perception which has psychotic qualities of this kind, because of the break-down, in our world, of those capacities for 'making present' and 'meeting' of which Buber speaks above.

This is why Mahler is such an important creative artist in our time. *It is of this possibility of irreversible disintegration of which Mahler's 'hate theme' speaks*, and it is against it that he successfully strives—and wins. All these possibilities of loss of touch with the world had been seen by Mahler over the edge of the chasm of madness. There is a sense in which he lived in an inner world—and yet knew that his only hope was to 'find' the 'other' and the real world (to which one is responsible) as he does, agonizingly, in the *Ninth* and *Tenth*. But in hope of what, since he was doomed? Winnicott indicates a danger that is far more terrible to us than death. Death may revive in us the Humpty-Dumpty feeling of being 'perched on a wall', 'notoriously in a precarious position'. But more terrible than any physical catastrophe is the threat of 'irreversible disintegration' *of the psyche* so that *it could be as if we had never been*. This is the most dreadful thing we can imagine—and what it means phenomenologically is that it could be that we *are* nothingness: our life could have no meaning whatever, and so it could be as if we *had* never been. Later Winnicott says how the problem with the psychotic is to enable him to discover 'what it is to be human': entering into his madness is to enter into the horror of the possibility of never discovering this. The chromatic turn of Mahler's horns threatens not mere death, but the 'spoiling of the source of life' itself and with the source the meaning of human existence itself, utterly.

Melanie Klein believed that envy was the most destructive form of hate:

There are very pertinent reasons why envy ranks among the seven 'deadly sins'. I would even suggest that it is unconsciously felt to be the greatest sin of all, because it spoils and harms the good object which is the source of

111

life. This view is consistent with the view described by Chaucer in *The Parson's Tale*: 'It is certain that envy is the worst sin that is; for all other sins are sins only against one virtue, whereas envy is against all virtue and against all goodness.'[8] The feeling of having injured and destroyed the primal object impairs the individual's trust in the sincerity of his later relations and makes him doubt his capacity for love and goodness.

Envy and Gratitude, p. 20

—and makes him doubt the meaning of his life. At worst it can mean insanity.

One point we may note in passing here and that is the connection between envy and idealization—a theme I explore below in an Appendix. Melanie Klein emphasizes that a degree of splitting is natural, and, indeed, the basis of those inner dynamics which make us human. Nor can a clear distinction be made between 'good' and 'idealized':

> In the exploration of early splitting processes, it is essential to differentiate between a good object and an idealized one though this distinction cannot be drawn sharply. A very deep split between the two aspects of the object indicates that it is not the good and bad object that are being kept apart but an idealized and an extremely bad one. So deep and sharp a division reveals that destructive impulses, envy, and persecutory anxiety are very strong and that idealization serves mainly as a defence against these emotions.
>
> p. 25

With Mahler, as we have seen, his idealization of Alma as 'Marie' was deeply divided from the destructive impulses and envy as expressed by his ban on his wife's composing, and his neglect of her as a person, while his persecutory anxiety is obvious in his tendency to attribute misfortunes to persecutory demons and apes, which he would attempt to thwart by magic. Melanie Klein's subsequent paragraph not only links these elements with Mahler's capacity to confuse himself with his wife (and his sister) but also helps to explain what he sought in his music: 'ego-integration' and 'object-synthesis':

> If the good object is deeply rooted, the split is fundamentally of a different nature and allows the all-important processes of ego integration and object synthesis to operate. Thus a mitigation of hatred by love can come about in some measure and the depressive position can be worked through. As a result, the identification with a good and whole object is the more securely established; and this also lends strength to the ego and enables it to preserve its identity as well as a feeling of possessing goodness of its own . . . when

---

[8] This anal-sadistic element, demonstrating an envy of creativity, is now manifest in many attacks on art itself in our time, not least, alas, in Pasolini's pornographic film of Chaucer.

things go wrong, excessive projective identification, by which split-off parts of the self are projected into the object, leads to a strong confusion between the self and the object, which also comes to stand for the self. Bound up with this is a weakening of the object, and a grave disturbance in object-relations.

p. 25

In life the latter complex was Mahler's predicament: in his music he sought ego-integration and object-synthesis by seeking to 'restore the good object'. Although there is idealization in this, it is also a 'condition of life', as Melanie Klein admits:

> I also found that idealization derives from the innate feeling that an extremely good breast exists, a feeling which leads to the longing for a good object and for the capacity to love it. [*Footnote* in the original: I have already referred to the inherent need to idealize the prenatal situation. Another frequent field for idealization is the baby-mother relation. It is particularly those people who were not able to experience sufficient happiness in this relation who idealize it in retrospect.] This appears to be a condition for life itself . . . Since the need for a good object is universal, the distinction between an idealized and a good object cannot be considered as absolute.

The 'Thou' of *Das Lied von der Erde* is an idealized object who becomes the earth, giving and creating life for ever. The mother whose lullaby is the *'ewig'* song in the *Ninth Symphony* is the ideal mother whom Mahler never experienced. Elsewhere in his work the Virgin Mary stands in the mother's place as object. But there is a moment when he needs to find the capacity to love an object which is more real than ideal which, by the end of the *Ninth Symphony*, he does achieve. It would not be possible to express generosity of giving in love more forcibly in music: *'Lieb' und Leid, und Welt, und Traum'* as Diether says, 'Through the mind and heart of a man.' And at the end of the *Tenth* we are beyond the 'depressive position' in an agony of 'the capacity to love': the idealization of Alma has become the capacity to love her.

As Melanie Klein points out in her next chapter, 'one of the consequences of excessive envy is an early onset of guilt', the only cure being reparation. This explains the anguish in Mahler's music—the music of the suffering of the earth. The anguish arises from concern at the harm one's envious hate may have caused:

> When the infant reaches the depressive position, and becomes more able to face his psychic reality, he also feels that the object's badness is largely due to his own aggressiveness and the ensuing projection. This insight . . . gives

113

rise to great mental pain and guilt when the depressive position is at its height . . .

p. 31

The depressive position is of course the dawn of ruth in normal infancy: or it can be a stage worked through in analysis. But one can also say, I believe, that in reconciling himself to the voices of envy or hate and accepting them as being within himself Mahler becomes, as the *Ninth Symphony* progresses, increasingly aware of the problem of the consequences of his own hate, and so experiences all the agonies of concern, as he becomes capable of love. There are many places where this anguish is expressed—not least is the episode which begins at the 13th bar of the final *Adagio,* where, even after so many attempts to integrate envy, it returns with terrible intensity, as Diether points out (Example 111, p. 212), yet out of this version of the chromatic turn immediately arises a revision of the principle triumphant statement 'extended in a new direction': the pain of depression goes with 'feelings of relief and hope'. Or, I believe we can say, it expresses feelings of being more alive and real, in complex with a deepening of the valuable capacity to feel concern: both being involved in a richer recognition both of one's mortality, and what transcends our mortality: i.e. gratitude for having existence, gratitude even for the agony.

Melanie Klein is relevant here:

> But it also (i.e., the insight) brings about feelings of relief and hope which in turn make it less difficult to reunite the two aspects of the object and of the self and to work through the depressive position. This hope is based on the growing unconscious knowledge that the internal and external object is not as bad as it was felt to be in its split off aspects.

p. 31

This is what happens in the First Movement of the *Ninth*. The music discussed on p. 180 conveys the sense of coming closer to the reality of (ambivalent) existence. And so, the threat of annihilation in the envy (hate) theme is largely overcome, at the cost of pain—but with joy, that the object is restored:

> Through mitigation of hatred by love the object improves in the infant's mind. It is no longer so strongly felt to have been destroyed in the past and the danger of its being destroyed in the future is lessened; not being injured, it is also felt to be less vulnerable in the present and future . . .

p. 31

With these developments, of course, go feelings of confidence in the capacity of the self to survive. Of course, as Melanie Klein emphasizes,

114

any such triumph is only temporary: 'such results . . . (can) . . . be temporarily undone.'

> Strain of an internal or external nature is liable to stir up depression and distrust . . .

And, we can add, life is always bringing strains, so the problem is insoluble: what counts is the work done. But this is real work, by contrast with unreal work:

> By contrast, the frequent way of dealing with depression by hardening one's feelings and denying depression is a regression to the manic defences used during the infantile depressive position.

Mahler's regression has the tremendous courage and strength of that creative reparation that accepts our human weakness and dependence. What he gains is a sense of that vulnerability that makes death unimportant: 'Death, thou shalt die!' But Melanie Klein's phrases explain why Mahler uses his linear structure, establishing 'islands' of 'work achieved', and then dealing with 'manic defence'—and rejecting it.

In his creative engagements with such ultimate problems of existence, Mahler is by no means 'morbid' or merely 'valedictory'. Today, when there is a heavy taboo on death (which has taken the place of the Victorian taboo on sex), we feel it is 'morbid' to dwell on the subject. However, to contemplate death may well sharpen a man's search for meaning in his life, and Alma Mahler records as we have seen how Mahler seemed even more capable of joy during his last year, when he knew death was approaching (see above, p. 24). Discussing Mozart, Wilfred Mellers says that he saw death as 'the context in which we exist': that is, existentially. And Mellers quotes a marvellous letter from Mozart to his father:

> I need not tell you with what anxiety I await better news from yourself. I count upon that with certainty, though I am wont in all things to anticipate the worst. Since death (take my words literally) is the true goal of our lives, I have made myself so well acquainted during the last two years with this true and best friend of mankind that the idea of it no longer has any terrors for me, but much that is tranquil and comforting. And I thank God that he has granted me the good fortune to obtain the opportunity (you understand my meaning) of regarding death as the key to our true happiness. I never lie down in bed without considering that, young as I am, perhaps I may on the morrow be no more. Yet not one of those who know me could say that I am morose or melancholy, and for this I thank my Creator daily and wish heartily that the same happiness may be given to my fellow men.
>
> Quoted in *Man and His Music*, 3, p. 51

In Mahler it may have proved to be too late for him to employ such existential resignation as he achieved, in his living—his mortal existence was already doomed. (How poignant is Alma Mahler's account of the moment when Mahler, on his death-bed, could no longer hear!)

But the very structure of Mahler's *Ninth*, with its Rondo-like return to the same themes, and thus to engage with the same problems, marks the persistence of his quest, which has that determination expressed by T. S. Eliot in *Four Quartets*:

We shall not cease from exploration . . .

The structure of the symphony (like the structure of *Four Quartets*) is like a series of therapeutic sessions or attempts to re-experience growth, round the same essential problems of existence: this structure, in itself, represents, too, a certain kind of engagement with the problem of Time.

Although it symbolizes an intense subjective exploration, the value of the creative achievement of Mahler to our world lies in this willingness to undergo exploration for what he wrestles with is that primitive hate which could, exported into the world, by its annihilating impulses, end it. Jack Diether, relevantly, sees a threat from the thermonuclear age even to Mahler's joyful sense of the world's eternal continuity. Because of its persistent engagement with this hate the *Ninth Symphony* is about the end of the world in terms of the potential universal loss of a sense of the point of life—and the possible triumph of the collapse of meaning and values.

The nuclear bomb may be seen in one sense as an ultimate symbol of our ontological insecurity, and our compensation for this in hate. How shall we link Mahler's expression of collapse and destruction with the problem of identity—and the Bomb? From philosophical anthropology we have to say that *even the hydrogen bomb is a product of distorted love*—of the paranoid-schizoid dynamic. Mahler (like psychoanalysis) shows us that hate itself seems to emerge from love, and from the very fount of identity (as does Example 13 from Example 33). The dilemma of ambivalence is the price of consciousness—of being human and alive in the light of the blue horizon. Hate is inseparable from love, even as it burgeons in the exploring vitality of bodily and psychic being—hate is bound up with joy, because it is a manifestation of hunger. For Mahler love and libidinal joy are pregnant with distrust: hate springs out of the libidinal urge itself.

Any gains must be exposed to the ultimate forces of manic denial and to derision, as of the sense of schizoid futility. They must be tested

116

against the hate we feel for the 'regressed libidinal ego'—the unborn infant within us, who reminds us of our dependence. It must be tested even against the hebephrenic giggle, which asserts that we have no problem at all ('Of course we are alive: guilt and hate need not threaten us, because they don't exist, nor does our need to make reparation, nor does our weakness . . .') Only by such 'tests' can confident resolution be achieved, for otherwise we may be merely ensnared by 'pretend' or 'manic' reparation: in the third movement we test beyond the manic, to the near-psychotic. By crying as Lawrence did, 'Let me not deceive myself', Mahler achieves a sense of true gratitude which can be celebrated, because nothing has been found that can eradicate all meaning. Yet this gladness in the continuity of life can be only held for a moment. But it is followed by poignant yet peaceful satisfaction in having had the experience of such utter resignation, (though the struggle must go on again, in the *Tenth*). Only by such creative effort to solve the problem of existence is the pain of the apprehension of the true nature of things turned to a glad paean that things are what they are—and that one has existed, and has been capable, because of one's consciousness and love, to convey meaning on the universe even though one is weak and mortal. That is the message of the *Ninth*.

8

Towards The Still Centre: How Psychological and Philosophical Themes become Music

How can such complex philosophical themes become music? Musical analysis confirms the nature of Mahler's progress. His is the progress of the soul, and does not belong to 'Time before and time after', but to the 'moment in and out of time': so, his music moves towards a new feeling about time. His quest for integration is episodic and grows continuously, not by conflict but by resolution: so, this is the form of his music. Diether is aware of the connection when he says of the *Ninth*:

> The development section gets away from the tonic key, not by modulating rapidly and freely without ever touching the home key, in the usual manner, but by setting up alien 'islands' which crumble one by one, each succeeded by futile gropings to 'attain' or 'remember' the song of peace.
>
> Diether, p. 79

Diether discusses the episodic structure of the symphony in such a way as to make it clearly possible to discuss the work in existentialist terms. He sees the music as a creative groping to 'attain' or 'remember' the song of peace which is the song of love—or, more significantly, the song of being, of original being-at-one-with. What has to be remembered, in order to maintain a sense of survival and continuity throughout the 'crumbling islands' of anguished experience, is the core of being which was experienced (albeit weakly) in the first stages of primary identification. So it may be possible to make 'the end accord with the beginning.'

Of course, we are not trying to substitute a psychological analysis for the music. Diether warns us against his own criticism. Though he had studied Mahler's life, letters and music for twenty-five years before he wrote his essay, he believes that the symphony is so complex a work that there is danger in trying to simplify its meaning in explicit terms. One must always go back to the music, not least because the music has a direct emotional meaning about which any explicit statement can be no more than a rough generalization. Yet because of Mahler's particular way of developing, and because of his own interest in words, we can, I believe, understand the music better if we are trying to understand better what it is 'about'.

Diether emphasizes that the symphony is 'one of the most heart-rendering utterances in all music', a comment one would fervently endorse. This comment serves, for my purposes, to emphasize the amount of true reparation in the work: as Diether says in another essay, 'loss, estrangement, guilt, and anxiety' are profoundly felt in this work 'as they are in Kafka'. Moreover, by contrast with the attempts we have looked at to see Mahler's work as a referring to 'outside' events, Diether's insistence is that Mahler's musical technique is comparable to the 'stream of consciousness' technique in literature, and he sees the conflict as an inward one: 'Instinctively, Mahler recognized that the true life of musical creation is largely subconscious.' So, despite the explicit verbal origins of some themes and preoccupations the music as experience is 'more emotionally compelling than mere words can ever be'. And in the *Ninth* especially Mahler 'goes beyond "the word as bearer of the idea" ' :

> The 'message' is implied rather than stated, and so the more direct emotional meaning which music can impart is totally freed from the original verbal inspiration.

p. 69

Making connections between the life and the work are not here reductive. The more we know of Mahler's life and his music, the more poignant the *Ninth* and *Tenth Symphonies* become. We can often trace Mahler's meanings because of his facility for conscious and unconscious self-quotation. Bruno Walter says that *Das Lied von der Erde* and the *Ninth Symphony* are 'without musical connection'. But Diether establishes that in fact they are connected in a subtle, allusive way, while other links may be made with earlier works, especially the *Gesellen* cycle, the *Kindertotenlieder* and the *First*.

Often Mahler's self-quotations have a philosophical, or perhaps it would be more useful to say an existentialist meaning, which is transformed from one work into another. Here Diether gives as an example the 'motor rhythm of *Das Irdische Leben,* composed before 1892', which 'turns up in the 1910 sketch for the *'Purgatorio'* movement of the *Tenth Symphony*'.

119

We recognize the rhythm of the 'Mill of Life' which accompanies the ballad of child starvation, and we feel, perhaps without verbalizing it, as Gloucester in *King Lear* did . . .

> As flies to wanton boys are we to the gods;
> They kill us for their sport . . .

. . . Perhaps, in the cosmic view of our planet, all mankind is allegorically a child starving in the midst of plenty . . .

p. 71

This 'starving child' is surely the Regressed Libidinal Ego whose yearning to be was associated in Mahler's mind with the child Ernst swept away by Death, before he could realize his potentialities? The need to be reflected, and the failures of reflection: these themes belong to the existence problems of all men whenever they feel *'abandonné'*, as when we experience the death of loved ones, or are made in some such way to confront the problems of meaning in our lives that we normally forget. For those of us who have no faith, all we have to begin with is our own resources. All we can find is our own immaturity and emptiness starving for a sense of meaning, and the opportunity to be. Mahler's achievement is to have been able to accept the ultimate reality of death and to swallow the terrible implications that we have nothing more substantial to set against nothingness than the brief existence of a 'poor bare fork'd animal' with a childish ego-weakness at the core, able to find meaning only through his dependence and his need for 'confirmation'. How can a composer who has relinquished God and a transcendental reality believe that 'in my end is my beginning'? How is it that all that has been painfully constructed in the First Movement 'will disintegrate again'? What does the 'painful construction' consist of anyway?

Diether's analysis of the key-relationships can provide a clue, I believe. He says that Mahler discovered with the writing of the *Fifth Symphony* that the 'polarity of (the) semitone shift satisfied his sense of overall tonal progression'. The *Fifth* and *Seventh* move a semitone upward and 'the fact that only the *Ninth* moves a semitone downward acquires a special and poignant significance'. The *Ninth* is also his only symphony of which *each* movement inhabits a different tonality from the others: D, C, A, and D flat.

Even so, the tonal relationships of the first three movements is classically simple. A minor is the dominant minor key of D major, and C major is the relative major key of A minor.

If the symphony had ended in D after C major and D minor this would have been 'a scheme common enough in Haydn's time': it is the D flat which is Mahler's stamp.

But there is also in the *Ninth* a special quality in the tonality that is Mahlerian. No other symphony begins with two sharps and ends with five flats: Diether relates this to Mahler's love of enharmonic relationships. He compares the development of key relationships in the *Ninth* with those in the *Fifth*. The *Fifth* moves from a 'desolate funeral march in C sharp minor'—'prostrate'—to 'a lively, bustling D major implying *an acceptance of life's challenge, an unquenchable optimism even in the teeth of the cruellest oppression*'. The *Ninth* 'depicts a retirement from life' (or, I would say, is *said* to depict such a withdrawal). But what happens?

> It sinks once more *from* D major—to what? Initially to D flat major, for it is a voluntary retirement, and so the tonality suffers a sea-change . . . a willing renunciation of life and acceptance of its end . . . This is more positive—a step further, so to speak, than the sweet nostalgic regret in the first movement, but it is no less subject to reversion. So the *Adagio*'s second subject is pitched in that very enharmonic minor, that C sharp minor of the *Fifth*'s desolate opening, and the music passes easily from one dimension into the other, back and forth, without visible movement. This is music truly on the threshold of infinity. Thus the ubiquitous tonic major-minor complex is present in the *Adagio* in a newly enhanced context, through the use of enharmonics. Tonally we have the progression of the *Fifth* in reverse, and partly something altogether different, *reflecting the ambiguity of Mahler's feeling*. The '*ewig*' cadence and the chromatic fate-motif are here too, fully integrated into the new musical fabric. Thus the whole *Adagio* translates into pure music the poetic ambiguity of *Der Abschied*, with its lingering sensuousness and overwhelming passion of its outburst apostrophizing '*Schoenheit*', '*ewigen Liebens*', and the '*Lebens-trunk'ne Welt*'. It is music imbued not only with the utmost sadness of leave-taking, *but with a deep love of life and a feeling for life in every fibre*.
>
> pp. 96–7 (my italics)

This piece of musical analysis reveals that in the depth of the texture Mahler's symphony is a massive achievement of a positive *hold* on life, a positive existential impulse, even under the most imminent threat of death and disintegration. It is truly tragic: it moves forward by accepting nothingness; but then builds bridges over the chasm. It is not 'valedictory' but gropes for transcendent meaning and values.

So I am still not satisfied with the terms being used. Diether's analysis is of course far more satisfactory than Dr Redlich's 'Union of life and death'. I still want to dig beneath these terms, and to explore the 'ambiguity of Mahler's feeling'. Wherein lies the strength of Mahler's capacity to convey a triumphant 'feeling for life in every fibre', in three great valedictory works?

The answer is, I believe, that Mahler dares in the *Ninth Symphony* to accept his need for a *massive regression*. He accepts the need for the re-birth of the regressed libidinal ego, and goes back to primary identification with the mother to re-experience the source of the sense of being and to the original creative reflection. That is, he needs to refind the sources of the 'core of being'.

The piece begins, sepulchrally, with quiet low notes on the horn and cello. But the rhythm which is established is also that of the primaeval heart-beat

EXAMPLE 6

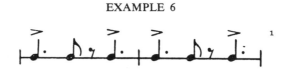

felt through the belly wall or at the mother's breast. But it is also a funereal drum. The rocking of the cradle (or the mother's arms) is the 'eternity' figure of *'ewig'*. Death and psychic birth are here combined we begin to listen as if with our attention riveted to the quiet primaeval beat of our bodily life and to our most primary consciousness of being.[2]

> But hark! my pulse, like a soft drum
> Tell thee I come . . .

The symphony is to explore how *'dans ma fin est mon commencement'* : so we have regressed inwardly from the threat of death in the world, to the primal beginnings of consciousness, when one was but a pulse, and no more. What is the significance of that pulse being created? As Diether indicates, these opening themes derive from the *'ewig'* theme of *Das Lied* and are both valedictory, and *longing* : we have regressed out of time to a time before birth and a time out of time ('once below a time') in which alone the sense of a meaning-that-has-been can exist.

[1] Later to become

EXAMPLE 7

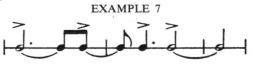

in the violins—the last movement enacting the truth that 'Death is omnipresent and inescapable' (as Diether says). See below, p. 224.

[2] Cf. 'Sit on my finger, sing in my ear, O littleblood', *Littleblood*, Ted Hughes, *Crow*, p. 80. Or, in Sylvia Plath's work, 'I am I am I am'.

Under the threat of death Mahler seeks to be reborn in the sense of becoming invulnerable, existentially. To do this he must 'recreate the object' and re-experience 'confirmation'—to find himself whole, to a whole Alma; to make peace with himself and the whole earth. So, he returns to the first experience of at-one-ness, from which the core of being derives. He mothers himself. From there he begins at once to explore the discovery of the self, of the me and the not me, so that the suspension in a recaptured sense of eternity quickly gives way to movement, expansion, exploration and discovery. From the sense of unitary being (at-one-ness, *ewig*) of subjective identification with the feminine element he moves towards the discovery of the object, and so of object-relations—the mother, the woman partner. From this inevitably rise the problems of hate and existence anxiety, since he is treading the path towards painful ruth and concern.

The first orchestral song has the hesitant and expanding shape of a primal exploring awareness. It is a breathing

EXAMPLE 8

Andante comodo

—and it is also an echo and a tender groping—a musical expression of 'togetherness' seeking 'a presence in the being of the other', to quote Buber again.

To say that passages of music enact 'encounter' is bold, and, of course, this kind of interpretation is very subjective (yet, for example, the poetry and music of *Das Lied* are full of images of reflection, echo, seeing and being seen, and being heard). Surely this figure in the melody of the orchestral song—

EXAMPLE 9

Andante comodo

may be seen as the musical equivalent of something like the inarticulate communication between mother and infant? The echoing theme is obvious too in Example 10, overleaf:

123

EXAMPLE 10

where the imitative response between object and subject (or perhaps between subject and subjective object) seems also to be enacted as *'creative reflection'*. Or to put it another way, the music speaks of the first primitive grunts and cooings of mother and baby, in symbiotic at-one-ness, and 'primary maternal preoccupation'. Here in music is a deeply moving statement of the experience of *liebende Wirheit*, even of primitive play—in the rocking movements as if in the mother's arms (or at the heart of the deepest moments of shared being in making love as an adult). As Mahler needed to listen to his wife's breathing through open doors it is here the breathing of the self *as echoed by the object*. It is, I believe, a musical enactment of that murmuring exchange one can hear between mother and neonate before there is any question of communication—even at the telepathic stage of primary identification. Soon, the tentative steps of exploration, of feeling of space, are encouraged, step by step, as a mother responds to her child's giving, as his fingers uncurl.

EXAMPLE 11

The last phrase (marked *molto express.*) is like an expanding thrill in an infant's body, as he employs the discoveries of the first tentative touches to make a significant discovery of himself, and of the world in which he finds himself. The creatively reflected new psychic I AM explores his existence as a network in space.

The melodic phrase curls round the richness of this gain with deep satisfaction: linked by rhythm with the heart, it is a touch and gain of love, and makes tender references to erotic parallels in the rhythm and movements of physical love. Yet the melody is poignantly nostalgic and broken: for the recollection of a child's love is overlaid by the sad lament on the horns, as for the death of childhood innocence, for in the background is an adult knowledge of the death of a child—such as Mahler renders in the *First Symphony* and the *Kindertotenlieder*. The poignancy in Mahler's music surely comes from the sense that he was faced with death while still overcome with awareness that he had not yet found the secret of meaningful existence, despite titanic efforts to bring the core of the self to birth. (When he watched Ernst die as a child he must have been miserably aware that a child has no philosophical capacity to come to terms with death.)

EXAMPLE 12

The developing vocal melody at the opening surely marks (as by its richer and richer orchestration) the advance of the tentative explorations of love from the primal to maturity?

This music at the beginning of the *Ninth* re-enacts the discovery of space by the child, and it echoes from earlier works the forces of creativity and love. It moves towards the expanding joy of existence, and picks up themes from *Das Lied*. The dominant symbols are Mother Earth, the perfection of the circle of the blue horizon (blue is 'Mary's colour', the sky, heaven, infinity), and blooming, spring, eternal greenness, everywhere and 'for ever'. Relevant concepts are eternity, completeness; also yearning, and longing. The peacefulness is in conflict with falling, sinking, and sorrow *('leide!')*. But predominant are the rhythms of the quiet heart, of breathing and the echo of breathing, and of the soft funeral drum which is both the mortal pulse and the rocking arms of the mother. The essence of the 'love song' or 'peace song' in the *Ninth* is its feminity—it belongs to the primary experience of *being* in the mother's arms, cradled, rocking, crooned to: and it echoes the rocking peace of *Der Abschied* (which is also the peace of at-one-ness with Mother Earth that Mahler achieves under the contemplation of death).

But in the *Ninth* the pulse of love, as it grows, takes in adult passion, sorrow, love, the need for freedom. As when one was an infant, this excitement brings *hunger*, the hunger to be, and so that incorporative hunger that is hate (or envy). Out of Example 33 (p. 153) emerges hate.

What I call the hate-theme first appears in the First Movement, early on (pocket score, pp. 6–7). Its essence is that it is chromatic, and curls back upon itself, as if to circumnambulate one's defences, to tread one down, or undermine the soul. It slides and yaws, as if to menace with emptiness. If we compare it with the musical forms I have described above as '*mandalas*' of security, the 'hate' theme unwinds what they create, and opens a chasm into which one might fall beneath the structures they establish. Yet as Diether points out, the hate theme is merely a chromatization of the '*ewig*' theme, combined with a major-minor alteration and the rhythm of the opening funereal heart-beat. It is (like hate) a distortion or inversion of love, developed into a fierce cry of anguish:

EXAMPLE 13

The end of the theme resembles a barbed tail, which thrusts at us as we are cowed by the outburst of disintegration. The yawing effect is emphasized by the *diminuendo* opening again to *forte*: the theme often sounds like a beast-voice snarling, or an aggressive male voice—expressing the oral (and perhaps anal) sadism of hate. The rhythms are dotted and off-beat, the theme is punctuated by abrupt rests as if by angry indrawn breath. The harmony is unnerving, the intervals include the tritone, the *diabolus in musica*.

Because this theme emerges from primitive paranoia, it sounds as if it is 'out there' in the world. The savage horns or trombones are 'apart': and speak like ferocious animals, menacing ghosts, or the voices of death.

EXAMPLE 14

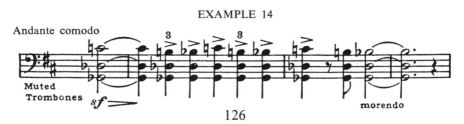

126

In certain psychoanalytical studies of Mahler, it has been suggested that one main-spring of his music is unconscious guilt at his brother's death. But such a theory is too reductive, as is much Freudian analysis, which often seems to concern itself with 'unmasking' 'surface' emotions —to show the 'true' feelings underneath. Why should not Mahler's primary feelings here be grief? Of course, his guilt may well have had to struggle with unconscious hostility. Maybe there was sibling rivalry; maybe Mahler's mother did have another child too soon after Mahler's birth; maybe he did feel in some way that, when his brother died, he had brought his death about, by his own unconscious hatred. But anyone who has listened to the music must surely know, from its effect upon their deepest feelings, that Mahler's anguish over his brother's death was one of the most important experiences in his life—and his *loving grief* was the most real thing about this dreadful experience.

Of course, there may be a strange mixture of hate, guilt and love, even in grief: when anyone close to us dies we fear that our outbursts of hate towards them in the past, or in fantasy, have at last had their effect. So, we may say that when Mahler explored love he found it menaced by death, and that this menace was too appallingly like hate— his own hate, his father's hate, the destructive elements in all experience. The inescapable reality of death made the struggle with hate and destructiveness within seem futile: yet unless this struggle was success- ful, life would go on seeming a cruel joke. So we might say that all his music emerges, like the music of the tragic flute in *Das Klagende Lied*, from the bones of his brother. This brother's ghost haunted him all his life—offering from the shadows a joyful encounter, from the world of the dead:

Again the song of yearning *(das Lied der Sehnsucht)* sounds in my ears, and again we wander together over familiar fields. There stands the organ- grinder, holding his hat in his withered hand, and in his music, so out of tune, I hear the greeting of 'Ernst von Schwaben'. Now Ernst himself appears, holding out his arms to me; and as I gaze at him, I see it is my poor brother.

(Letter to Steiner, June, 1879)

('Ernst von Schwaben' is the name of an opera which Mahler abandoned.)

The reference to the organ-grinder here is uncanny, especially the reference to the fact that his music is out-of-tune, for it shows that chromatic, 'turning' music of that out-of-tune kind was associated in his mind with ghosts that came towards him from the world of death, child ghosts, such as we encounter in the *Kindertotenlieder*, which question the point of human life.

From all of Ruckert's poems (literally hundreds) Mahler selected those which were about the death of his little son, who was also named Ernst. We may also note that one of these poems refers to the reflection of the child in the mother's face, while their general effect is to colour our feelings about the world of reality itself, seen either covered with darkness, or illuminated with the light from human eyes. This problem of 'seeing reality' was obviously also experienced by Mahler in a special way: he needed to concentrate on images of trees and flowers, at times, for instance, in order to resolve his own agonized feelings. While composing the *Klagende Lied*, he concentrated his view on a corner of his room—only to see a strange (paranoid-schizoid) image of his own face breaking through the wall. This story, bizarre as it is, suggests that Mahler's confusion of self and wall at that moment was seriously schizoid, and brought on by distress caused at the remembrance of his brother's death, and the existential dread associated with it, explored in the symbolism of the *Klagende Lied*. The ape that mocks (like the monkey sitting on the barrel-organ) is identical with such a menacing face —it is his own face, his own capacity to be menacing, ugly, and hateful. It is the split-off hate projected away from oneself, but then menacing.

To Mahler to be ugly was an 'insult to God':

All creation adorns itself continually for God. Everyone therefore has only one duty, to be as beautiful in every way in the eyes of God and man. Ugliness is an insult to God.

Mahler, quoted in Gustav Mahler, p. 184

By contrast, the true reality of life was 'soul'—in the meanings of consciousness: in this letter he shows himself a true existentialist:

(To Alma, 5 December 1901)
. . . music, mysterious as it is, often illumines our souls with a flash of lightning, and you will feel that the only true reality on earth is soul. For anyone who has once grasped this, what we call reality is no more than a formula, a shadow with no substance—And you must not, please, take this for a poetical metaphor; it is a conviction which can hold its own at the bar of sober reason.

Gustav Mahler, p. 206

So, if meaning and symbolism are threatened by being insulted and made coarse (as in our culture today) then life loses its reality, and 'sober reason' should be appalled.

Mahler's imminent death evoked all the fears of annihilation which he experienced as a child when his world seemed threatened by the savagery and vulgarity of his father, in aggressiveness or sexual arousal. These moments seemed to him like the threatening impingement of 'false male doing', and thus an attack on being. In that this savagery and vulgarity were in himself (for, as we all do, he had internalized his father), these elements seemed to threaten the quest for (female element) being, and the possibilities of ontological security altogether. They threatened both creativity and meaning. And so, since he 'lived in music', they threatened existence itself (just as today's attack on consciousness in a nihilistic culture menaces our survival—while, to use Hamlet's words, 'reason panders will', as intellectuals plunge into sensualism).

Against this dissolution, Mahler draws on 'natural being'—remembering the solace he gained, when his father left him in the woods. Donald Mitchell has pointed out the use of birdsong in Mahler, which anticipates Messaien. Five pages before the end of the *First Movement* we have (at *Plötzlich bedeutend langsamer und leise*, p. 56, *'Misteroso'*) a passage which enacts a man listening to a bird, while a contrapuntal Bach-like ground rises to a pitch of glad gratitude (after *Nicht mehr so langsam*, bar 386, through the *crescendo* to double *forte*). It enacts the Biblical phrase, 'He shall rise up at the voice of the bird'. After the gladness we again re-experience the threat of envy (at *Etwas belebter*, bar 393): but at once—at *gehalten*, bar 395, there is a statement of the possibility of the 'inclusion' of hate by the introduction of the resolving D natural (see Example 3). Everywhere in Mahler the resolution of dread and hate are associated with benign influences from the natural world—the linden tree in the *Gesellen* cycle; the moon, autumn and the blue horizon in *Das Lied*; even (in the *Kindertotenlieder*) the gale and wet weather that drenches the bones of the dead children—while their souls are in heaven. This return to Nature is a regression to the healing power of the Mother ('He lay us as we lay at birth on the cool flowery lap of earth', as Shelley said of Wordsworth).

By regression to 'memories of feeling' the composer, like a patient under analysis, develops 'a different attitude to his earlier frustrations' and envy comes to be 'included'.

The effect of this regression is to remember 'reconsidered passion': if one goes back to the primal encounter, and asks what emerged from it, hate is bound up with the very growth of freedom itself. The aggression in hate is to be seen as the assertion of life. The musical developments which enact these processes are embodiments of Mahler's subjective experience of the embracing of one's own aggression—such as Winnicott refers to in a discussion of its origins. We can find our hate (as aggression) a source of strength, in that it emerges from our energy to be ourselves:

> Put in a nutshell, aggression has two meanings. By one meaning it is directly or indirectly a reaction to frustration. By the other meaning it is a source of an individual's energy . . . actual aggression in one sense is seen to be an achievement.
>
> 'The Roots of Aggression' in *The Child The Family and the Outside World*, pp. 232ff

The embracing of one's aggression, and the discovery of its hate-dynamics as an 'achievement' is at one with what Melanie Klein (above) calls 'allowing the all-important processes of ego-integration and object-synthesis to operate'. *'Thus a mitigation of hatred by love can come about in some measure and the depressive position can be worked through'*—but (as we have seen from Melanie Klein) with much suffering.

The first achievement in the *Ninth* is the beginning of this 'working through' towards becoming able to bear the pain of responsibility towards the 'other'—the 'object' who has become 'synthesized' (or 'found'). This is what happens in Example 3 above.

This must be one of the greatest moments in modern music. Its poignant triumphantness and peacefulness were achieved at the cost of anguish—the anguish which gives the moment its power to move us so deeply, and belongs to the 'stage of concern'. The new vision of love here is also an awareness of the universal human predicament, now seen in its wholeness for the first time, and not wished away by magic or omnipotence:

> The more integrated ego becomes capable of experiencing guilt and feelings of responsibility, which it was unable to face [previously].
>
> Winnicott, *op. cit.*

The resolution happens, of course, in a wide context, of which Diether writes:

> a cadenza that flutters and quivers on the threshold of that haven of peace . . . as the last spectres scatter and vanish . . . the chromatic fate-motif is caught up in this resolution, united and reconciled . . . in a piquant and magical piece of tone-painting.
>
> Diether, p. 80

130

As Diether points out, in this reprise, instead of the expositionary climax with the hate motif *('for we have been through all that and more')* it remains in a partial state of suspension, interrupted only fitfully by attempts of the more passionate music to break through. Formally this represents a cadenza leading to the coda,[3] with a classical if much elaborated cadential trill. (Note, he says, how the minor third tone is raised to the major again just before resolution):

EXAMPLE 15

It is in the first part of the coda that the hate motif is caught up in the resolution. It is united, and reconciled, with both the figures in Example 16 overleaf:

[3] *Footnote* in Diether: 'Compare the cadenza on the dominant of F sharp minor in the finale of the *Second Symphony* (Cue 30)'—*Chord and Discord*, p. 79.

EXAMPLE 16

This is the first figure to introduce the D tone, and continues to stress the fifth and sixth (already sparsely stated: see Example 25) by means of an 'echo', which reaches upwards between the little shuddering figure on the violas.

It is also reconciled with this outcry:

EXAMPLE 17

This shrill lament comes before Example 13 and anticipates the chromatic figure in its first bar. As we shall see, this 'quotes' the chromatic existential theme at *'Du aber, Mensch, wie lang lebst denn du?'* from the most anguished passage from *Das Lied*. (See below Example 20, p. 139, and p. 157, Examples 17, 37, and 20 compared.) So, in the 'mitigation' of the hate motif, we find the palpitating viola figure become ethereal—and the acceptance of mortality, yielding a change which has been long desired.

Diether sees it as parallel to a passage of resolution in Wagner:

> The aesthetic effect, though quite different, is analogous to that wrought by the upward resolution of the chromatic motif of desire at the end of Isolde's *Liebestod*. As in *Tristan*, Mahler's chromatic motif of anguished protest is heard literally dozens of times before it is finally resolved in this passage.

p. 8

How simple in essence is the perception by which hate is resolved by love! Yet how much creative anguish and courage is behind this coming-to-terms with hate. The motif Example 16 belongs to 'togetherness' and primal being. So, this astonishing transmutation is possible, because love can mature, as hate cannot. This truth, pointed out by Michael

Balint, is of great relevance, to the arts today. To take the path of hate can only lead towards greater and greater desperation and negation. But this path is taken by some, because the pain of acceptance (Example 17) is too great to bear. Yet to accept such pain of being human is our only way to solve our problems. The symphony is thus at once both a great work of regression, and at the same time a great achievement of maturity.

I do not wish to imply that Mahler's music merely represents a therapeutic activity to resolve problems of infancy: but rather that in the face of the adult problem of existence, in a Godless universe, among crumbling social order, we need to ask 'What is it to be human?' in full recognition of our deepest needs, bound up as these are with encounter and ego-weakness. In a sense what Mahler had to do was to 'manufacture a sense of being' he did not possess: but his music is, in lieu of a 'lap' to help us regrow a sense of being, the nearest we can get, through symbolism, to the re-experience of primary life, and the discovery there of the potentialities created by *liebende Wirheit*.

As Guntrip says,

> The mother first supplies the baby with his basis for 'being' while he is still in the womb, and must be able to prolong that secure experience of 'being-at-one-with-her' after birth, so that as the baby begins to experience his physical and psychological separateness from the mother at a conscious level, he is protected, by the unconscious persistence of the feeling of 'being at one with', from the shock of what might otherwise be experienced as a feeling of being 'cut off', lost, dying.
>
> *Schizoid Phenomena*, p. 266

Mahler was dying: so, he seeks to re-enact the sense of being-at-one with the mother which, being inadequately experienced in his own infancy, has left him feeling 'cut off' and lost. He strives to develop a fully male—a true male—strength, rooted in being, to bear his predicament:

> The conscious ego is the ego of separation, of 'doing', of acting and being acted on, and in that sense is the location of the male element in personality. It must derive as strength from the deepest unconscious core of the self that has never lost the sense of 'being-at-one-with' the maternal source of its life.
>
> *ibid.*, p. 266

His music enriches our souls with that kind of strength (by contrast, 'pseudo-male' black art merely leaves our ego-weakness betrayed, if not more withdrawn).

For related reasons, Mahler had to go beyond the musical conventions of 'acting and being acted upon'. Tonal music, traditional structures, and

Western time, all belong to these, and thus to the dissociated male element of doing, split off from 'being'. This predominance of doing as a pathological pseudo-male manifestation[4] is the characteristic of our culture: this is but a culmination of a traditional neglect of being. Mahler renounces the traditional forms because their apparent philosophical security no longer satisfied him. He pursues a new existentialist development. He discovers in his escape beyond tonality, in Oriental stoicism, in his linear, episodic structure, and in a new feeling about Time, an original musical art which enables him to bring new resources to bear on our problems of life. One of the major elements in human nature which he brings to bear in this way is 'female element being', with all its capacities for 'Primal Maternal Preoccupation', or the feminine capacity in us to forfeit our self interest, to bring new worlds into being, and to confirm meaning in the unique existence, by creative reflection. In this he finds the way to the discovery and release of *potentia*—as Nietszche said, *Wie Man wird, was Man ist*—'how one becomes what one is'. (See Kaufmann, W., *Nietzsche*, 1950, p. 133).

Mahler seeks an existential security that belongs to

> Release from action and suffering, release from the inner
> And outer compulsion . . .

—but this is no forfeiture of life or consciousness, but rather a quest for the still centre, where an unextinguishable sense of authenticity may be found.

*

By what agencies in music, however, could Mahler arrive at his goal? Here, we can look back to *Das Lied von der Erde* where musical elements are made explicit by association with the words. As we have seen, in *Das Lied* is foreshadowed the possibility of achieving gratitude for having existed. In that work, envy has been touched on—as in the song *Youth*, which is almost bitterly nostalgic for 'vanished youth and scattered love', while in the drunkard's song the composer explores the possibility of a nihilistic indifference to life. He explores the problem which Melanie Klein discusses, of the impulse to 'devalue' in the individual tormented by envy, who sinks into destructive confusion:

Was geht mich denn der Frühling an!?

Later, in the *Ninth Symphony*. we hear the man 'learning' something profoundly illuminating from a bird's song: the drunkard—who hears

4 See Guntrip, *op. cit.*, pp. 255ff.

134

the birdsong—is unable to draw on the natural resources of joy in life because of his envy (which has taken the oral-aggressive form of the alcoholic). So there is a poignant sadness of contrast between what is offered by life, and the inability of the manic drunk to take it. The next song, however, opens with bird-trills over a grave pedal note, and the calmness of heart in reconciliation—'*warum es müsste sein*'—is achieved by what is taken in from the natural world, in gladness. The ghost's gratitude for having lived is inseparable from the trills of the birdsong of continuing life:

EXAMPLE 18

Grave

This is another kind of turn in Mahler, and it can be associated with the turn in the bass which underscores the major reference in the last song to the symbolism of continuing life, the grass on the paths on which the wanderer walks and sings his songs (as Mahler walked on his mountain paths, composing in his head).

EXAMPLE 19

Tranquillo

The word underscored by this figure is '*weichem*'—translated as 'tender' (the word has a flavour of 'feminine'). The emotion conveyed is of a glad compassion for the humblest of manifestations of the continuing cycles of life, as in the folksong *The Trees they do Grow High*, where human mortality is placed in the context of ever continuing natural love and growth. A favourite theme in his life and work is that of *listening*—as to the voice of the bird, or even to the thunder. For Mahler even found joy in the most destructive noises of nature:

(To Alma, 23 June 1904)
thunder and lightning, and claps so loud it's a joy to hear them . . .
Gustav Mahler, p. 237

—and this was at a moment when he was also writing about his

miserable efforts to assemble the scattered fragments of my inner self . . .
ibid., p. 237

Separated from her, he wrote:

(To Alma, 1 December 1901)
It (going away) makes me very unhappy, yet it is almost like the voice of the Master, the Teacher. (I say that to avoid saying 'God', because we have said so little on that topic and I could not bear it if mere phrases passed between us). The voice summons us to be brave, enduring, patient . . . even if the Teacher's voice is heard in the thunder, we must still understand it . . .
ibid., p. 208

To Alma, he wrote that she must *question*:

(To Alma, 9 December 1901)
Sometimes I shall pause and have that mistrustful look which has so often surprised you. It is not *mistrust*, in the ordinary sense, but a *question* addressed to you and the future. Dearest, *learn to answer*. It is not an easy thing to learn—you have first to know yourself thoroughly. But to *ask* is more difficult still. Only by asking can one learn one's whole and inmost relation to others Dearest, dear one, *learn to ask*!
Gustav Mahler, p. 207

In the *Third Symphony* the nightingale urges men to listen:

> *O Mensch! O Mensch!*
> *Gib acht! Gib acht!*
> *Was spricht die tiefe mitternacht?*

—and this *'Gib acht'* theme becomes the *'ewig'* theme in *Das Lied* and then the opening song of the *Ninth*.

'Listening' was also a question of listening to the 'breathing of the Earth' and to the breathing of 'the significant object':

The door of our two rooms, which were next to each other, had to be always open. He had to hear my breathing. I often work in the night and found him standing at my bedside in the darkness, and started as at the apparition of a departed spirit. I had to fetch him from his studio every day for meals. I did so very cautiously. He was often lying on the floor weeping in his dread that he might lose me, had lost me perhaps already. On the floor, he said, he was nearer to the earth . . .

Gustav Mahler, p. 173

But not all that one heard from such listening was pleasant—sometimes it was terrible. Alma writes:

One day in the summer he came running down from his hut in a perspiration and hardly able to breathe. At last he came out with it: it was the heat, the stillness, the Panic terror. It had gripped him and he had fled. He was often overcome by this feeling of the goat-god's frightful and ebullient eye upon him in his solitude, and he had to take refuge in the house among human beings and go on with his work there . . . 1907, while working on *Das Lied*.

ibid., p. 116

This 'listening' and 'asking' enabled Mahler to explore the nature of hate, so that he could eventually find it as having a meaning in itself.

But what Mahler chiefly learnt from 'natural being' was a sense of continuity, that he was able to take into himself. Despite man's sorrow, and despite death, the birds sing on, and the grass grows: the horizon is forever a blue circle where heaven meets earth, and life goes on. This becomes for Mahler a symbol of the eternity only achievable by the soul in terms of a transcendent sense of being. In aspiring towards 'eternity' Mahler is aspiring towards an inner completeness that is invulnerable to dissociation. Despite its resemblance to the '*Lebewohl*' figure in Beethoven's *Piano Sonata*, Opus 81A, it is not only '*farewell*' but '*ever*', and so attempts to 'make the end accord with the beginning'. It can be associated with that whole ambiguity by which in this symphony, as Diether says, we begin 'with the distant tread of death, and which (having) examined every aspect of its proximity to life, ends as nearly and truly reconciled to both as seems possible for a man of Mahler's tremendous and clear-sighted intellect to become'. In *Das Lied* experience has been that of a 'wild delirious world'—of supreme joy. Despite the threat of personal death, '*Die liebe Erde all überall und ewig, ewig blauen licht die Fernen, ewig, ewig*'. Here is a vision of the 'good object', who is now the whole world, Mother Earth, in our experience of whom lies the clue to that gratitude which promises escape for ever from destructive envy. Envy belongs to time and manic-depressive conflict. As we escape from it we escape from tonality into a vision of Eternity. For when a sense of being is achieved, the meaning felt to be in existence is timeless, and can no longer be threatened by the guilt and sorrow expressed by the minor key, or by the implications of the 'male doing' confrontations implicit in diatonic structures. These belong to tension and resolution—in time. 'Only in time is time conquered', but once time is conquered in the realm of being we are beyond time.

In the Chinese poems which he set to music Mahler found a symbolic expression of the problems of existence which beset him dealt with from a stoical point of view which he found sympathetic. Life is full of gleaming 'golden enticement', yet one was bound to sing of sorrow, against which the 'laughter within your heart gives answer': this poem states the manic-depressive problem of Mahler's attitudes to experience. Bitter experiences threaten even the quest for a sense of meaning through symbolism:

> When such sorrow comes,
> Dry is the soul, its gardens are withered,
> Fading and dead the pleasure of our song.

Depression can come from actual life experiences: or it can arise from intra-psychic conflict between love and hate, and the ensuing guilt. This depression from within withers one's perception of the world, and the sap of one's search for a feeling of at-one-ness with life. Yet at the end of *Das Lied* there is an achievement of reparative feeling parallel to that in *The Ancient Mariner* in which the Mariner 'blesses' the water-snakes 'unawares':

> On pathways that are paved with tender grasses
> O beauty!
> O life of endless loving, wild delirious world!

This offers possibilities of gratitude and the sense of 'the continuity of life' that transcends mere individual existence. Both life and death are no more than 'twilight'.

> *Dunkel ist das Leben, ist der Tod.*

Wine and song counteract this despair 'when hearts beat faint', in a merely manic way. But the increasing poignancy of the music convey that even hedonism and the stimulation of the senses with wine merely deepen the despair: and the core of the poetic philosophical problem is reached:

> *Du aber, Mensch, wie lang lebst denn du?*
> *Nicht hundert Jahre darfst du dich ergötzen*
> *An all dem morschen Tande dieser Erde!*

138

Here there are two existence problems. One is that man only lives less than a hundred years, and then dies. The other is that if he merely enjoys, this *yields no confirmation of his existence*. In the songs about youth and maidens we have an idealization of a joy Mahler felt to be denied him: the ape of Envy arises out of this golden dream.

Because of its association with sexual violence the 'ape' not only asks about the meaning in life, and mocks brief joy. It mocks the impulse to find confirmation, expressed in all the symbolism of reflections, and encounter in *Das Lied*.

> The wish of every man to be confirmed as to what he is, even as what he can become, by men: and the innate capacity in man to confirm his fellow-men in this way.
>
> Martin Buber, 'Distance and Relation', *op. cit.*, p. 68.

Moreover, because the ape arises from envy (and the infant's desire that the parents' sexuality should be sadistic) it represents a terrible desire to 'destroy the object'. But if the object is destroyed, all hope of confirmation and meaning will be lost. Mahler feels he will go mad—and lose all hope of that potential sense of continuity, of life or of cultural meaning, that alone can solve his problem. As Winnicott says of his psychotic patients, they, all the time

> are hovering between living and not living [and so they] force us to look at this problem, one which really belongs not to psychoneurotics but to all human beings . . . what is life about? . . . these same phenomena that are life and death to our schizoid or 'borderline' patients appear in our cultural experiences. It is these cultural experiences that provide the *continuity in the human race which transcends personal existence*.
>
> 'The Location of Culture', *Playing and Reality*, pp. 99–100

To the schizoid individual the solution of existential problems is a life or death matter: and to answer the question 'What is life about?' requires creative effort—itself a kind of encounter, helping provide 'continuity'. So, Mahler's last works are an attempt to answer the question

EXAMPLE 20

Allegro pesante, appassionato

Du a-ber, Mensch, wie lang lebst denn du?

which is itself expressed in a chromaticism that must be resolved, if the question can be answered. Its most poignant expression is Example 17.

The chromaticism is sweetened by an inward development—by insight: for the existential problem is within, and to overcome it requires the achievement of a sense of transcendence. This may be seen happening as Mahler transforms his own themes. For instance, the statement in Example 16 is quoted again and again throughout the work. In bars 343–344 it is the same as in the opening bars:

EXAMPLE 21

Wie ein schwerer Kondukt

But later it becomes transformed, at the very moment when the 'hate' theme itself is undergoing transformation. Can we discuss the way in which notes below are altered so that the melody is fundamentally transmuted? It certainly seems to have taken on a new poignancy, as of the voice of one who knows more about human suffering.

EXAMPLE 22

Schon ganz langsam

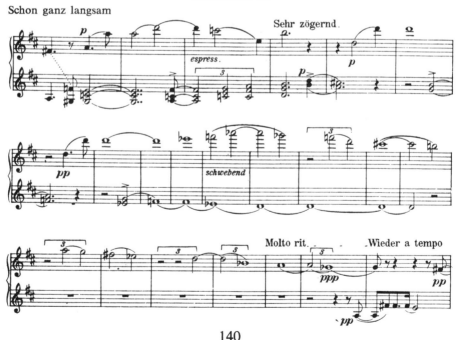

So, with the 'hate' theme, as Boys says:

It is as if its significance had utterly changed and what had appeared as terrifying is in reality, or when seen in another light, a comforter.

Embraced within oneself hate can be seen not as a threat to existence and the meaning of life but a desperate expression of the need for existential security. It is the possibility of *loving oneself* so that one can love others, because one has come to see that their problem, like one's own, is also fear of ego-weakness and arises from existential dread. The ape that seemed to be on the hurdy gurdy, and associated with the barrack bugles, and the threat of violence and hate in the father who did to the mother what one wanted to do oneself (and worse)—all these are not malignant predators outside one. They are not impulses towards vulgarity, sadism, raucousness and destructiveness at whose mercy one is, even in one's symbolic struggles to find a point in life—but they are all manifestations of one's poignant need to feel that I AM, with the sound of one's beating heart. Embraced, they become one's own existential impulse: not only a 'comforter', but that human poetic-philosophical quest that *is* the point of life.

Mahler was intelligent (and intellectual) enough to know explicitly that this was the quest he was making. He wrote:

(To Alma, 29 June 1909)
Man—and probably all forms of life—are unceasingly productive . . . pro-duction . . . is accompanied by an act of self-realization; and hence its creativeness is heightened on the one hand, and on the other is manifested as a challenge to the moral being. This then is where we find the source of all the restlessness of such men (i.e., men of a higher development) In between the brief moments in the life of a man of genius when these challenges are answered, there are the long barren stretches of existence which wring the soul with unanswerable longings. The 'works' of this person or that . . . are, properly speaking, the ephemeral or mortal part of him; but what a man makes of himself—what he becomes through the untiring effort to live and *to be*, is permanent. That is the meaning, my dear Almschi, of all that has happened to you, of all that has been laid on you, as a necessity of the growth of the soul and the forging of the personality . . . exercise your-self in beauty, in goodness, grow unceasingly (that is the true productive-ness), and be assured of what I always preach; what we leave behind us is only the husk, the shell.

Gustav Mahler, p. 322 ((my italics)

Whatever we may make of this as a philosophy, it is clear that the continual productiveness in Mahler's music was felt by him to belong to self-realization, and that creativity for him is thus bound up with the challenge to the 'moral being'. These are the 'unanswerable longings'—to become that which one is capable of becoming: 'What a man makes of himself—what he becomes through the untiring effort to live and to be.' This emphasis shows Mahler to be a true existentialist, and also shows how his existentialism belongs to that of the positive movement, utterly different from the nihilism of contemporary art, which speaks neither of joy nor the moral being, nor of goodness, beauty or love, as Mahler so creatively does.

9

The Ninth Symphony:
A Detailed Analysis

In much musical analysis we often find such terms as 'enthusiastic figures', or 'optimistic development', 'the mood changes' or 'weird, sinister emptiness'. But these criticisms seldom embark upon a discussion of *what* the music might be 'enthusiastic' or 'optimistic' about, or what the 'emptiness' refers to, or what *kind* of 'moods' music evokes in us. Of course one cannot put the music into explicit terms: but the way critics of his music write shows that intuitively they *know* that Mahler's work moves between positive hope and nihilistic despair. What existential struggle is going on? And how can we discuss this *musically*? With Mahler, happily, there are words scribbled on his manuscripts which give us clues; and in some of his preceding works, which he 'quotes', there are words set to music. Moreover, one may trace in his music a whole personal history (with its own individual symbolism) often indicated by comments written on the scores, or by his choice of words, as we have seen.

Of course it is possible to write vaguely about 'love' or 'death' in music, and yet come nowhere near illuminating its meaning. In order to analyse convincingly we have to discuss the symbols by which these themes are explored in the art, in detail, and try to show how in Western musical idiom, they speak of experience in life.

So, in trying to show the deeper meanings of the *Ninth Symphony*, I must demonstrate that I am aware of the major elements in its *musical* structure. Then I must try to show that the composition speaks of the human realities which I believe it to be about. I have not forgotten the lady who asked Schumann, after listening to him play a piece, 'What did it mean?'—whereupon he played it again. The music is the music is the music.

However, Mr Deryck Cooke, who is also (significantly) a leading Mahlerian, has shown us that music speaks a language and that this

143

language can be interpreted in explicit terms. While the music remains music, speaking directly to our body-life and consciousness, it stirs and organizes feelings: when it symbolizes hate we feel hate, and when it symbolizes love we become more capable of love even as we listen. The art flows into our actual lives and enriches them. So, we can connect the musical form with the message the music creates within us as we listen and make its general drift explicit. By doing so, I hope, we may both enrich our understanding, and develop our concepts of what art is and what it can do for consciousness and freedom. Mahler's stupendous achievement, I believe, offers us a path to the future—by which we can find meaning and a new sense of the potentialities of being.

*

All Mahler's work is closely integrated, and the *Ninth Symphony* needs to be seen in close relationship to two previous works—the *Eighth Symphony*, for chorus, soloists and orchestra, and *Das Lied von der Erde*, a symphonic song cycle.

The *Eighth Symphony* was Mahler's final attempt to express a religious faith: despite its impressiveness, I find it empty. The *Song of the Earth*, the *Ninth*, and the *Tenth* are attempts to find a meaning in life without God. To Mahler 'God is dead' as for Nietzsche: Donald Mitchell has pointed out the effect on Mahler of Nietzsche's philosophy.

The link between the last act of faith and the final acts of assertion of existential meaning is the *human voice*. In *Das Lied*, the 'I' of the poems is pre-eminent and there is 'another' who is yearned for

> *Ich stehe hier und harre meines Freundes . . .*
> Here will I stay and tarry for my friend . . .

As we have seen, the 'I-Thou' is integral with the search for a meaningful relationship with the universe as ultimate 'object': this truth, increasingly emphasized by psychoanalysis and existentialism, is at the heart of Mahler's music. Not only is there 'another', but the last works are integral with the struggle to 'find' and love Alma, as the inscriptions on the scores show. This quest for love itself is integral with Mahler's feelings about the *Moon*, the *Earth*, and the *time-rhythm* of the universe.

> *O sieh! wie eine Silberbarke schwebt*
> *Der Mond am blauen Himmels see herauf . . .*
> O see, like some tall ship of silver sails
> The moon upon her course, through heaven's blue sea.

The moon is the mother, and, as in Coleridge's poem *The Ancient*

144

Mariner, casts a benignity over the world of *Der Abschied*. And as I have implied, the internalized mother is a pervading benign force in the *Ninth*. The music of the *Ninth* is thus in the dimension of the I-Thou, and so has an essentially *vocal* quality.

Mankind, grown weary, turns homeward *(Die müden Menschen geh'n heimwärts)*—Mahler is dying, and seeking resignation to death. However, his dying is but a weakness of mortal flesh: his spirit does not want to die—and is aware only too poignantly of the need to find a sense of meaning before death comes, and aware too of the Spirit's weakness for this task. But the problem of how one resigns oneself to becoming nothing is integral with discovering how, in relationship, one *was* (or *is*) something, *being something*, a potentiality.

> *Ich sehne mich, O Freund, an deiner Seite*
> *Die Schönheit dieses Abends zu geniessen.*
> *Wo bliebst du? Du lässt mich lang allein!*

In this we may sense Mahler's isolation, that he sought to overcome by listening to the breathing of the Earth, to natural being, and his wife's breathing. Hearing, being heard, echoing are essential elements in this music. The 'breathing' of the earth is felt as part of a whole attempt to relate to the Earth as we have seen, and the 'listening' and seeking are a positive impulse exerted against sinking and dissolution, resolution against disintegration. Sharing, love, gratitude, joy in the beauty of existence—all come together at the end in a sense of the continuity of existence that transcends mortal existence, in which (in *Das Lied*)

> *Still ist mein Herz und harret seiner Stunde!*

—the English translation, 'My heart is still and waits for its *deliverance*' does not quite catch the implication of that *'seiner Stunde!'* with its emphasis on time. After this moment, in the music, the theme of *endless continuity*, focused in the word *'ewig'*, is associated with an escape in the music into the dimensions of being which are outside time. It becomes 'eastern'. As Wilfrid Mellers says,

> in the 'Farewell' appear strange linear arabesques—sometimes pentatonic, sometimes in chromatically inflected modes, sometimes almost as non-tonal and inhuman as bird-calls; while in the ineffably protracted suspensions on the word *'ewig'* music strains to release itself from harmony and metre.
>
> *Man and his Music, The Sonata Principle*, p. 131

Beethoven, says Mellers, saw that he must free himself from Time and the Will: Mahler's music dissolves into Asiatic immobility, escaping from the obsession with Time.

Mahler lingers on those suspended dissonances, his last hold on the life he loved with all his richly attuned senses . . .

p. 131

As is already clear, I disagree with Meller's interpretation of the meaning of this dissolution. It seems to me, in truth, no dissolution, but a new and important beginning, a new vision. It is true that sensual life is relinquished unwillingly. But more important is the escape Mahler achieves, into a plane of meaning in being that can make the imminence of death unimportant, and can resolve the torments of the time-and-place-ridden obsession with 'doing' of our world—finding peace in the realm of 'being' and what one is able to *become*.

In the *Ninth* there is a close connection of theme and style with *Das Lied*. In the *Ninth* the human voice is replaced by the orchestra—which continues to 'sing', but has, of course, more rich and varied 'vocal' resources, while in the structure the linear progression, with its timeless feeling, is developed in the symphony.

The usual Sonata and Rondo form is given up, in favour of a form which arises from the essentially 'vocal' quality of the music, which gropes towards the renewal of life through love and joy: *'O ewigen Liebens—Lebens—trunk'ne Welt!'* thus becomes both theme and structure: the musical structure *is* itself one of *loving encounter*—and if there is confrontation it is with that which threatens encounter: hate. But here there is an essential break away from the forms to which his earlier works such as the *Eighth* belong. The new form is a philosophical dialogue very different from the earlier expressions of *faith* against *doubt*. What we now have is the engagement between the possibility of *meaning* (bound up with love) and the possibility of *no meaning at all* (bound up with schizoid hate). This parallels the whole trend of 'continental' philosophy, from Kant, Nietzsche, Buber, and Kierkegaard, to Binswanger, Buytendijk, Plessner, Marjorie Grene and Rollo May. The structure of this symphony can be seen as parallel to a course of existential psychoanalysis, or indeed the intention of the whole existential movement, to find, step by step, how potentialities may be drawn out from the self *in relation*, to others and the world.

As F. Stiedry says,

One extended melody gives birth, time and again, to new melodies. These melodies are more frequently sung by the orchestra as duets and terzets than as solos and are supported, as are many lieder, by a lavish accompaniment.

The structure, which is of very great clarity, is melodic and conveys the sense that life exists only in individual lives, yearning for tenderness, tormented by dependence. The 'accompaniments' convey the richness of joy and suffering. These forms and modes are *not* (as Mellers suggests) a movement towards the 'inhuman': even when Mahler is 'listening' to a natural sound, it is in a spirit of learning from the universe as Eliot learns from the bird in *Four Quartets*:

> And the bird called, in response to
> The unheard music . . .
> Go, go, go said the bird . . .
> Quick, now, here, always . . .

The *bruitisme* is not an 'escape' from being human into 'nature', but an attention to the voice of the *ahnung*, the voice of a natural conscience in the 'nisus', to which one belongs. The 'voice of the bird' which helps with the final resolution is one which sings of human joy and sadness in the universe out of which life springs: its antecedant is the moment when the father left the child Mahler alone in the forest, and he experienced an oceanic feeling of at-one-ness on which he drew all his life.

The First Movement

The First Movement of the *Ninth Symphony* has three parts:

I. The 'orchestra song'.
II. Interludes and melodies appearing alternately (p. 18, *score*, Universal Edition).
III. The 'orchestra song' (p. 51).
  A cadenza (p. 56).
  A coda (p. 58).

The creative theme of this movement is the resolution of the menace of hate and nothingness,

> In the completion of its partial ecstasy,
> The resolution of its partial horror . . .

The hate and nothingness arise out of the love, encounter and meaning themselves—a terrifying enigma, the psychology of which we have examined.

Part I: The first five bars state with simple clarity three important motifs:

—a rhythmic sequence, Example 6.
—a harmonic sequence reminiscent of *The Song of the Earth*, Example 25.
—and an introductory theme, Example 40.

We need have no difficulty in recognizing Example 6 as a *heartbeat*. The heartbeat—strong or faltering, or joyful, or a fatal heart stroke—these recur throughout the last works, and their origins are in *Das Lied von der Erde*. As Diether points out, at a critical moment in the last movement of that work, we have an underlying minor third *ostinato*, 'almost identical with that heard in *Der Abschied* and initially scored for the same instruments—clarinets and harp in unison'

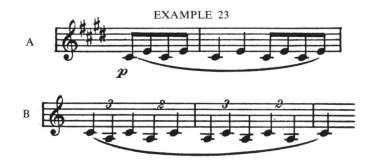

EXAMPLE 23

The implications of this gentle beat are clear in those words it introduces in *Das Lied von der Erde*, p. 85.

Still ist mein Herz und harret seiner Stunde . . .

At the end of *Das Lied*, the heart reaches its quietus, and here (I believe) the musical inheritance is from the Aria *Ah! Golgotha!* from Bach's *Matthew Passion*, in which we hear Christ's heart slow down and stop, in the beating pluck of a harp, beneath the painful minor sevenths played on the *oboe da caccia*.

EXAMPLE 24

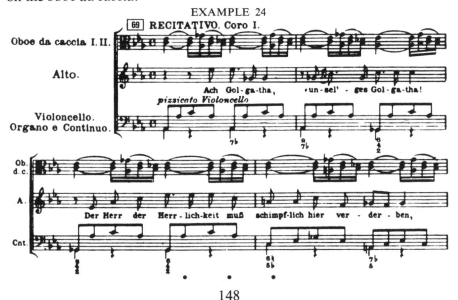

The 'rocking' bass, the chromaticisms, the sense of suspension at the close (ending on the mediant) are surely influences on Mahler's late consciousness (as is the theme 'the innocent must die as well as the guilty')?

The next motif in the *Ninth* is a *harmonic sequence*:

EXAMPLE 25

This harmonic sequence, which pervades the whole movement, is reminiscent of the last bars of the *Song of the Earth*. As Diether has pointed out, this figure (marked Z)

EXAMPLE 26

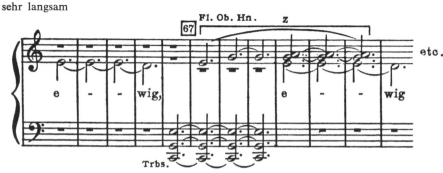

(Der Abschied, Das Lied)

is the same as Example 25 except that the last two notes in Example 26 are sounded simultaneously:

> without as yet touching the tonic D, Example 25 already outlines the third, fifth and sixth tones which are so prominent in Example 26.

The next figure, the introductory theme Example 40, already discussed in its context in Example 16, introduces the D tone and continues to stress the fifth and sixth by means of an echo, alternating with the little shuddering figure in the violas.

The concluding figure of *Das Lied* is called by Deryck Cooke 'infinitely yearning': so, the figure we pick up with this sparse harmonic sequence 25 belongs to the 'major-minor antithesis', the sixth. But in *Das Lied* it is a *major* sixth which is a mild dissonance in a state of flux. Quoting the *'ewig'* figure that the last fragment resolves, Cooke says

EXAMPLE 27

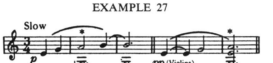

> The major second that will not resolve down to the tonic, as well as the major sixth that has been trying to push up through the major seventh to the upper tonic *and failed*, and still will not resolve on the dominant, remain suspended on the air at the end of the work, expressive of an infinite yearning, at once glad, peaceful and sorrowful. The second phrase is the same procedure carried forward into the main theme of the First Movement of the valedictory *Ninth Symphony*, the work which followed.
>
> *The Language of Music*, p. 79

The major second, says Cooke, is 'largely a neutral note, common to both major and minor systems, bridging the melodic gap between the tonic and the third, and strengthening the context, but not functioning expressively in its own right'. It is found to function similarly to the major sixth (see below, p. 229).

Mahler used the major second in this way at the end of *Das Lied*. But while this may be in a context of 'finality', *Das Lied* ends on a *'musical depiction of eternity'*:

> a cadence figure; but the most memorable cadence of all, as repeatedly begun by the singer and completed hereafter by the orchestra, the celebrated tonic chord with added sixth which so haunted Alban Berg persisting for no fewer than 74 bars . . .
>
> Jack Diether, p. 73

Besides being a *cadence* figure, this is also, as Diether says, used to *begin* the vocal phrases of *Der Abschied*, including the recitatives (though in different parts of the scale and in the minor mode). This 'endows the vocal music with a feeling of finality, even at its highest passion'. We take off, then, in the *Ninth*, from this 'endless yearning', still unfulfilled, for meaning: in a state of 'non-possession, non-acceptance, need'.[1]

This combination of finality and eternity conveys the feeling 'in my end is my beginning'—or, to put it another way, 'confronted by my death, I concentrate on the problem of finding a meaning in my existence'. The simple third figure of the opening (Example 16, horns) thus expresses a feeling of bitter regret that life must be given up, but yet a hope that the problem of meaning may yet be solved. Its repetition at crises in the first movement confirms this—it is unfolded like an existentialist banner, at moments of intense philosophical application (e.g. bar 343, p. 51).

The falling cadence complex, either completed

EXAMPLE 28

—or uncompleted

is used in the symphony as in the *Song of the Earth*, not only to end but to begin themes. Diether traces it back to the vision of spring and the blue ring of eternity:

EXAMPLE 29

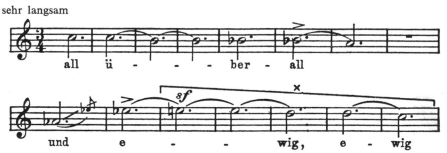

[1] See Deryck Cooke on the major sixth, *The Language of Music*, p. 69.

It is a 'common enough musical conceit', as we can see if we see its strong resemblance to the use of the *'Lebewohl'* figure in Beethoven's *Piano Sonata*, Opus 81A. As Diether points out, this *'ewig'* figure is elaborated into a variant of one of Mahler's chief motto-figures, variously employed in nearly all his symphonies from the *Second* on:

EXAMPLE 30

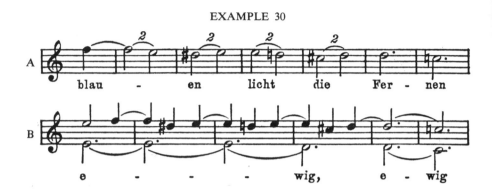

So, with the sparse statement, Example 25. This is both valediction and beginning, seeking gratitude and continuity, in the sense of each word as used by Melanie Klein—seeking a sense of having lived, in the flux of life in the Universe, a meaningful life.

By the time the D is finally established in the bass at the seventh bar, the orchestral song proper has begun, the principal melody, in D major (see Example 8 above):

EXAMPLE 31

Later the first violins continue and develop the melody (second last

EXAMPLE 32

bar, page 4). In the following bars it reaches the 'falling cadence' which is one underlying motif of the symphony. As Bruno Walter says, '*Der Abschied* might have been used as a heading for the *Ninth*'. All that is to be constructed in the First Movement is to end only in the single falling second which opens Example 31, slowly fading away in the oboe, at the conclusion. This brings us to the strange paradox of music itself. It may be true, as Jack Diether says, that 'all that has been painfully constructed will *disintegrate* again, until nothing remains'? It is true that 'all that is living must die'. But the music does not die: it has been constructed as itself a living meaning, and does not 'disappear', because it can be played and heard again. Music is (as Wilfrid Mellers has said) a 'freezing of moments in time'. The sense of 'in my end is my beginning' lies in the construction, which is an elaboration of possibilities, seized in the moment before all is consigned to nothingness by time. It is, thus music of ultimate 'intentionality', creating an inexpungeable meaning out of the chaos. At the beginning, death, the end, is implicit, even as the music enacts life's primitive beginnings in the mother's arms or rocking cradle: the end of life (at the later funereal moments) is declared in the simple rhythms of the beginning. The death of the body is symbolized by the sinking tonality, which echoes the falling cadences of the opening. Important themes now emerge against the falling-cadence complex in D major, with its 'feelings of gentle nostalgia and resignation' as Diether calls it. There is a note of rising passion in D minor

EXAMPLE 33

Andante comodo

Just as the beginning hovered between the sixth and the neutrality of the second, picking up the '*suspension*' of time and *becoming* (in D major), at the end of *Das Lied*, now we enter the world of 'tension' between major and minor, the more recognizable (manic-depressive) world of everyday experience, of relationship, of hope and disappointment, of passion, and conflict.

As I have argued, out of this passionate energy of love itself springs hate. Out of that encounter which seems most confirming and belonging to becoming, as we emerge from primal being, also arises the possibility of defeat and disintegration. As I have tried to show, this feeling arises psychologically from our very hunger to exist. Musically, this emergence

of the threat of emptiness, chaos, disintegration, and all that we associate
with hate, out of the heart of love, is fascinating to trace in Mahler.

It can obviously be related to his impotence, which arises from a fear
of love. His own dreadful experiences of being stricken by fate, even at
moments when joy and love promised their highest flights, seems to be
merged with the consequences of his experiences of adult sexual sadism.
A fear of hurting the other by the aggressiveness in passion, a fear of
being castrated because one has opened oneself to joy, surely have
beneath them an unconscious fear of implosion or 'loss of inner contents',
arising from a schizoid fear of love as harmful.[2]

In the final verse of *Das Lied*, the melody which begins with a falling
tone from the mediant reaches its falling cadence in the second of its two
clauses. An echo of this appears in the *Ninth* at this moment. No sooner
has it been sounded than the violas repeat the *'ewig'* figure twice more
without its resolution, as Jack Diether says, 'as though reluctant to let
it go after all'. (*Molto espress.* at bottom of p. 4.)

As the key signature changes, the second horn echoes this in the minor
with further variation: that is, the nostalgia for primal being is given an
anguished quality, as if of one final, backward-looking sob, on the threshold of adult passion, from which, with foreboding, trouble seems inevitable. But Mahler does not withdraw—rather, he goes on with courage
to suffer the pangs of ambivalence. He does not retreat into selfpitying
Oblomovism, or a sentimental indulgence in giving oneself up to the joys
of futility as Beckett does in *Krapp's Last Tape*. The heavy brass sound
the D minor triad as a dark foundation to a rising chromatic theme.

EXAMPLE 34

---

[2] Freud had a similar dread of giving in love: see *Human Hope and the Death
Instinct*. See also R. D. Laing's first book, *The Divided Self*.

As Diether says, this is another variant of the 'ubiquitous falling tonic triad' that mirrored the 'sudden clouding over his features after he had made a cheerful remark' (see above, p. 61). This is an expression of the manic-depressive mood swing, in which guilt emerges from a surge of joy, out of the fear that one's love-hunger might harm the object, or lead to a loss of self.

So, we have in Mahler both schizoid and depressive elements—and the *Ninth Symphony* itself represents a massive step towards reparation and the achievement of the 'depressive position' or (to give it Winnicott's more positive name) the 'stage of concern'. The minor triad here has the same function as it has in the *Sixth Symphony*, as Diether says, while the 'whole D major paragraph tells us explicitly to what it is counter-poised here—not life, but the calm acceptance of its ending' (p. 76). But this calmness is imbued with a new depth of suffering, which is integral with adult encounter, and belongs to concern.

As I have implied, the opening music represents the primary stages of encounter, perhaps of relationship with the 'subjective object'. We begin in the Garden of Eden to which the individual sometimes yearns to return, perhaps feeling that death will be a return to this primal state of simple being. Dylan Thomas said, towards the end of his life, when the indirect suicide of alcoholism was overtaking him, 'I want to be for ever unconscious'. Death is conceived of as ultimate regression—to that at-one-ness, from which a new life or meaning can be born.

But the new broad theme of the song after a modulation to D minor is the voice not of the mother, but of adult passion, that fares forth into the world, and whose objects are objective. One voice begins it, but a second voice (1st trumpet, p. 6) joins in at the 10th bar, and this, soon becomes an important new theme in two forms: the 'hate' theme (see 13 and 14 above):

EXAMPLE 35

Andante comodo

Throughout the whole movement, against whatever positive structure can be established, this hate theme in various forms bursts out from time to time, as a passionate protest. As Diether sees,

It is the interrupter, the grim destroyer of unfulfilled ambitions, the crouching ape of *Das Trinklied* whose 'howls pierce the sweet scent of life'.

Yet this 'gesture of ultimate despair' grows as we have seen (p. 126 above) directly out of the 'farewell' figure and the major-minor alternation, and rhythmically from the opening funeral tread.

The ape is not merely Death, however, as we see if we look up the music of *Das Lied* where the howling ape is described *('hinausgellt in den süssen Duft des Lebens')*: he mocks the sweetest moments with something more than mortal sadness or resignation:

EXAMPLE 36

Allegro pesante

As Diether shows, this 'Ape' theme in its turn emerges from the *'ewig'* motif: it is like a distorted form of healthy cells—which is what hate *is*, a distorted and inverted form of positive emotion. Mahler takes the D major second inversion, and places a semitone between the third and second degrees of the scale, chromatizing the *'ewig'* complex, and implanting a desperate new rhythmic impulse in it.

As we have seen, Diether shows how the shrill lament in the violins that anticipates the hate theme

156

Molto adagio (EXAMPLE 17)

which later becomes this (bar 107)

EXAMPLE 37

Andante

is also a version of the melody for 'But then, Man, how long livest thou' from *Das Lied*:

Allegro pesante, appassionato (EXAMPLE 20)

Du a - ber, Mensch, wie lang lebst denn du?

Musically, as Cooke says, such a falling cadence stands for falling, despairing, and sighing. It expresses the *normal* (manic-depressive) sorrow against which we set joy ('In expressing the normal emotions of life, man has to undermine the joy of the major system by means of the pathetic 4–3 and 8–7 suspensions, or by chromatic tensions . . .' p. 154).

But in discussing descending chromatic scales, Cooke says that slow gradual painful sinking, through the chromatic scale, *'expresses the feeling of life ebbing away altogether'*. This brings us to the schizoid problem.

Mahler's chromatic descent in the 'hate' theme is quick in tempo, and repeated in turn, thus increasing 'the element of pain by every possible chromatic tension'. Thus the effect seems less that of life ebbing away, but rather of life being quickly eaten away or undermined—or, as I believe, of identity and *meaning* being threatened with dissolution.

The chromatic element threatens to dissolve that tonality which has been established in the opening pages and has given a feeling of security, love, and a groping towards freedom. There has been some conflict of major and minor but that corresponded to the 'normal manic-depressive' relationship with life. The chromatic threat now points beyond this to the schizoid problem of a deeper tonal break-down.

157

The association is thus made clear between the mood out of which the paranoid threat emerges and the philosophical problem of man's mortality the possibility that the 'fruit' of his life is 'rotten'. Of course, in the anguish of this theme is the suggestion of a sudden ebbing of life—as by a heart attack. But there is a deeper menace, the threat to all achievement, which is the schizoid sense of futility underlying the manic-depressive anguish.

How is it such a disturbing theme of hate can emerge out of passion and love? We can illuminate the origins of this chromatic turn further, if we imagine the vulgar tune *O Du Liebe Augustin!* played on a barrel-organ, out of tune, with a monkey on the top. To be confronted with a hurdy-gurdy playing an out-of-tune 'all-is-lost' at such a moment left him for ever in fear of being overwhelmed by ugliness and coarseness.

Is this not the source of the hate theme of the *Ninth*?[3]

EXAMPLE 38

---

[3] And are not the 'turns' of the barrel organ redeemed in the majestic turns of the last movement? This theme emerges again in a new form in the *'Purgatorio'* movement of the *Tenth Symphony*!

EXAMPLE 39

sehr langsam

158

Since Mahler lived 'in' his music, he felt that such crude and disruptive 'male' noises could destroy him there.

But of course, since the reminiscence had come to be bound up with fantasy, and fantasies are dramatizations of 'endopsychic structures and situations' as we have seen, this hate-ape theme symbolizes a dynamic *in himself*. The menace thus arises out of: (*a*) his problem of identifying with his father; (*b*) problems of the male-element, which is felt to be aggressive and destructive, 'pseudo-male doing' in lieu of 'being'; (*c*) problems of the assault on 'female element being'; (*d*) problems of the primal scene and inward sadistic fantasies—i.e. the desire for parental sexual intercourse to be painful; (*e*) fear of love leading to impotence.

How shall this be resolved? It is resolved, as we shall see, not by an 'escape' from tonality (which would be collapse into dissociation) but by moving beyond that kind of conflict altogether, into the inclusion of hate, by understanding it as a twisted form of love, and by persistence in the 'construction of something upon which to rejoice'.

'Hate' that is, is 'cured', by love: a 'schizoid diagnosis' of it is made, by seeing hate as an identity problem, and its aggressiveness as having a positive meaning.

To describe the struggle we may use John Bowlby's useful term, 'psychic tissue': Mahler's engagement was with something that was part of himself, stubbornly destructive: a basic weakness. As Deryck Cooke says, Mahler is intensely preoccupied with the 'discrepancy between aspiration and weakness'.

> His persistent theme is 'the spirit is willing, but . . .'—no, not 'the flesh is weak', rather, the spirit is willing, but is undermined by its own fatal weakness—faced by life's frustrations, it is prey to discouragement, bitterness, emptiness, despair.
>
> *Mahler, 1860–1911*, p. 8

Later, Cooke speaks of Mahler as a 'restless seeker for the naked truth (whether "beautiful" or "ugly"), ridden with doubt and perplexity, ill-at-ease in an unfriendly cosmos' (p. 12).

It is out of this conflict that Mahler's 'programmatic' structures develop. The paranoid-schizoid problem is that of not collapsing under the feeling that the cosmos is malignant, and that the identity is too weak to endure: the ape, the laughter, the coarse military noises, the thuds, snarls, and thunders of death not only speak of the breakdown of values or tradition, nor are they 'only' Death—they threaten the utter extinction of meaning. They are worse than insanity: they hint at the possible total collapse of all structures, forms and values, into nothingness. It is this that makes Mahler a modern artist; what makes him an artist of the future is that he had the courage to overcome all these threats, not give in to them!

What we call 'insanity' can be, as Laing and others have shown, a 'strategy of survival.' An individual feels he could collapse, or suffer extinction of his existence, unless he acted in what to us is a mad way. But to allow oneself to go through a kind of madness and chaos may be the way to complete a certain journey, towards emerging from madness: this seems to be the kind of interpretation put on much madness, by those who have examined its meanings, phenomenologically, like Laing, Marion Milner, and Winnicott. Mahler 'allows' himself to encounter madness, often savagely destructive—but with a positive purpose. He never gives himself up to the joys of dissolution, and as for pushing hate into the world, he was most concerned about the effect of his music on others ('What do you think? Is it at all bearable? Will it drive people to make an end of themselves?'—see Bruno Walter's *Memoirs*). But there was always the possibility that he might encounter a nihilism so profound that no kind of recovery would be possible—and this threat persisted until the end of the *Tenth*.

The musical structures are elaborated programmatically, to build meaning over such chasms. This accounts for their incredible subtlety— to which no analysis can do justice. Here, for instance, after the 'hate' or 'non-being' theme, the D major duet (Example 31) returns in F. The introductory theme—

EXAMPLE 40

appears in the melodic stream. After a variant of the main orchestral song (Example 32), the melody modulates to B flat major with this short transition motif:

EXAMPLE 41

160

and this leads to another new melody in two parts

EXAMPLE 42

Andante comodo

This 'absorbs' some of the painful chromaticism of the threat of dissolution, into the other 'positive' songs, making them touched with poignancy and tension: but richer. After each catastrophe, each threat, each episode of despair, the melodic flow becomes richer and more suffused with human *potentia*; this is Mahler's great achievement: he continually redeems the most dreadful suffering. By the first bars on p. 12, one might imagine no man might be happier.

Yet absorbed into this is an experience of sorrow which makes the gladness richer, as if we are moving towards a sense that a life which has experienced and overcome sorrow and despair is more capable of gratitude for having done so. Thus in the viola here we have a meditative chromaticism underlying the re-emergence of the main song (p. 10 bottom line, last 2 bars). And later a chord on the harp underpins the song's climax with the memories of pain (p. 11 middle)

Diether points out that the exposition already contains a preliminary suggestion of Rondo style. Like many of Mahler's it is a double exposition, in which the two main sections are repeated with alternations, instead of the classical repeat patterns. 'But the fullest close within the exposition', says Diether, 'is that which separates the re-statement of the first subject from that of the second subject.'

In the initial statement the D minor music (chromatic hate theme) flows back into the D major song so smoothly that we have a suggestion of Rondo form with its ternary form A–BA. In the first seventy-nine bars, we have a *maggiore* theme with a *minore* in the middle, all 'in the relatively brief, evenly distributed bar ratio of 26–20–30'. The only harmonic movement out of D is a momentary excursion into B flat Major in the re-statement, where a new subsidiary is inserted between the two main D major clauses.

The principal melody (Example 31) began in D major. There is a modulation to D minor for the passion theme (Example 33). Then, after the chromaticism, the D major Duet returns, *forte*. But, as Henry Boys says, 'the characteristically wide intervals lend this restatement its ecstatic, urgent, quality', with sudden contrasts from *piano* to *forte*, from note to note. Without any transition, the melody modulates to B flat major, and we have two tranquil themes played together—leading to the new melody in two parts (Example 11). Integrated into this is a version of Example 12 (p. 125).

Discussing the structure here, Jack Diether suggests there is an amalgam of Sonata and Rondo forms. This movement contains a regular exposition, recapitulation and coda, but also an unusually long, multiple development section which alternates extended episodes in subsidiary tonalities, with Rondo-like returns to the main tonality and partial subject-matter, 'analogous, if you like, to the classical *fausses reprises* of Haydn, Beethoven, etc.' We have just seen the return of the 'orchestral' Song in D major, after the chromatic intrusion of the 'fate' theme.

But then, 'after the full close, with a D major cadence once more turning to a D minor in the next bar, the key-signature itself suddenly changes out of D major-minor for the first time, and the second subject erupts anew' (p. 78). It accelerates to a 'ferocious *Allegro*', bringing the exposition to its close with a 'desperate, warlike peroration in B flat major' (Diether, p. 79).

According to Deryck Cooke, D major is a 'brilliant' key, which he discusses in Beethoven's *Missa Solemnis* as expressing 'jubilant praise', associated with 'glory', being the 'trumpet and drum' key of his predecessors. It is the key of 'the trumpet shall sound' in *Messiah*: by contrast the minor is despairing, and redolent of urgent despair, and passion. This language of key relationships has been used by Mahler— but not to express 'jubilant praise'. Rather the home keys are established as firm bases, expressing secure *liebende Wirheit* (D major, the basic term of vitality 1–2–3–4–5) on the one hand, and the passionate minor on the other—so that explorations may be made, into other areas of experience, by which existential security may be found.

As Diether says, 'the classical Sonata form is at once observed and turned inside out, as it were'.

The development section gets away from the tonic key, not by modulating rapidly and freely without ever touching the home key, in the usual manner, but by setting up alien 'islands' which crumble one by one, each succeeded by futile gropings to 'attain' or 'remember' the song of peace . . .

p. 79

As I said above, I don't believe 'futile' is the word. I believe we can rather say, the crumblings are *surprisingly* followed with *successful* achievements of the song of *love*. In the end, as Diether says, in the third and last episode (the number three recalls the three sledge-hammer blows of fate in the nihilistic *Sixth*), the music leads amid mounting tumult to a catastrophic climax which *'sunder everything'* and 'finally ushers in the real reprise'. We can call this 'testing to destruction'—except that the capacity to achieve the conclusion at all is a triumph over chaos.

The development section is twice as long as the first exposition which has combined Sonata and Rondo form (i.e. the first 107 bars). After one more nostalgic return to the main key, it sets forth into three extended and well-defined episodes in other keys: *Allegro risoluto* in G minor, beginning with the chromatic motive in the bass (p. 25); *Appassionato* in B flat minor (beginning with Example 33, pp. 32–3ff); and *Quasi allegro* in B major (beginning with both themes in combination, p. 41ff). The brief returns to D major or minor which separate these episodes are broken, fragmentary and evanescent.

All this amounts to an 'unprecedented concept' which takes longer to unfold than normal developments: but, in terms of the psychology of culture, we can say that the symphony could not have been written without such a complex and lengthy 'testing', by episode after episode, of the *possibility of sustaining meaning* under such duress. If one has lost one's faith (of the jubilant secure D major kind), and finds only disintegration and hate emerging from one's passion (D minor yearnings of the heart)—then, one may ask, 'What shall I say in the face of this menace?', 'Supposing I find myself abandoned thus?', What if I swallow the full reality of Death?', 'Can anything hold in the face of this nothingness?' It is such questions that are asked here—and the progress of keys relates to such questionings.

As Diether says, there is no movement out of D at first: Mahler is, as it were, belaying his rope to what rock he can find: but even the tonal progression of the exposition, not unusual in Sonata writing, 'encompasses a secondary tonal relationship' (relative major of the subdominant minor) in which the implicit link is initially missing: the two keys D major-minor and B flat major are juxtaposed directly. G minor has no place in the exposition, occurring only in the development.

Part I of the First Movement emerges from a duet between motives Example 33 and Example 35 which, with the help of other motives like Example 40, always in simple B flat major harmonies, reaches the apex of the song with a crowning sustained B flat as in the passage overleaf:

EXAMPLE 43
(bars 92–104)

But the opening phrases of this are the melody of *'Du aber, Mensch . . .'* except that the question *'wie lang lebst denn du?'* is phrased differently, in a way which moves towards the later resolution of hate by love. It becomes a counter statement to Example 17, the shrill lament in the strings (bars 39–40) which anticipates the dramatic figure of dissolution.

Part II (bars 108 onwards)

The second part consists of three interludes and two orchestral songs. The first interlude (p. 18) restates the opening material—the beat motive Example 6, the harmonic sequence Example 25 and the opening of the main orchestral son. But now, emotionally, these motives are all charged with apprehension and dread and the material is surrounded with spectral sounds: it is as if the grown man now recollects the primary reminiscences with a bitter awareness of their remoteness. The heart-beat (on four horns) has a fearful trend: the harmonic sequence is set out on drums; the introductory theme (Example 25) is shown to lead on easily into the spectral threat of disintegration:

EXAMPLE 44

Bars 114–116. Score p. 19

The clarinets seem to be trying to rise as if to the surface to breath (p. 20 top); while the horns express the snarling possibilities of chromatic disintegration (bars 124–128).

Against this muttering, of what I would call 'male element doing' which has taken over from primary encounter, with all its consequent dangers, there emerges a melody on the cellos which has all the plangent qualities of the mother's voice, as if soothing after a nightmare (bars 123 126). There is a firm statement of the persistent harmonic sequence of the *'ewig'* theme, and an insistence on the harp of the steady pulse—of 'Littlesoul', the awareness that one is still alive.

EXAMPLE 45

After this lovely vocal line (expressing tender encounter), Example 10 (derived from Example 12, related in its turn to the main song) appears as a solo. To this the horn contributes a series of significant comments, collected as memories of 'work done' and leading to a new love-lyricism on the oboe.

The first fragment is from the first cadence of the orchestral song (bars 6–7 of the symphony): the next from bars 8–9, the next bars 9–10, the next bar 17, and so on. But then the horn 'quotes' in the same breath from the chromatic, 'fate' or 'hate' theme—but in such a way as to suggest a reconciliation between the opposing forces. It is as if for the first time the fact that hate and love are both rooted in the same existentialist need is *recognized*, and the solution is glimpsed—which is to 'embrace' hate.

This seems to me, in terms of *meaning*, one of the most important moments in the Symphony. The solo horn here brings together a number of links, which may be examined in detail to see the rich complexity of Mahler's 'self-quotation' and modification of his melodic themes.

EXAMPLE 46

This obviously echoes the original lullaby, modifying it:

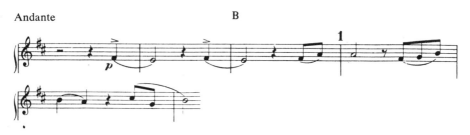

The solo horn goes on, picking up memories:

The 'memory' is of a phrase (bars 72ff) where earlier a solo horn attempted the love song, but could not sustain it:

There are many other echoes of previous 'work done' in this horn solo.

This rich echoing of fragments takes us a courageous step forward, in the progress towards discovering how the 'answer' to the problem lies at the heart of the weakness itself. In our most anguished existential moments we find the clue to the *Dasein*: by the leap into the chasm we find security.

Thus the orchestral song now progresses more confidently, combining Examples 41 and 42 both prolonged. In the oboes we now have a most expressive statement of a yearning confidence in love. This seems to grow out of the enrichening, by the horn solo discussed above, of the main love-song. This theme has now incorporated 'adult passion', and has moved beyond the original primitive, simple encounter. This too takes into the structure elements from earlier 'yearnings' emerging from the lullabies and songs, such as this (bars 34–36).

EXAMPLE 47

But the oboes now are yearning in an 'adult', sexual way:

EXAMPLE 48

And as one might expect, out of this lyric eroticism emerge again the bugles of male aggressiveness—and madness again, the crazy heart gone wild.

The subsequent martial section is built from a combination of the 'hate' theme—and the first song: a combination, we might even say, of the Father and Mother.

Although at the conscious level we speak of a 'martial' episode, what we have at the unconscious or phenomenological level is Melanie Klein's 'combined parents'. There is male violence, mad hate (p. 29) sinking to the squeaking and gibbering of psychic ghosts, diabolic laughter, chaos and despair (pp. 30–1). Utter disintegration seems to threaten, and leads to consternation. At last (p. 32) the passion motive (Example 33) breaks out in a new form.

Musically, pp. 26–32 are a G major quartet which is a combination of four motifs:

EXAMPLE 25

the harmonic sequence related to the '*ewig*' theme;

EXAMPLE 40

which counter-states against peace, speaking of sorrow to come, and evoking antithesis;

EXAMPLE 13

Andante comodo

—the 'hate' theme of chromatic dissolution; and Example 49 overleaf:

EXAMPLE 49

—a theme from which the oboe love song above derives.

This quartet begins with an *entrata,* over a double *forte* pedal C (*Allegro risoluto*, p. 25), combining Examples 33 and 35, ending in the dominant (double bar, p. 26), and then developing as follows:

EXAMPLE 50
(bars 184–189)

Allegro risoluto

After this, the mood changes—G minor sets in (p. 29) into two outcries of Example 43 (p. 30, French horns) and Example 33, the 'passion' motive (p. 31, trumpet). Later the song seems to break off (p. 31) but Example 33 in repeated diminution intervenes and broadens out into the original form, this time in B flat minor, opening the only solo song of the movement with an extended new very passionate passage (pp. 32–3ff).

The quartet is thus of four voices, in which all Mahler's major preoccupations are, as it were, locked in mortal conflict, as if the 'combined

EXAMPLE 51

parents' were locked in mortal sexuality. At this moment, the music seems most impressionistic, and to slide raucously and even madly into chaos: in truth, of course, on examination, it is closely organized. At bars 188–199 (full score, p. 28), for instance, the trombones and drums seem to be uttering the blows and snarls of masculine hatred: yet the drums are actually beating the harmonic figure derived from the *'ewig'* theme while the trombones are playing the yearning antithesis, the existential theme Example 49. The horns seem to be expressing insane hatred: yet what they say is part of the texture of the G major quartet.

In my terms I believe we may say that Mahler is here moving towards recognizing the truth that the problems he is dealing with are integral with the identification with, and internalization of, the father and mother. The male hate he fears will destroy his world is part of the father whom he has taken into himself, along with the good and feminine (and loving) elements of the father: the four voices (love and hate in mother and father) must be studied together. Mother love is the orchestral song: the possibility of eternity in the 'I-Thou'. To use terms from W. R. D. Fairbairn for a moment, the mother as exciting object does not satisfy, but is experienced as rejecting (Example 33), leading to the threat of disintegra-

170

tion, and this in turn is associated with the father's hate. The solution is to try to find and love the regressed libidinal ego, or infant self, which suffers these fears—and, at the same time, to understand male and female in the parents and in oneself, not least the origins of hate (Example 35).

But as the conflict progresses, we seem to hear mocking, diabolical laughter scorning any possibilities of solution. Yet these mocking voices (as on the horns on p. 30) are in fact stating Example 37 which says *'Du aber mensch . . .'* and is striving to complete this phrase from Example 43

In the end, this phrase will be resolved as in Example 3, p. 79. But here it cannot be, and it ends in disintegration and frustration. The chord at [11] on p. 31 seems one of utter despair. But in the consternation the trumpet and clarinet, as if at the moment of defeat, utter Example 33— the rising theme of passion, and the cellos strive in repeated diminution of that example, to express this theme.

In my terms, this says that the solution is 'in' the adult passion itself: in the rich need to love, we find the solution to ambivalence, as we take it into ourselves in infancy. Existentially, we need to examine our needs and creative impulses in the here and now and not be defeated by the menacing internalizations of the Super-ego. (Mahler thus anticipates the path of existentialist psychotherapy by half a century).[4]

So, a new, extended passionate solo song emerges, a richer version of Example 33 in B flat minor:

EXAMPLE 52

Allegro risoluto
Leidenschaftlich

On p. 34 a second voice in the trumpet resolves the gloom into D major again, using the motive B from Example 50 and Example 33—the 'hate' theme, surrounded by enthusiastic figures in sixteenth notes.

[4] See Rollo May in *Existence: A New Dimension in Psychiatry*, Chapter 2.

EXAMPLE 53

Plötzlich langsamer (Das tempo so weit mässigen, als nötig)

Mahler is moving towards 'loving the father' despite his aggressive military-bugle associations, and his vulgar, sadistic impulses. He is coming to love maleness, even the pseudo-male-doing, in himself—recognizing it as a 'strategy of survival'. The happy moment in the strings (bars 235–6) at the foot of p. 35 is reminiscent of the happy moment towards

EXAMPLE 54

Ninth Symphony, p. 35

EXAMPLE 55

First Symphony, Miniature score, p. 44

172

the end of the First Movement of the *First Symphony* (which Deryck Cooke says is perhaps reminiscent of a time when Mahler's father left him alone in the woods: see Examples 54 and 55 on previous page).

But there can be no optimistic development here: the second interlude begins on p. 36, consisting of repeated combinations of the first two chords of orchestral song, Examples 33 and 35 and other fragments. The 'hate' theme reappears again and again as a subdued snarl in the trombones. The lively figure in Example 54 goes over into the minor, and the next page is full of tension again. But these tensions have an inclination to *rise*. The motive I have called the 'passion' motive is there in the first violins (at the top of p. 36 of the score), seeming to be lifting depression. The 'hate' theme snarls chromatically, but the trombones sound a sequence of chords in sequence, the last of which is D major, but is also the beginning of another snarl which, however, ends more in sorrow than in anger. Meanwhile, in the horns, a sad cry, originally expressed in bar 27 as a herald to the passion theme, full of foreboding as to where this would lead, speaks here over the conflict, and brings in the *'ewig'* interval to redeem its sighs with elements from the outburst of love on p. 23. Its tenderness redeems the intervals we have previously associated with hate:

EXAMPLE 56

EXAMPLE 57

The chromatic snarl remains, but it is subdued, and its last chord, while marked *morendo* (bar 251) has a secure quality, being on the verge of resolution into the D major triad. Elsewhere the same potentialities of the resolution are expressed in the trombones, as we have seen.

There is a statement of the falling *'ewig'* in a new way (p. 36)—which anticipates the coming orchestral song on the horns. Moreover, there is a sudden chord struck on the harp (at *'Schattenhaft'*), whose tonality suggests not disorder, but the possibility of integration and resolution (p. 37, Bar 253). (Interestingly enough, this chord is much more strongly emphasized in Bruno Walter's later recording.)

Pages 36–7 are enormously important. For some time, this section (Part II) has seemed to be dominated by hate. But beneath these catastrophic assaults there has been an underlying sweetening and strengthening of the lyrical mode. In bar 185 there emerged the tune marked B in Example 50 above, p. 169. This is obviously related to the 'hate' theme of chromatic decline, and has its rhythm, though here in a form closer to a sob than a snarl. At the same time it incorporates a fragment of the original love-song. And this phrase later emerged on the oboes at bar 234. where there is a modulation into D major, becoming the lovely 'optimistic' development above (this again echoes the 'forest' moment in the *First Symphony*), made out of B and more of Example 35.

This 'optimistic development' is 'nipped in the bud'—but not before it has caused a radical change in our attitudes to the hate-Ape theme. On pp. 36 and 37 we feel, for the first time, 'couldn't this aggressive energy be a good thing?' 'Couldn't we love our own aggression?' 'Couldn't our destructive energy that arises from our fear of nothingness be seen positively—as a quest for meaning?—and if it is seen like that (whether in my father or myself) it must then *cease to be destructive?'*

Thus the snarl in the trombones at the top of p. 36 ends as if it were about to resolve into the chord of A major. What follows in the bars after Example 50 opens in A major and moves towards D minor. The falling *'ewig'*-type fall on the horns moves back towards D major: the harmonic form is underlined by the harp. The next subdued snarl on the trombones, at the top of p. 37 moves towards B flat major, a change again emphasised by the harp. These are no more than hints at the transformation that is to come—but on these pages *menace* is transmuted to sorrow, and fear is changed to compassion. The fragments of the passion theme enable this to happen, moving upwards, if to combat the falling tendency of disintegration.

The chord on the harp seems to express a new confidence in the possibilities of resolution—setting off a new trend. We have just learned that the 'hate' theme *can* be transmuted: now (the music seems to say) it is only a matter of more work on the problem. There is a shadowy reassumption of the love song—as if in timid assertion of the possibilities glimpsed: on the next page, the song is stated boldly and sweetly on the horns (largely associated up to now with menace and male aggression). The solo mother's voice (in the violins) anticipates a very clear and strong statement of the main song, in D major, in thirds and fifths—the menacing military voices now become triumphant bugle calls.

There are many new melismas, including this version of Example 32 (See above p. 152—*Full score* p. 38).

EXAMPLE 58

Schon langsam

But still the 'ape' menace is not put to rest—and on p. 39 shows it can't yet be trusted, and still threatens disintegration (horns, bars 275–278).

The song then returns to the melody, derived from 'But thou O man', Example 36 treated with new melodic material, but always combined with Examples 33 and 34:

EXAMPLE 59

Schon langsam

EXAMPLE 60

Bewegter (quasi allegro)

After this passage, the horn is still playing the dramatic 'hate' theme in terms of the extremest threat, but this is now part of the pain of joy in living—that beneath it always lies the menace of non-existence: the greatest joy of life is *in* its temporality. The threat of the end of our time continually threatens us with meaninglessness—out of which fear arises our hungry hate: but the same voracious hate-hunger is itself man's most glorious if painful gift, to suffer the quest for meaning ('sorrow is my only consolation'). Pp. 45–6–7 are thus about the painfulness of consciousness, which is both consciousness of joy (experienced with *Höchste Kraft*) and of death, which suddenly appears *fff mit höchster Gewalt* (p. 47). As Alban Berg said,

> The whole movement is permeated by premonitions of death. Again and again it crops up . . . most potently of course in the colossal passage where this premonition becomes certainty, where, in the midst of the almost painful *höchste Kraft* (highest power) of joy in life, Death itself is announced *mit höchster Gewalt* (with the greatest force).
>
> Quoted by Deryck Cooke, p. 44

Death can *become* a 'certainty', because the music is now 'ready' to come to terms with it: it is no longer the same as the paranoid fear of inner hate and collapse. This is now recognized as emerging from the internalization of the aggressive and destructive father who annihilated the mother, in sex and aggression: as the menace at the heart of love and joy.

Death is 'out there'. For the hate element in the father, in the self, and the world, there is only (now) pity and compassion, and the desire to redeem hate into love: to love and embrace the destructive distortions of the will-to-meaning, and find freedom and authenticity thus. This interlude says, 'The way is hard', even at the pitch of 'being alive'.

Death is seen as a natural force, implicit in one's existence, in one's birth. 'In my beginning is my end' and 'in my end is my beginning'. The opening syncopated beat of Example 6, the infant heart, becomes the syncopated beats of the death-stroke (the heart attack), and in the next section this takes on a new role.

In the third interlude (*Wie ein Schwerer kondukt*), the motive Example 25 (which derives from the '*ewig*' cadence) serves as *basso ostinato* under Motive A from Example 31 in muted string phrases and then a new trumpet call, of military death-panoply (recalling perhaps the cheap band that plays in a toy fantasy to the dying brother in the *First Symphony*). The drums play Example 25 without the '*ewig*' fall—this is given to the Glockenspiel—'eternity' is not the funeral toll. The horns and trombones echo it, in a wail of sadness:

The Ninth Symphony: A Detailed Analysis

EXAMPLE 61

Wie ein schwerer Kondukt

But then Part III of the First Movement opens—with the orchestra song on the horns. As we have seen, Mahler once spoke of the 'sure foothold' which 'love alone gives'. The child has a clear existential sense of meaningful at-one-ness: the adult can only recapture that existential security through love, while love of the 'significant other' is linked to love of the earth. By 'learning' we may penetrate beyond 'the turmoil of appearances' to regain 'the clear eyes of childhood'.

> It is almost like the voice of the Master, the Teacher. (I say that to avoid saying 'God' . . .) The voice summons us to be brave, enduring, patient . . . even if the Teacher's voice is heard in the thunder, we must still understand it . . .   p. 208

This 'listening' is a central theme of his work: *'O Mensch! . . . Gib acht!'* was the nightingale in the *Third Symphony* (what the Night tells me . . .)—and this *'Gib acht'* theme becomes the *'ewig'* theme in *Das Lied* and the lullaby song of the *Ninth*.

> Sometimes I shall pause and have that mistrustful look which has so often surprised you. It is not *mistrust*, in the ordinary sense, but a *question* addressed to you and the future. Dearest, *learn to answer*. It is not an easy thing to learn—you have first to know yourself thoroughly. But to *ask* is more difficult still. Only by asking can one learn one's whole and inmost relation to others. Dearest, dear one, *learn to ask!*   p. 207

So, the quest for love, for the security of the 'I-Thou', go with asking the existential questions, and listening to the answers from the Teacher. This Teacher is obviously not God, 'out there' in an objective, separate heaven: but the *'ahnung'* in our nature and the universe, while the answers may come from the thunder—and from pain and disaster.

So, it is absurd, as so many critics do, to call Mahler's work 'pessimistic' or even 'nihilistic' as in the case of the last movement of the *Sixth*. In such movements the music continues with the quest for meaning, with its *asking*, even though everything else is given up—the reassurances of traditional faith, the conventional God, traditional securities of harmony, structure and tonal organization. Temporality, death, and the possibility that all is meaningless are courageously encountered: even in the *First* and *Second*:

> The spirit of unbelief and negation has taken possession of him . . . He despairs of himself and of God. The world becomes a witch's brew; disgust of existence in every form strikes him with iron fist and drives him to an outburst of despair.
>
> <div align="right">'<i>Programme</i>' of the Second Symphony, p. 213[5]</div>

But this is not nihilism: it is an *existential* despair—and the effort to *learn*. The closing bars of the *Sixth* are rich with a new learning, as all the old securities are smashed under the hammer. But it is a mistake to regard this as an end, a collapse, a throwing up of the sponge, as pessimism or negation, for it is a beginning—a beginning to learn *how to be*, when all the existing forms of being have proved unsatisfactory, while the world is menaced with a longing for non-being.

So from p. 36 onwards we have had a stage in the *learning* which is eventually to yield pp. 58–9, and the conclusion to the First Movement.

In the strictly technical sense, we have a conclusion to Part II: a second interlude, bars 237ff, p. 36, leading to the second orchestral song, p. 38 (bars 265ff) and a third interlude, pp. 48–50—the *schwerer Kondukt*, military funeral. But these interludes and songs are not experienced as being in opposition as in a classical symphonic form, but rather in a dialectic of 'asking and learning'.

When the orchestral song appears again at the opening of Part III (pp. 50–60), it is abbreviated and compressed but the heart-beat is strong, and the melodic texture is rich. The initiatory motive (which became the death blows in the funeral passage) is absent, but the melisma Example 49 is prominent in the introductory bars—picking up memories of its relationship to the oboe love-song on p. 23 (Example 48).

EXAMPLE 62

[5] 'Disgust of existence' expressed in trivial and offensive forms with no creative goal, *is* the essence of British culture today, even to such an extent that someone like myself has often felt it hardly worth completing the present work, so anti-life has taste become.

178

The Ninth Symphony: A Detailed Analysis

Example 32 is incorporated in the D major principal melody. Examples 41 and 42, the B flat episodes, slightly varied, became a melody of compassionate richness, of great poignancy and tenderness.

But even here, we find irrepressible hate still arising from the upsurge of passion: examples 33 and 35 appear combined in bars 372–373, leading into the cadenza, on p. 56.

This cadenza is the final act of redemption of this fear of nothingness emerging out of the heart of joy, or negation out of sexuality, or insane and empty derision out of the heart of 'finding' and giving—the schizoid dread has many varieties. Yet again it enacts the *listening*. On this page I wrote, when I first heard it 'He shall rise up at the song of the bird'— later to find this refreshment at natural sounds a recurrent theme in Mahler. 'What the birds told me' is expressed in the woodwind: 'what *music* told me' is expressed in the marvellous piece of counterpoint, referring to the whole expansive structures of the world of classical music, and Bach's unfolding structures. The strings are silent at first, but then, beginning with a sigh of deep suffering (bar 386), play the most exalted bars of the whole movement, reaching their pitch of glad gratitude in bar 291 (p. 57)—related to the hopeful upsurge on p. 35:

EXAMPLE 63

The upsurge there did not 'come off'. On p. 57 this paeon *does* come off. And although it is assailed by motive 14, so 'hate' is still there, at the second assertion there is an emphasis on the tonic D which suggests a new possibility of the final 'inclusion' of hate. At once, motive is brought to bear, endorsing this inclusion, and ending softly: the 'passion' theme

179

here leads not to an outbreak of disruption, but to peaceful harmony (Example 3).

The new harmonic possibilities (previously hinted by the chord struck on the harp, on p. 37) are now emphasized softly in the trombones. And the horns now blow softly a combination of Examples 35 and 43. The latter, we remember, is derived from the phrase *'Du aber mensch'*. The recognition of man's tragic predicament is thus suffused into the motive of disintegration, so that outbursts of negation, despair and destructiveness in man (in ourselves, the 'hero', the father) may be seen as manifestations of the dynamics of meaning. (Perhaps even the voice of God speaking in the thunder may be seen—as Job found them in the end—as manifestations of the meanings of things which are beyond us?)

The hate theme is thus transformed into pure gold—into love and security, in D major. As if in glad amazement, the moment is crowned with Example 40, which has haunted us all through with its references to pain, on the E flat clarinet, while the flute and oboe play the same gentle sighs once played by the horns. The woodwinds sigh, a flute plays a descending phrase, broken and poignant. This is met on the way by a muted chord from the formerly menacing but now also subdued trombones. Then as Boys puts it 'the strings very quietly give again the balm of the metrical song-like tune', and terror is changed to comfort. A solo violin plays Example 58 and motive A from Example 31 leads us towards the close. While much in the *Ninth Symphony* (as Newlin tells us) belongs to the nineteenth century, this page, like the end of *Das Lied Von Der Erde*, moves forward beyond traditional tonality toward Schoenberg, atonality, other new potentialities in music. This close attains eternity, and the peace of the sense of continuity: the resolution on the previous page is secure tonally, but after the long act of the exploration and embracement of hate what we hear is the lullaby again, the mother's voice and the response of love—in utter simplicity, but with a new meaning. It recaptures for us, after all the adult passion, despair, and conflict, the 'clear eyes of childhood'—but not in mere regression. We are beyond 'the turmoil of appearances' and we have found a profound truth: we have achieved, even in this stillness and poise, 'the sure foothold which love alone gives . . .', that 'condition of complete simplicity, costing not less than everything'.

Technically, this is expressed by what some have even believed to be an inadequacy in orchestration. As Diether says:

On the last page, the lyric theme slowly evaporates in D major, in a broken dialogue for solo violin and winds, in which the oboe keeps repeating its '*ewig . . . ewig*' as described before, till the final *morendo*. And this time the falling cadence is completed only by a very tenuous high D in the piccolo, flageoletted harp, flageoletted plucked violins and violas (on the G string) and flageoletted bowed cellos.

Footnote: Orchestral violinists are wont to complain that the *pizzicato* simply 'won't resonate' implying that in this case Mahler's quest for extreme sonorities exceeded for once his knowledge of the instrument employed. It is true that the sound cannot be heard more than a few feet away when demonstrated by a single player. But as flicked by all the violins and violas in unison, it does make a very soft 'effect'; and that, as the late Dimitri Mitropoulos pointed out, is all that Mahler wanted, definitely nothing more.

Chord and Discord, Vol. 2, No. 10, p. 81

The Second Movement

Why, then, did Mahler have to write further movements, after such an achievement? Or, rather, since he was writing a symphony, why did he put so much—perhaps his major effort at redemption—into the First Movement? Listening to all Mahler's symphonies, I believe we are confronted with this problem of getting proportions right. Mahler was confronting problems which no man had yet fully phrased—and which we have not begun to solve. He could only go on dealing with them before they could even be seen in proportion. Again, we have to say, the existential problem is never solved. The nature of the real questions of existence is that they require continual application:

we shall not cease from exploration . . .

In the 'Programme' for the *Second* Mahler wrote:

The Spirit of unbelief and negation has taken possession of him . . . disgust of existence *in every form* strikes him with an iron fist . . .

Supposing one turns to 'blissful moments in life' now—after that First Movement—will the iron fist strike? Supposing one turns to traditional happiness, in country and city, says farewell to them and still the dance of music's meaning—will the negation overcome again? So, we have the Second Movement, the *Scherzo*. This is composed of four sections:

   I. Three peasant dances.
  II. Repetition of second and third dances.
 III. Development of first and second dances.
 IV. Return to beginning and coda.

EXAMPLE 66

The first dance is a *Ländler* in C major. The two opening motives are as follows:

EXAMPLE 64

In Tempo eines gemächlichen Ländlers
Etwas täppish und sehr derb.

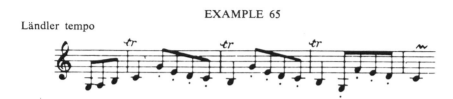

The main theme is a stamping movement in the strings

EXAMPLE 65

Ländler tempo

—and these are combined. The movement is linked to the opening of the first by the echo of the *'ewig'* cadence as noted by Jack Diether and marked here at X (see opposite page, Example 66).

These opening themes are repeated in counterpoint. Two other important phrases are these:

EXAMPLE 67

(oboes)

A   B

These opening themes are repeated in counterpoint.

Diether compares this first *Ländler* Dance with the openings of the other two dances in this *Scherzo*:

A
1st time (*a*)

EXAMPLE 68

B
2nd time(*b*)

It becomes obvious from this comparison that each begins with a version of the falling figure which pervades the whole symphony.

A *Ländler* is a peasant dance *(Etwas täppish und sehr derb)*. The waltz that follows it is perhaps an 'urban' dance—between them they represent the traditions of the organic Austrian community, and of Vienna, as a centre of popular musical life. Farewell to these, as aspects of worldly joy in being! But, what can one find and hold in one's hand as meaning, from this area of art and vitality?

Diether suggests that the *Ländler* first dance and the third dance stand in classical relationship to one another, the third dance being its Trio, a minuet in the normal subdominant key of F major—but 'before the minuet can even enter the waltz interposes itself'.

This second dance is in E major, a waltz in Rondo form. It enters without premodulation, in sharp contrast. The main theme is as follows:

EXAMPLE 69

Poco piu mosso

This is related to B, the second opening motive of Example 64. This waltz consists of a main theme, followed by two episodes, and one subsidiary theme, as follows:

FIRST EPISODE (6 bars):

EXAMPLE 70

C above is identical with Example 69 above, and is related to 64B again.

The SECOND EPISODE begins on p. 68:

EXAMPLE 71

Poco piu mosso

The SUBSIDIARY THEME (p. 70) is in E flat major. This is connected with the second episode through its octave steps and the phrase marked in the second bar here:

EXAMPLE 72

This is a bizarre theme, and leads, in fact, on to certain grotesque elements in the Third Movement, the *Rondo-Burleske*. Note at the end of this theme the chromatic sequence, Example 72D. Here, again, chromaticism causes confusion. First, Motives A and B from Example 64 are combined with the first episode, Example 70. Then (p. 72) the subsidiary theme Example 72 is combined with the second episode (Example 71) and a new short motive on the trumpets:

EXAMPLE 73

p. 73

Under these invocations of the problem of hate, the dance tries to proceed as if nothing was wrong—but it cannot. Everything is disturbed. And when the third dance turns out to be a version of the orchestral song of the First Movement, we can see that we are still dealing with the same problems, even on the dance-floor.

The resumption of the first episode leads through the transition phase below to the third dance:

EXAMPLE 74

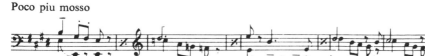

The third dance is a very slow *Ländler* (p. 75). This, as we have seen, is in F major, the normal subdominant key. At its beginning and its end the main theme is a melodic counterpoint to the first main theme (Example 65) but it is also, of course, closely related to the orchestral song of the First Movement:

EXAMPLE 75

Ländler tempo, ganz langsam

In the middle section this main theme appears in its original, much faster tempo. Its importance as the expression of the redemptive forces of love (as in the First Movement) is at once emphasized by the descant of an oboe phrase *(espress)* reminiscent of the love-descant on p. 23 (bars nos. 163–7) at an important moment in the First Movement.

This concludes Section I (pp. 61–78).

Section II (p. 78) is a short repetition of the second and third dance. The repetition of the second dance consists chiefly of six variations on the second main theme (Example 69) prolonging its six bars alternately into eight and seven bars, each fifteenth bar with an ironical cadenza, frequently quoted later on.

As Diether points out, the version of the second dance that enters on p. 78 is significantly different—having been modified by the influence of other motives we have experienced so far in this movement: that is, there has been 'learning'. The *'ewig'* complex is still growing, enriched by its contemplation of the world of experience 'out there' and the suffering within.

In the E major first appearance of the second dance the descending figure began on the tonic, and the melody descended through six tones of the E major scale to the mediant G before turning upward again in the third bar (Example 68A). In the D major entrance on p. 78 the descending figure begins on the mediant tone F♯, the *normal starting place for the 'ewig' complex*, and the new melody works its way down a whole-tone scale to the next F♯ (enharmonically written as G♭).

The harmony is related to the melodic form: see Example 68B. The new melodic form is extended into a fifteen-bar musical statement which is repeated several times with variations.

The Ninth Symphony: A Detailed Analysis

As Diether points out, it is extremely symmetrical, being in four-bar periods and a cadential three-bar period. The first completes the whole-tone descent: the second answering period introduces a chromatic turn. The third period repeats the whole-tone progression, with embellishment, except that the melody lands on G instead of G♭ over a Neapolitan sixth chord. And this prepares for the perky cadence of the final period.

EXAMPLE 76

Ländler tempo

This final 'snap' has a chromatic turn repeated on the dominant.

This whole sentence, 'carefree and debonair' as Diether calls it, is 'destined to be transformed into the first five bars of the *Adagio* theme of the finale'—except for the perky cadence figure, which serves to round it off and dismiss it 'with a shrug'. Diether also points out that this turn contains the three chromatically descending tones which formed the basis of the 'hate' motive of the First Movement.

What Stiedry calls a 'bizarre subsisiary theme' (Ex. 72) is in fact the intrusion of the chromatic hate complex, introducing a new rhythm, but *disguised with such an innocuous harmonization* that its derivation passes unnoticed. However, as we have seen, it introduces not only grotesqueness here but also anticipates the Third Movement's bitter irony.

On p. 82 this motive is heard in a more definite shape—still rationalized by its harmonization. It is doubled with woodwind, interrupting the

EXAMPLE 77

Ländler tempo

bouncing cadence, and becomes increasingly more aggressive.

We may say, I believe, in my terms, that we have in these derivatives of the 'hate' theme the element of pseudo-male doing, arising from the

187

passion and vitality of the (doomed) dance. The 'hate' theme of a desperate quest for meaning, the father's aggressive sexuality (lurking in the dance), do not, however, threaten a total catastrophic loss of meaning. Instead, as the physical vitality and joy of music and dance are relinquished, the recognition of hate yields, instead, poignancy, rather than chaos: compassion rather than madness and despair: pity, rather than cynicism.

Section II is completed with the following combination of the first episode:

(EXAMPLE 70)

with the chromatic sequence D.

(EXAMPLE 72)

. This leads, as previously, over to the third dance:

(EXAMPLE 75)

Ländler tempo, ganz langsam

p. 85; this time as a sort of variation without the middle part. This brief reprise is in F. The last appearance of this key in the *Scherzo* is full of lingering retards and ends suspended on a long sighing pause on an unresolved cadence as if sadly unwilling to reach a resolution (p. 86).

Section III opens with a development of the first dance (p. 87) in different modulations and combined with motives D from Example 72, 67 and 74. This is the C major *Ländler*. The tempo is *wie zu Angang*, but nothing else is the same. Instead of introducing the main theme Example 65 the first part wishes to modulate as it did in the waltz and is haunted by a spectral rocking figure derived from Example 81 below. Instead of stopping on a tonic chord as in Example 66 the *'ewig'* figure has a tendency to land softly as a submediant chord, interrupting the cadence:

EXAMPLE 78

Ländler tempo, wie zu anfang

This harmony (already heard in Example 68) is to prove very significant to the rest of the symphony, as Diether points out.

The 'stamping' fiddle tone from Example 66 returns, but it is a pale reflection: a contrapuntal inversion, in solo viola ruefully taking the former counter-voice over subdued cellos with the main theme:

EXAMPLE 79

Ländler tempo

(p. 87)

This evokes the chromatic motif, in its rhythm heard in the waltz, but now more exposed, with an up-beat derived from A in Example 81 overleaf.

189

EXAMPLE 80

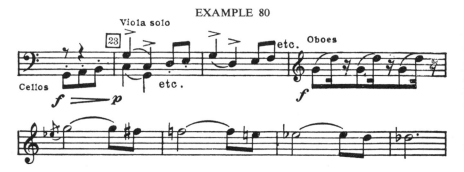

The viola is replaced by a solo violin: the chromatic motif is repeated higher with the upbeat figure inverted, downward instead of upward sevenths.

EXAMPLE 81

On the next page (90) this is displaced by the explosive theme Example 82 from the waltz, as though evoked by the repeated sevenths.

The first episode (Example 70) and Example 73 serve as sinister bridges to the development of the second dance which begins on p. 90. There are bridges of this kind earlier—on page 75 for instance, and page 84. This second dance development is a grotesque spectral *Scherzo* in itself, always in *ff*. The subsidiary theme (Example 70), opens this section with chromatic sequence D. On p. 92 emerges a trio-like, parodistic melody in G flat major:

EXAMPLE 82

Ländler tempo

This is developed from the motif played on the trumpets at the reprise of the first dance (p. 73).

(EXAMPLE 73)

The origin of this is thus associated with the moment when the first dance is mingled with elements of the second. Just before this, at the end of the waltz-rondo, the 'hate' theme, with its chromatic falls, had suddenly appeared in the strings (p. 72)—in a new rhythm, disguised by innocuous harmonization. This influence thus lay behind the sudden emergence of this new motif, out of a dance in which the country dance is mingled with the sophisticated one, the short trumpet motif emphasizes the new impulse to modulate freely, discussed by Jack Diether.

On p. 95 there are imitative entries of the subsidiary theme, fantastic and bizarre. On p. 97 begins a fifteen-bar reprise of Example 69 the second dance main theme in B flat, in intensified tempo and expression, with somersaulting figures, reaching at the end a frantic trill (p. 99).

But here the six-fold acceleration is interrupted by a *(klagend)* trumpet call, turning the music back to C major with the *'ewig'* motif—actually using one of its upbeats from the First Movement. Everything is stilled —the last instruments sent sprawling by the tuba in *fortissimo*.

The *Ländler* begins again—Section IV. But its rhythms are limping, and it gets nowhere: the stamping feet do not advance. Instead the C major (p. 101) suddenly turns to a stern C minor, with the horns playing a sombre series of falling chords, full of sadness, but expressing also a Humanistic determination to face the truth.

Diether quotes Walter, 'one feels that "the dance is over"'. Here I believe, there are a number of themes being explored. As Diether says, imminent death 'alters all perspectives': so, what can one feel about the physical vitality which is our normal way of 'feeling alive'. Despite his deep relish for physical vitality, Mahler must have felt sadly that it was not futile to attach a sense of meaning in life to a failing body, for 'what is living can only die'. Yet where else can gratitude and a sense of the continuity of life come from except from relish in the senses:

> . . . only in time can the moment in the rose-garden,
> The moment in the arbour where the rain beat . . .
> Be remembered . . .
> Only through time time is conquered . . .

To attach one's sense of being alive to the dance, however, is to attach it to desire—for the manic hedonism of dance is, as Winnicott implies, both 'the Primal Scene' and 'life'. So the attitude to dance is bound to be equivocal, as it is in Eliot's *Four Quartets*:

> Desire itself is movement
> Not in itself desirable:
> Love is itself unmoving,
> Only the cause and end of movements . . .
> . . . music moves
> Only in time . . .

Yet Mahler is

> Caught in the form of limitation
> Between un-being and being . . .

Diether shows how the waltz melody moves towards a perky assertion of vitality that both leads forward towards the profound main *Adagio* theme of the finale, and contains the 'three chromatically descending tones which formed the basis of the fate-motif of the First Movement'. What began at the trill of the bird and the movement of inward gladness at the tender grasses is here but a hedonistic flourish, but from which later gratitude for life is to be wrested.

The episode is reminiscent of the dancing in *East Coker*:

> Round and round the fire
> Leaping through the flames, or joined in circles,
> Rustically solemn or in rustic laughter
> Lifting heavy feet in clumsy shoes . . .
>   . . . keeping time,
> Keeping the rhythm in their dancing
> As in their living in the living seasons . . .
>   Feet rising and falling,
> Eating and drinking. Dung and death . . .
> Dawn points, and another day
> Prepares for heat and silence. Out at sea the dawn wind
> Wrinkles and slides. I am here
> Or there, or elsewhere. In my beginning . . .

As with Eliot, the recognition that the dancers all go under the hill, throws the artist back on himself, his need to discover meaning from the natural world that speaks to him of his end and his beginning.

The coda vacillates between major and minor—in a characteristic Mahlerean way: the major returns after 14 bars, but there is a low, ominously rising bass. The last pages comprise fragments of phrases 67A and B, 70C and 72D of the second dance, and a melisma of the third. The subsidiary theme appears *pianissimo*, the chromatic sequence 72D, and the transition theme Example 74.

When the interrupted cadence occurs, instead of the soft, pensive, flat-submediant chord we get a loud rasping one with added seventh (p. 103) to introduce the 'hate' chromatic music—which is, as Diether says, like the howling ape itself this time. The rocking figure rises distended and transformed, and this 'contrapuntal grimace' ends in a 'naked tritone'.

This is the moment when one might expect a cadenza, classically preceded by a six-four chord. But Mahler's is, as Diether says, an anti-cadenza. A drone-like bass is taken from the stamping, earthy *Ländler*. Over this the woodwind figures alternate with the next pair in the major and minor modes. The woodwinds make a series of short shrill utterances derived from the rocking figure. A fragment from 25 is played sepulchrally on the horn, and spectral fragments follow, from all the dances: rocking limbs, sad forlorn cries, wailing, ghostly pluckings, chromatic disintegrations, wisps of song. The horn on p. 104 seems almost to cry 'My God—why hast thou forsaken me?' These ghostly noises all finally settle into a repeated dominant-seventh chord with *appoggiatura*. The dance is over, as Diether says, with no transfiguration

—only a 'ghostly cadence with plucked strings, a "unison" piccolo and contrabassoon five octaves apart.'

The learning of the First Movement—its spiritual peace—the spiritual peace—has to be tested against the truth of mortal existence in the world. The life of conducting, of joy in the vitality of the *heurige*, in the sophisticated concert hall and dance-room, must come to an end: these are temporal joys. It is no good saying 'I live in my music' for the music dies. What existential achievement can then endure? The end of the *Ländler* is not bitterness or nihilistic despair: it is only a sepulchral relinquishing, of music as belonging to the 'bustle' that 'distracts one from the problems of existence'. The noise and confusion have to be given up:

> (To Alma, September 1908)
> Unfortunately, this wonderful entering-into-possession-of-oneself is undone the moment one returns to the noise and confusion of everyday life. The only thing then is to *think oneself back* into that blissful state, and to make it a practice at every opportunity to look back at that other world and to draw breath of that other air—I have now done at last with the special rehearsals . . .
>
> *Gustav Mahler*, p. 305

Mahler was trying to say in the Second Movement 'I have now done at last with the special rehearsals' in a different and more profound sense. But the plaintif compassion and sadness in the movement are not nihilistic: they bewail that it must be so.

The 'most advanced disorder' is like the spectral disintegration of the inhabitants of the court in *Das Klagende Lied*. Hate emerges to destroy the world, culminating in the 'anti-cadenza', because if we build our sense of identity on manic vitality, the only consequence can be the triumphant dance of death.

And yet, as we have seen, the orchestral song and the trill of joy have been experienced, with all their potentialities. Indeed, it would not have been possible to 'place' the manic denial without their presence: what we have, after all, is not dust and inanition, but a piece of compelling music about these!

> . . . only by the form, the pattern,
> Can words or music reach
> The stillness, as a Chinese jar still
> Moves perpetually in its stillness . . .

The Third Movement

The middle movements of a symphony, in Classical form, are usually slow and reflective. But Mahler's *Ninth* has two slow and reflective 'outer' movements, and two fast, ironical, ones in the centre. He follows the Second, with its sad irony, with a bitterly sardonic *Burleske* in the Third Movement which drives his existentialist 'testing' to the verge of insanity. If the despair in the Second Movement is manic-depressive, the exposure to 'disgust for existence' in the Third is hebephrenic: 'hebephrenic disdain' seems to me the phrase from psychoanalysis that describes it. It is also comical: but with the bitter comedy of those moments in Mahler when a jaunty parody gives the impression of a skeletal dance (see, for example, the episode marked *'Mit Parodie'* in the Third Movement of the *First Symphony*, Score p. 81, line 6, when the child is dying to tin soldier music that cannot touch his tragedy).

We hear this mood in Mahler's letters:

(To Alma, 10 September 1908)
I have to revise parts and meditate on how to make a side drum out of a fish-kettle, a trumpet out of a rusty watering can, a concert hall out of a wineshop. I have extracted only one bit of consolation out of all this turmoil —one of the trumpets asked Bodanzky in despair: 'I'd just like to know what's beautiful about blowing away at a trumpet stopped up to high C sharp.' This gave me an insight into the lot of man, who likewise cannot understand why he must endure being stopped to the piercing agony of his own existence, cannot see what it's for, and how his screech is to be attuned to the great harmony of the universal symphony of all creation.

Bodanzky answered the unhappy man very logically: 'Wait a bit! You can't expect to understand it yet . . . when all the rest come in, you'll see what you're there for . . .'

Gustav Mahler, p. 304

The Third Movement can be said to be about this 'insight' into man's predicament, in the same vein of ironic serious playfulness.

But the irony is not destructive in its direction. All through the First Movement there were moves towards the redemption of the 'hate' theme: all through the Second we have noted a deepening pity—and the emergence of those turns which are to become the solemn paeans of the final movement. For in this Third Movement we will also experience the most heart-rending tenderness, even the iron fists rain their blows. In it we move through deep sorrow towards a timid, tentative, display of the most triumphant statements of existential security, which is to flower in the *Adagio*.

The amazing thing about the Third Movement is its enormous energy, combined with its contrapuntal mastery. Yet, at the same time, while a reckless abandoned irony is displayed, the positive direction is not lost. There are three important motifs which open the movement:

EXAMPLE 83

Allegro assai. Sehr trotzig.

B is a quotation from the First Movement of the *Fifth Symphony*, which is the expression of funereal despair, and related in its existential themes to the First Movement of the *Second*.

> There is the great question: 'Why hast thou lived? Why hast thou suffered? Is all this only a great and ghastly joke . . . ?'

The Third Movement of the *Ninth* explores the possibility of life being a great and ghastly joke.

Having stated the three motives, Mahler then gives the principle subject of the Rondo (p. 106, 15 bars)

EXAMPLE 84

Allegro assai.

This begins with motifs marked A and B above in Example 83. This subject has a counter-theme:

EXAMPLE 85

Allegro assai.

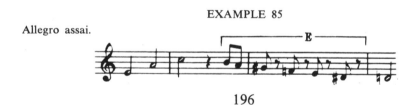

It also has a bass:

EXAMPLE 86

and a continuation:

EXAMPLE 87

Allegro assai.

Diether's terms for this movement are 'daemonic, sardonic, savagely nihilistic'. As he points out, the movement is in Mahler's 'tragic' key, A minor, the relative minor to the C major of the preceding movement. In his previous symphonic Rondos Mahler is joyfully extrovert—the Rondo in D major in the *Fifth*, and the Rondo in C major in the *Seventh*. This movement is set in contradiction to those, with savage intent.

There was much in the Second Movement of the manic-depressive confrontation between major and minor. The Second Movement deals with problems of sorrow and loss, the triumph of hate over joy. The Third goes more deeply into the underlying schizoid problems, and approaches the possibility of there being no solutions at all—not even in music: the triumph of hate over consciousness itself. It approaches schizoid futility and hebephrenic dissociation: it dares to contemplate the possibility of utter loss of hope of overcoming envy and of ever establishing a sense of meaningful existence. It verges on insanity. It was dedicated in bitter irony to 'my brothers in Apollo', it is marked *Sehr Trotzig*, 'very defiant'. It is an exercise in ironic use of the structural form of the fugue, of that form which one perhaps most closely associates with 'order'.

There are many complex elements here which Diether notes, one of them being the presence in the principal Rondo theme of the augmented-fourth tone itself—of which Deryck Cooke says,

Its relationship to the tonic is that particular tension which we have mentioned earlier as embodying the 'flaws' in the harmonic series, and in the whole musical scheme of things *diabolus in musica* . . .

197

In taking this interval 'when it is exposed without resolution of any kind', says Cooke, it becomes an 'essential' note, a tension in its own right, 'it becomes *diabolus in musica* indeed, for it acts as a "flaw" which destroys the integrity of the tonic key—thus removing the music outside the categories of human joy and sorrow inherent in the major and minor systems.'

The presence of this interval, then, takes us beyond depressive towards schizoid problems, in a 'devilish' way, on the verge of total disintegration. The augmented fourth occurs, as Cooke shows, in many portrayals of the devil: and so, it expresses the 'paranoid-schizoid position', or being 'confounded'. Yet, the movement overcomes disintegration by the magnificent logic of its construction in *fugato* style.

So it is offered in a spirit of expressing the worst that can be done, to subject musical meaning to nihilism. The ape is present from the beginning, as Diether makes clear. The ghastly tritone in the coda of the previous movement (p. 104, top) which ends a chromatic passage reminiscent of the 'hate' theme in the First Movement is echoed here, and it is turned into a mocking sneer in the next bars by muted trombones (bars 8–9)—the interval is the same.

At the same time, the rhythm is the martial iron boot of male aggressiveness—as in the *Sixth Symphony*:

EXAMPLE 88

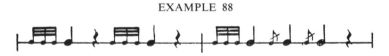

The note D♯, here the augmented fourth tone itself, is very prominent in the ensuing music. Figure B in Example 83 recalls the A minor movement of the *Fifth*, and C contains a suggestion of the 'hate' chromatic motif, grotesquely distorted. This reference, as Diether points out, becomes pointed when the horns state its turn:

EXAMPLE 89

Allegro assai.

and when the strings take it up:

EXAMPLE 90

Later, when there is a contrasting theme in the major, the martial tread is still there—and, moreover, not only is 'male doing' satirized—but also the *'ewig'* theme itself.

EXAMPLE 91

Figure X here outlines the falling cadence once more, in the key of F major. But also, as in Example 68B of the Second Movement, the harmony is diverted into the flat submediant. The opening chord, as Diether points out, is exactly the same as in 68B: tonic-dominant flat submediant. (I–V–♭VI): it is almost a variation on 68B. He says

> Of the latter's seven whole-tone steps from mediant to mediant we now get five in the first half of the tune, after which the second half sarcastically

199

resolves itself into the dominant at the seventh bar, while the bass continues to sink and the whole thing is ready to start again.

The 'sarcasm' or 'testing' (as I would prefer to call it) is indeed very deep, in the texture of the music. Again, we have the elements of parody such as we experience in the Third Movement of the *First*—expressing a kind of angry scepticism at all efforts to overcome the nihilistic message of death. But, just as there, opening himself to the horror of death leads (pp. 84–5) to poignant lyricism, so here the bitterness breaks, as if into a flood of tears. Both Example 68B and this tune are preparing (as Diether points out) *for the great themes of the finale*. Hate, transformed, becomes the *strongest* love: or, rather, ambivalence and mortality, experienced fully, yield the *firmest* sense of meaning, based on love and the swallowing of *the worst that fate can do to one*: the embracing of darkness, nothingness, and pseudo-male, inauthentic doing, as manifestations of the attempt to discover meaning in being. All that bitter mockery was itself a manifestation of the urgent human need to find meaning in life: hate and nihilism are manifestations of love and hope. Despair is the path to transcendence: so, this music is truly tragic, in that it seeks ultimate meaning.

Mahler himself seems almost conscious of this progress: he wrote to Natalie Bauer-Lechner about the final *Adagio* of his *Third*:

> In adagio movements, everything is resolved into quiet being; the Ixion's wheel of outward appearances finally becomes still. But in fast movements, in minuets and allegros (even in andantes, these days) everything is flow, movement, change. So I end my *Second* and *Third*, contrary to custom— although, at the time I was not conscious of the reason for it—with adagios, as with a higher form in contrast with a lower . . .
>
> Bauer-Lechner, p. 50–1

In the *Rondo-Burleske* he is beating his fists against 'the Ixion's wheel of outward appearances' but later becomes able to reach into the still heart of being, further on in the movement and in the final *Adagio*.

Indeed, the second subject of the second double *fughetta*, which seems to be dragged into the whirlwind, is this:

EXAMPLE 92

But, of course, on close inspection this turns out to be the turn from the previous (second) movement coming a few bars before Example 76:

which is to become the great paean of gratitude in the final *Adagio*. And this itself is presaged by a theme which 'quotes' Mahler's Pan theme from the *Third Symphony*:

EXAMPLE 93

Allegro

Again, we may detect the position of 'listening,' to the forces of the natural world. In the *First*, the agonies of grief are assuaged by the linden tree, as they are in the *Gesellen* songs. In the *Third* Mahler was listening —and he listened so intently that he became very frightened—of Pan himself! Here he even satirizes this awe. The *Third* is very much about listening, and this again is related to *enquiring into the nature of love*. But this is not romantic love of woman—rather that capacity to love the world which needs to be sustained despite the most dreadful blows of cruel fate (such as the death of Ernst). It is thus, as in Job, a listening to the nature of the world, the *ahnung*, in such a way as to come to terms with one's mortal existence in its vast dynamics. In his letters Mahler wrote:

> the symphony is concerned with another kind of love than that which you imagine. The motto of this movement (No. 7) reads
>
> > Father, gaze on my bed of pain!
> > Let no creature be lost again.
>
> . . . It is supposed to symbolize the peak, the highest level from which one can view the world. I could almost call the movement 'What God tells me!' —in the sense that God can only be comprehended as love . . .
>
> Mahler *Briefe*, p. 161

As Diether says, the *Adagio* is to take some of the ideas explored in the Third Movement and it:

201

Constructs from it a courageous affirmation of life in the very face of death —surely the most sublime embodiment of the variational principle in music imaginable . . . ?

So *'Gib Acht'* becomes a principle throughout the *Ninth Symphony*— and we have brought to bear a life-time of listening for meaning, which has its origins in the deep, tragic experience of enduring the triumph of death over childhood. In the *Burleske* we have a citation from the Second Movement of the *Fifth*, which is in the same key and not unlike it in spirit.

EXAMPLE 94

And also besides the Pan theme, the Life Theme from the *Third* (or what may here be called the 'continuity' theme).

EXAMPLE 95

These themes emerge in a complex Rondo structure. The principle subject is followed by a first Interlude (pp. 108–9) based on Motive C in Example 83. On p. 110 the principal subject turns up again, in a varied form. It leads over the anticipated motive on the French horns on p. 111:

EXAMPLE 96

Allegro

There follows a second interlude, based on fragments from Examples 84 and 85 above:

EXAMPLE 97

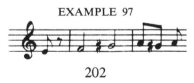

This is combined with the bass from the earlier passages in Example 86.

The following principle subject is centred on the counter-theme Example 85, with A and B from Example 83 as counterpoints. Example 100 serves as a transition again, to Episode 1, p. 119. Example 96 is now extended to twenty-two bars in length, repeated several times, with slight alterations, and combined with the continuation Example 87.

The fourth appearance of the principal subject on p. 119 is a repetition of its second appearance (p. 11) in A flat minor in an inverted setting. The second interlude that follows (p. 122) is the bridge to the first double *fughetta* (p. 122–5). Its first subject is the main theme Example 84 and the second subject is built on D from that example and E from Example 85.

EXAMPLE 98

Allegro

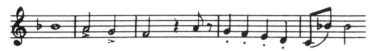

Episode I (p. 126) follows: Example 96 is combined with Example 87 and it is here that the Pan theme from the *Third* turns up.

Following these references to the influence of natural life, we have an anticipation of the main subject (p. 131), followed by a second double *fughetta* (p. 132). The first subject of this is related to the second subject of the first double *fughetta*, Example 98. But an important note is added at the beginning, and the theme continues differently:

EXAMPLE 99

Allegro

This is later asserted more and more stridently and assertively, on the horns. The second subject of this second double *fughetta* which is thrown against this figure is new. The first two bars of this theme are replaced by a turn: and this is to become the main melody of the last movement:

EXAMPLE 100

Allegro

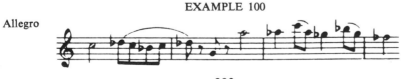

This moment of recapturing a confidence in 'life' is thus of great importance (and once we see this it bears out my invocation of the Kleinian concept of 'continuity').

This second subject is to grow into the deeply moving, lyrical section of this third movement. As the new falling figure A becomes increasingly insistent in the brass:

EXAMPLE 101

Adagio

—the violins become shrill and high, and this sound evaporates in a high tremolo and flutter-tongue on the dominant of D major.

This marks the entry of the second episode (p. 134). The thematic material is the same, but enriched. The augmented motive below is frequently combined with Example 113:

EXAMPLE 102

Adagio

There is a complete change of expression, and this presages the *Adagio-Finale*. This slower and deeply felt passage in the Third Movement is one of the most heartrending moments in the symphony, and must be one of the most moving passages in all music. Yet it occurs in the middle of this impish, ironic, and often devastating piece of contrapuntal parody.

Emotionally, perhaps, one could account for this in terms of the antics of the Fool in *Lear*, or the clowning in folk rituals: our only response to an intolerable anguish is to take resort to a kind of mad play. Mahler is really testing his own belief in any possible meaning in life, to destruction: he fears that the whole structure of his creative effort may break down, before he resolves his problems. So, he remembers moments of this kind in the past—the hopeless play with his dying brother, the silly barrel organ mocking his deep anguish in the family turmoil. He recalls the *parodie* of the *First*, and the drunkard in spring—when collapse into idiocy seems preferable to bearing the pain of being human.

But out of the structure he has created emerges, flowering, the possibility of the triumph of love: what we have is the sudden redemption of the 'turn' which, once twisted the other way in hate, threatened nihilism.

This 'redemption' is, psychologically speaking, the exercise of reparation, to overcome the deepest guilt and fear. As I have tried to show, Mahler discovers, as an existentialist composer, that 'Death' and 'hate' are within himself. The death of others, the loss of relationship, the nothingness of the universe, all these bring guilt, and fear into the soul, so that it feels most deeply troubled by its own anguished hunger for existence, experienced as envy and hate.

What needs to be done is to love these agonies—to see them as manifesting that very anguish that makes one a man, open to his world, and conscious of his predicament. Even as this pain is felt, a sweet gladness of being a creature capable of such suffering overtakes us. This explains the deeply moving quality of Mahler's work at such points: we are glad to be alive, even if it means such torment—indeed, not least *because* it means such torment.

This is how the falling chromatic cries of *'Ade! Ade!'* in No. 4 of the *Gesellen* Cycle:

EXAMPLE 103

205

are transformed into the gentle '*Alles!*' of '*Lieb' und Leid, und Welt, und Traum*' of the end of that song:

EXAMPLE 104

This is how the agonies of the loss of the brother (and Blumine) in the *First Symphony* (p. 83) are transmuted into the symphonic version of '*Lieb' und Leid, und Welt, und Traum*' here. There is a chromatic, falling passage of deep anguish—resolved into a calm, and resigned, sorrow. And this is how, out of the mad whirls of the *Rondo-Burleske*, Mahler develops the rich arches of his final existential structure. From the redeemed turn (p. 139) he soars to a high pitch of glad song—whereupon another major theme of the *Adagio* finale is struck almost in a giggle by the clarinets:

EXAMPLE 105

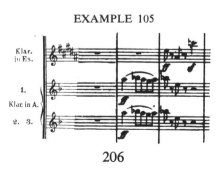

Some have interpreted this as a cock-crow. But it is rather like the attempts of a man to make a joyful noise, after being without voice or volition, because of some psychic catastrophe.

The manic, almost giggled utterance is immediately followed as if by nervous laughter. 'Can it be possible to be so positive?' the nervous little turn enquires. But it is to grow into the majestic and heart-rending theme on p. 169:

EXAMPLE 106

The little gasp of joy is repeated, in various forms, until on p. 144 it is asserted form and serious on the trumpet, and then comes to be stated in a viola solo that sounds like the mother's voice, in the early encounters that began the symphony (or, the voice of secure being, in the female element).

EXAMPLE 107

This is, of course, a highly subjective interpretation. Musically it is a transitional part of the Rondo, using the second subject of the second double *fughetta* (Example 98) combined with a variation of Example 101

above, from the second episode; Example 102, as well as Example 99. Diether sees this transitional slow episode as crucial—and a variant on something with which Mahler was much concerned. In the *Sixth* and the *Tenth* Mahler follows Beethoven in 'groping' his way into the finale

by seeming to search in the darkness for its idea, either through fragments of what has gone before, or 'phantoms' of what is to come, or both.

Bruckner works like this, too. But here, Mahler

incorporates the device into a central episode of the preceding movement, creating out of a sound structural principle, as he so often did, something uniquely his own and perfectly adapted to the altered form of the work in hand . . .

The first half of the episode (p. 132–41, ending just before cue [39]) sets two basic ideas in opposition. One is a series of passionate utterances in D major, each beginning with a slow version of the turn, sometimes diatonic and sometimes chromatic.

These may be said to represent the tendency towards 'giving way' to sorrow (moving towards hate and nihilism—the cynicism of the Rondo itself) and moving, by redemption, towards love and meaning.

In their engagement, as Diether says, they mount ever higher, but 'frustrated with varying degrees of vehemence depending on how far it gets'.

The other figure is one in D minor growing out of Example 101 (p. 204 above).

It is stern and forbidding and laden with doom: but, curiously, a bit of canonic writing seems to reveal its relation to a short motif of aspiration, like a fervently ascending prayer, from the *Eighth Symphony.*

EXAMPLE 108

This marvellous insight of Diether's points to the spiritual-philosophical struggle in the background. Mahler was menaced on the one hand by an appalling awareness of our mortal nothingness: on the other, he had an invincible impulse to find meaning in existence. At this time, the ambivalence was embodied in himself—a sensitive and noble consciousness in a diseased body.

This is first heard in the *Eighth*, significantly, in E flat minor at the point of resolution of an E flat major cadence (cue 17), after the final appearance of the words *'Imple superna gratia'* ('Bestow Thy heavenly grace') and leading to the sudden plunge into D minor for the contrasting section, *'Infirma nostri corporis'* ('The infirmity of our flesh'). Here is how the similar motif appears, by accident or otherwise, out of the counterpoint of the present passage:

EXAMPLE 109

(Top of p. 134 in score)

All this obviously has immense poetic-philosophical significance. The moment seems to have been reached at which Mahler must decide whether or not mortal death renders all one's idealism, all one's spiritual yearnings futile, just as his father's passionate hate seemed to threaten his world as a child. If one gives up the 'Holy Mary' ideal, does this mean one is left with nothing but a 'natural' voraciousness that will threaten the whole world?

As he dares to confront these questions, there emerges a strength of self-knowledge which also deepens his sense of at-one-ness with the natural world. Mahler comes closer to himself, and so to the 'tender grass', the birdcall, and the blue horizon, from which he is to draw a sense of life's continuity.

Diether says that the above passage in the brass is an example of the 'dichotomous pull' we so often hear in Mahler: 'the aspiration and its simultaneous rejection.' In my terms, this springs from the schizoid insecurity beneath Mahler's strivings. But it is also an indication of his immense artistic courage, in refusing to be satisfied with any aspiration until he had subjected it to the sternest tests of its authenticity. In this episode of the third movement, the 'testing' satisfies him, and the same ambivalent motif itself becomes redeemed—combined with the D major music at its most noble.

EXAMPLE 110

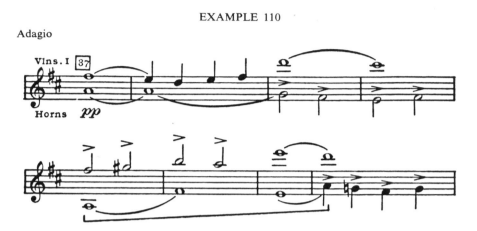

Immediately afterwards, the diatonic turn, repeated in descending sequence, becomes that most ubiquitous motif, essentially the theme of *'blau-en licht die Fernen'*—of 'continuity' itself, Example 29, p. 151.

But, even as gravity is achieved, the hebephrenic nervousness of the shrill turn on the clarinets (p. 141) seems to have set off the hobgoblins of the *Burleske*. The music moves through various keys, as the solemn turn develops and yet the daemonic elements are once more amused, trying to get the fast Rondo going again.

A kind of recapitulation begins on p. 147 with Tempo I, *subito*. The principal subject opens, without the counter subject (Example 85). There follows the transition passage Example 96 followed by the second interlude (p. 149) which is prolonged, as is the first interlude (p. 152). Even the turn (Example 100) appears (in the second violins and violas, p. 153).

On p. 154 the counter-subject (Example 85) appears combined with Example 87—this latter later becoming an independent theme. Finally, motif 'C' from Example 83 becomes a kind of cadenza leading to the coda—a wildly triumphant march. Once interrupted by this cadenza the main theme is repeated several times, until, again over C, the *Stretto* is reached (*Presto*, p. 162).

A second march, even more furious, sets in, with 'A' and 'B' from Example 83 in the middle parts. 'A' and 'B' are obstinately repeated, and there is a concluding quotation of 'C'.

As is clear from this account (based on Stiedry's analysis) the end is episodic and fragmentary—dominated by all the spectres of the ironic burlesque, and Mahler's A minor diabolism. Yet all this parodying nihilism is held in control by harmonic and contrapuntal mastery—the *'walpurgisnacht'* as Diether calls it, rides on, to its doom, just as the ruthless march of death sweeps away the sick child in the Third Movement of the *First Symphony*.

But what remains in our ears is the majesty of the meaning wrung from the mortal decay: and here, although our gallop into nothingness is recognized as real enough, what echoes in our minds is the elated anguish of existential dread—seeking the 'courage to be'.

Diether speaks of Mahler's 'invincible humanism' that 'dares to raise its head in the midst of these diabolic voices the moment they are silent' But as we have seen, there have been tremendous gains. This movement, which Diether calls a 'mad romp' is akin to that clowning which accompanies death in folk ritual and art. But the irony of (as it were) playing football with a skull, and submitting the possibilities of meaning to the utmost disdain, involve no forfeiture of essential gravity. On the contrary, the positive voice is the stronger for having tested the earlier gains by 'whirling madness': Mahler here takes a necessary 'voyage' *through* schizoid madness (to use some useful terms from R. D. Laing's attitude to therapy for the schizophrenic).

As the dances represented a manic affirmation of vitality in the second movement, here a sheer animal existence is asserted in a banal dancelike theme in A major, incorporating the descending chromatic motif, and related to the Pan theme from the *Third Symphony*. It is as if Mahler is wrestling with his paranoid fear of what the military barracks, and alll grotesque music stood for—false male doing: the monkey, the barrel-organ, the half-heard out-of-tune bugles, vulgar bands and inferior music, recognizing that he is like other men, all 'brothers in Apollo'—all 'poor bare fork'd animals', howling their attempts at meaning.

The Fourth Movement

We have seen how Mahler's 'hate' motif which symbolizes the menace of a sense-of-futility-in-life is transformed into a paean of praise-for-having-existed. Yet this cannot be achieved without tasting despair to the full. so, even the positive direction of this creative development takes on a profound poignancy, while a compassionate sorrow for man's predicament makes the sound richer in meaning.

As Diether points out, the last movement opens with a slow chromatic turn made lyrical. The first sweep up is on the dominant, and while this is a tribute to Bruckner's precept (in the E major *Adagio* of his *Ninth*) it is also reminiscent of many musical expressions of deep pain and sorrow, as in the *Crucifixus* of Haydn's *St Cecilia Mass* and (without the middle note) of the second *Kyrie* of Bach's *B Minor Mass*:

EXAMPLE 111

Molto adagio

f *lang gezogen*

                                   dim.

The music of the *Adagio* is permeated by this turn, in which the sub-limated chromaticism becomes a sob rather than a sigh, especially through the force of the added stress marks (the origin of this 'vocal' mode, as Diether says, being in the work of the Italian madrigalists).

Diether also speaks of the balance here between a 'sense of identity' and 'otherness'. Perhaps by this he means a resigned escape from melancholy over one's own death, into a sense of one's place in the continuity of life—for this is what the last movement conveys. And this raises, of course, the very large question of Mahler's use of tonality—the way in which the Symphony ends in D flat instead of D major, the key in which it opens: and the way in which this enhances the major-minor ambiguity in the work. (See above the discussion of key-relationships, pp. 192–4.)

The *Fifth Symphony* rises from a desolate funeral march in C sharp minor, from 'prostration' (as Mitchell calls it), into a lively, bustling D major. In this there is the expression of faith and hope—the assertion of an acceptance of life: challenge, and an 'unquenchable optimism', says Diether. But doesn't this unquenchable optimism sometimes ring hollow—because it brings to bear on the existential dread a mode of religious belief that is no longer convincing? This is my own impression of Mahler's explicitly Christian works, even the *Eighth*.

In the *Ninth* there can be no deception. It sinks from D major to D flat major—the composer is dying, and accepts his mortality. The tonality, as Diether says, suffers a 'sea-change analagous to that in the *Resurrection* chorus—a willing renunciation of life and acceptance of its end, an interim dwelling *"in einem stillen Gebiet"* '. This is more positive than the sweet nostalgic regret in the First Movement: but only because more of the inevitable dread has been swallowed in the subsequent movements, and more gains have been achieved. So, there can be further acceptance of ambivalence, and richer ambiguity. Here Jack Diether is not easily summarized, but must be allowed to speak in his own voice again:

> So, the *Adagio*'s second subject is pitched in the very enharmonic minor, the C sharp minor of the *Fifth*'s desolate opening, and the music passes easily from one dimension into the other, back and forth, without visible movement. This is music truly on the threshold of infinity. Thus the ubiquitous tonic major-minor complex is present in the *Adagio* in a newly enhanced context, through the use of enharmonics. Tonally we have partly the progression of the *Fifth* altogether different, reflecting the ambiguity of Mahler's feeling. The *'ewig'* cadence and the chromatic fate-motif are here, too, fully integrated into the new musical fabric. Thus the whole *Adagio* translates into pure music the poetic ambiguity of *Der Abschied*, with its lingering sensuousness and the overwhelming passion of its outburst apostrophizing *'Schoenheit'*, *'ewigen liebens'* and the *'Lebenstrunk'ne Welt'*. It is music imbued not only with the utmost sadness of leave-taking, but with a deep love of life and a feeling for life in every fibre.

> *Chord and Discord*, p. 97

What we have in this movement is the expression of the deepest sorrows of awareness of one's tragic predicament. The recognition of the suffering is at one with finding the unextinguishable fact of one's being:
I SUFFER BECAUSE I AM AND I AM BECAUSE I SUFFER.

This has involved the growth of concern—of compassion for all others, who have been 'found' by the growth of the capacity to love. The true 'reparation' here is at one with Mahler's discovery of his 'responsibilities' to Alma: but in a deeper sense it is a discovery of one's at-one-ness with the whole earth, in which there are both creative cycles and seasons, but in which the mockery of the ape's nihilism is a truth—since all must die, and the eternal regenerative cycles themselves bring death. This is 'the earth's sorrow', and the taste of this sorrow is also the taste of one's own destructive dynamics.

These, as Melanie Klein has told us, belong to very primitive and deep feelings that one may have caused harm to the mother: and, since the mother is the only object at first, to the whole world. Mahler's mother was a victim—of marriage to someone she did not love, of a man who resented her superior origins, of a man who was constantly brutal to her. She was a cripple—and Mahler identified closely with her in that. (Donald Mitchell believes Mahler had a tic of his own, and limped because of this.) She was also a victim of numerous tragic losses among her children, so

213

that Mahler himself (as several critics suggest) suffered from a deep guilt, arising from the inevitable feeling all siblings have, that the death of a sibling is the outcome of jealous and primitive fantasies, of wishing the rival sibling out of the way.

In referring to these biographical facts, I am trying to indicate the dreadful inward dynamics Mahler had to contest with, under the threat of death. It was as if his guilt at hating involved him in causing the earth's sorrow. Moreover, since moving towards love and reparation is bound up with deep and primitive sexual feelings, we can say that in the background, inevitably, is the troubled experiences Mahler had of sexuality. When his father ill-treated his mother, he seemed to be enacting the infantile fantasies in which (as Melanie Klein believed) a child unconsciously desires parental sexuality to be like that: so his guilt would have been deepened by love and desire. Mahler himself was aware that his own musical works had their origins in such parental conflict, just as his own origins were in their coition:

> They were as ill-matched as fire and water. He was obstinacy itself, she all gentleness, and without this alliance, neither I nor my *Third Symphony* would exist—I always find it curious to think of this.
>
> *Gustav Mahler*, 1958, p. 28

The musical works arise from the engagement with the 'internalized parents'—stubbornness versus gentleness, hate versus love, cruelty versus bitter subjection: in this inner world, Death takes on the role of the Cruel Father (who bullied the small boy about the tidiness of his drawer): the Mother is the source of resolution, compassion and peace.

The Cruel Father is the animus, malignant 'false male doing', in all its destructive banality. Yet these banal aspects of one's own being—perhaps the most dangerous threats to transcendent meaning—must, in some way, be embraced. That which is most feared must be found as only weak and human—and loved: if this can happen, the 'true male element' can be found, and taken into oneself, and the self can become whole. But in the process the pain of guilt is profound, about what one's hate may have done.

This Mahler achieves, astonishingly, in his *Adagio*, by taking some of the most banal tunes in the western world, and 'redeeming' them. As Jack Diether has pointed out (in a private communication) the opening bars contain several hymn and song tunes, utterly transmuted: tunes from *Abide With Me*, *Silver Threads Among the Gold* and *Poor Old Joe*, for instance:

214

EXAMPLE 112

At the same time, of course, the opening notes are the *'ewig'* theme again in a new guise, while the harmony that so transcends the melodies is derived from this passage in the Second Movement:

EXAMPLE 68B

and this in the Third:

(EXAMPLE 91)

This chord progresses, I–V–♭VI, with an intervening III chord occasioned by the dropping of the alto (viola) voice on the second beat,[6]

[6] Footnote from Diether here:
'The third bass note, though written A♭, is as truly the root of a flat-sixth chord as in the earlier examples, since this chord can be represented as B♭♭ D♭ F♭, the flat submediant of D flat major. As Mahler used the B♭♭ notation in the same context in

derives from origins in which the harmony is diverted into the flat sub-mediant: tonic-dominant-flat sub-mediant. The above figure from the Third Movement, as we have seen 'take the *"ewig"* figure, bypass its finality, and attempt to "laugh it off"'. Now, in the finale, the same harmonic idea is transformed into 'a courageous affirmation of life in the very face of death.'

> It is nowhere more difficult than here to find words to express adequately the profound effect of this use of altered harmony, structurally related to music otherwise utterly unlike it, in the predominantly diatonic opening of a solemn, hymnlike polyphony which is to become increasingly chromatic as it progresses. It immediately produces a warmth and deepening of the music comparable to the moving overall effect of the very remoteness of the key chosen.

Diether points out that the first five bars are in fact a metamorphosis of a figure from the Second Movement (just before Example 76):

EXAMPLE 113

It is by such metamorphosis that Mahler gives increasingly rich meanings to his melodies. He is not afraid to encounter simple and direct feel-

bar 17, and in the same contrabass register in bars 22 and 136, it is difficult to know why he used the A natural here, but it must obviously have had some practical rather than structural application.'

ing, and does not shrink from the recognition of vulnerability: that simplicity which exposes a childishness or innocence, which will be hurt and changed into experience by suffering. By some, who cannot bear such references to the 'commonest' melodic cadences (which express our most common aspirations for meaning and love), such direct simplicity may be taken merely to indicate Mahler's bankruptcy or sentimentality. But in these passages, surely, are transformed, in terms of adult spiritual anguish, the primitive yearnings of the child, such as we strive all our lives to understand? As Diether says:

> this *Adagio* could only have been conceived in the brain of one who knew that the most profound utterance that man can conceive is somewhere akin to the childish parable—one who could perceive the relatedness of all things, not just the differences of a few. 'One must use the most ordinary words to say the most extraordinary things'.

The path is that taken by George Herbert, and by T. S. Eliot:

> Through the unknown, remembered gate
> When the last of earth left to discover
> Is that which was the beginning . . .

And, as I have argued, at the beginning of the symphony we regressed to the very beginning of life. However, by now we are only too aware of the inescapable problems—and so follows the chromatically descending hate-motif, or 'nothingness' menace-motif, expressed (in Diether's words) as 'an overwhelming cry of grief and desolation'. Whereas in the First Movement the three initial descending tones are repeated immediately at the same pitch, here they are answered a third higher, with an even more terrible intensity.

Like the *Adagio* finale of the *Third Symphony*, this fourth movement of the *Ninth* has a Rondo-like structure, with a main melody interrupted by small episodic motives. The main melody originates from the second interlude of the Third Movement thus:

EXAMPLE 114

Molto adagio (main melody)

Third Movement, second interlude:

Allegro

EXAMPLE 100

Third Movement, augmented motif:

EXAMPLE 102

Adagio

There are two continuations of the main melody:

EXAMPLE 115
Molto adagio

EXAMPLE 116
Molto adagio

Before the second continuation the motive of the first episode in the Third Movement re-appears:

EXAMPLE 96

Allegro

This appears again together with the other three continuations, after the close of the long melody:

EXAMPLE 117

EXAMPLE 118

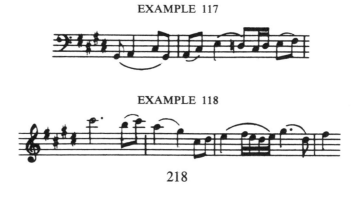

EXAMPLE 119

Plötzlich wieder langsam

After four bars, however, this passage resolves back into a varied restatement of the first clause, a solo horn suddenly standing forth with a majestic statement of the first two bars:

EXAMPLE 120 (p. 169, top)

Molto adagio

This expresses a paean of gratitude and the satisfactions of true reparation, the discovery of love, and the joy of 'having been'. This moves towards a significant expansive *crescendo* pitch (at the bottom of p. 171) culminating on a high A flat:

EXAMPLE 121

Molto adagio

Diether discusses the similarity between the themes of separation of spirit and flesh here and elsewhere in Mahler:

One may think that it is like Richard II's

> Mount, mount, my soul, thy seat is up on high,
> Whilst my gross flesh sinks downwards, here to die.

On the other hand, it may suggest the purely earthly ideals, and aspirations which continue to soar even as the flesh fails, just as Mahler is recorded to

219

have read philosophy (not the Bible) on his own death-bed, by tearing out the pages and holding them up before his eyes in a trembling hand. At any rate, there is a similarly aspiring violin figure in both parts of the *Eighth Symphony*, over a dominant pedal. It is heard thus at cue 22 in Part I

EXAMPLE 122

Molto adagio

to the words *'Firmans virtute perpeti'*, following *'Infirma nostri corporis'* ('The infirmity of our flesh invest with eternal strength'), and in slightly altered form after cue 79 in Part II, to the words *'Die ew'ge Liebe nur vermag's zu scheiden'* ('Eternal love alone can separate them'—i.e., the spirit from 'earth's residue'). The relationship of both to a crucial figure in the *Kindertotenlieder* will become clear on the final page of the *Ninth*.

p. 101

We may, however, take the implications further in the light of my analysis. Mahler's obsession with child death was not only an inevitable product of his disastrous childhood experiences, but also of his own pre-occupation with the regressed libidinal ego in himself, the unborn, regressed self, 'experienced as a fear of dying'. The most urgent need of this child-self is 'reflection', and its most terrible dread is separation, or loss of relationship. Yet here, this separation is accepted, and the 'separation from earth's residue' is tolerable because there is now a sense of meaning which can endure even such apprehensions of the abyss of being 'abandoned', of what the existentialists called 'thrownness'.[7]

In the *Adagio*, Mahler seems to stretch the web of his creative achievement over vast chasms. For instance, the change in musical texture, the evaporation of the rich polyphony, and the rarified expressionlessness of the passage at the bottom of p. 167 seem to represent a symbolic testing of the achievement of a construct *'upon which to rejoice'* over a huge span.[8]

[7] Cf., Sylvia Plath, 'I am too big to go backwards', in 'Poem for a Birthday', *The Colossus*.
[8] Aaron Copland, in his *Piano Sonata*, also asserts the sense of being human, with great tenderness, over a huge span, as against the dehumanized modern world and its emptiness.

EXAMPLE 123

When the chromatic turn is experienced again (on p. 171 of the score at *Etwas Unmerklich drägend*) however, it is magnificently *no threat*. There is a security of integration, in which the heart can beat quietly again.

The steps taken are gentle steps in a new world, of release from the threat of dissolution of identity:[9]

EXAMPLE 124

Plötzlich wieder langsam

The price of this recaptured innocence of the sense of at-one-ness with the universe, is that cost expressed by T. S. Eliot of utter humility.

So, the climax is one of great agony, followed by a glimpse of heaven maintained only for an instant: this is all we can ever expect to gain.

After the high A♭, the main melody returns as a variation (*Wieder altes Tempo*, p. 172), echoing the squeaky trill (p. 141) which nervously presaged the majestic themes of the *Adagio* and on this page we seem again to hear the mother's voice.

This changes into a very tender transition section, which in its linking mode resembles the moment in the *Gesellen* song-cycle when the singer refers to the linden tree: and in *Das Lied von der Erde* when, at last, the heart achieves peace. There are independent echoes of the melismas of the melody (p. 173), and this leads to a second appearance of the four episodical movements, to the accompanying 'heart beat' rocking motif of the last movement of *Das Lied*.

---

[9] This theme is actually an echo of the opening bars of the *Third Symphony*.

221

EXAMPLE 23A

This section is in C sharp minor, and has a sparse, chamber music texture, like *Der Abschied* (and is scored for the same instruments, clarinets and harp).

EXAMPLE 23B

This is now interrupted (on p. 174) by a passionate development of the 'hate' theme, developed into a cry of anguish:

(EXAMPLE 115)

Molto adagio

This, I believe, 'says' a number of related things:

1. There can be no peace in my heart, for I am dying, and it is appalling to leave the world.
2. The fear of becoming nothing, however, is not a menace 'out there': it is my own yearning for meaning.
3. Now I recognize my own yearning, to be, and to have a sense of having meaningfully been, it is very terrible, and fills me with sadness for all mankind.

The relationship of this cry of anguish to the initial chromatic threat is made clear by the trumpets and a full brass polyphony over a drum roll *crescendo* (p. 176). This, as Diether says, 'reverts for a moment to the catastrophic utterance of the First Movement'.

But, I believe, with this difference: the rising passion of this development *does not lead here to chaos* as such developments do in the First Movement, in an existentialist way, the music at the culmination of this moment says, 'Death thou shalt die!' This is not only the 'emotional

222

'crisis' before the point of reprise, as Diether says, but the moment of philosophical conquest of nothingness.

The final note of the turn is at last filled in *within* the context of [Example 115] and the harmonic sequel to this consummation is greeted by a shattering cymbal stroke at the conclusion of the drum-roll (*), over a tritone bass. The violins come in and then complete the introductory flourish (which we then see to be in the same key as [the opening flourish]) with its scale descent in augmented form, with utmost emphasis, and an octave higher than at the opening of the movement:

EXAMPLE 125

The culmination of the development is dove-tailed with the beginning of the reprise. Here the harmony disappears beneath a high C♭ leaving it exposed, and, as its triumphant ascendancy declines, the violins bow the opening funeral tread of the whole symphony: 'in my end is my beginning'. The opening tread

EXAMPLE 6

here becomes:

EXAMPLE 7

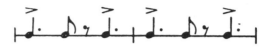

But now, as Diether says the chromatic motif is stripped of its anguish and terror, and is resolved (as it is at the end of the First Movement). It is now a 'sad but *accepted* corollary to the final song of yearning, which rises once more to the heights and then sinks back to be swallowed up in oblivion'. On p. 181 begins a coda, using the two combinations of the main melody above always very soft. Diether continues:

> the reprise itself is dominated by a statement and counterstatement of the main clause: the *minore* does not return. The statement is enriched by a flowing counterpoint for horns and cellos, again featuring the turn, as well as a noble figure (bracketed below) further recalling the *Eighth Symphony*. Compare the following, noting also the use of the stressed chromatic turn already in the texture of the *Eighth* (Part II, cue 20):

EXAMPLE 126

Molto adagio

EXAMPLE 127

This statement is *fortissimo*, and its urgency is emphasized by a cymbal crash, after which the percussion is silent. A pause at the end of p. 178,

224

embodying the transmuted 'hate' theme prepares for the counter-statement that begins on p. 179. Here the *'ewig'* motif may be heard in the horns and cellos. The turning figure groans in the bass, reinforced by bass clarinet, bassoons and tuba: a dissonant distortion of the polyphony increases, and reaches a poignant climax, with the violins and trumpets in excruciating bitonal conflict with one another. This dissolves in a rapid *diminuendo*, and there is a final accompanying cadenza for the high violas, echoing the flute cadenza of the First Movement. Again we hear what may be called the mother's voice, calm and reassuring.

Again there is a general pause (p. 181) before the coda begins, for *pianissimo* strings, *Adagissimo*.

The strings are muted except the violins, which offer a veiled remote statement of the 'hate' theme still. Again there is an echo of the *Eighth Symphony* and from the setting of the words *'Der Tag is schoen auf jenen*

EXAMPLE 128

Hoch'n' ('The day is bright on yonder height') from the *Kindertotenlieder*:

EXAMPLE 129

The final statement (in the violins) of the chromatic movement, or 'hate' motif, in the second violins is altered (Diether points out) 'so that the second half begins no higher than the first half, as though too numb or oblivious to move'. Again, 'Death thou shalt die!' or 'Nothingness, you shall be overcome!' Thus the symphony attains 'the peace that passeth all understanding' and a sense of meaning in being, 'at the still centre of the turning world'. If such a sense of intense meaning in human consciousness can be achieved, hate, death and nothingness themselves can be consigned to oblivion, for *we have existed*.

Diether's own commentary on the '*mandala*' of the end is impossible to summarize, and again must be given in his own words.

EXAMPLE 130

The repeated viola figure below transforms the chromatic turn about the dominant back into the diatonic form by raising the double flat with which it began in the movement's opening flourish. The final note shown above in the second violins, along with the open fifth in the cellos below, form the minor tonic triad, and this too is raised to the major triad when the second violins re-enter for the closing bars on F natural. Thus the tonic major-minor motif is reversed, in precise opposition to the closing bars of the *Tragic Symphony*, which asserts the minor triad with awful finality. In the two final bars, the diatonic turn of Example 130 is reversed, the violas die away on the dominant, the cellos repeat the open fifth, similarly dying away, and the resolving mediant tone in the second violins is far above the fifth which it resolves, as though it were a resolution on some ethereal plane, disembodied and not of this world:

This is surely a kind of Buddhist *nirvana* to which Mahler's contemplation soars, not the Roman Catholic resurrection of the two choral finales (II and VIII). All the familiar aspiring to heaven of the *Eighth* is there, but it is finally sublimated into this ethereal oblivion. Again the verbal clue to the instinctual meaning of such music seems to be provided by *Das Lied von*

der Erde. I noted above the resemblance of Example 17[10] to the phrase *'Du aber, Mensch'*. In the earlier work, the plaint 'But thou, man, how long livest thou' is contrasted with 'The sky is eternally blue, and the earth will long stand fast and blossom in spring' (*'Das Firmament blaut ewig'*, etc.) In our thermonuclear age, of course, not even that is literally certain. But our petty world is to the greater cosmos as the individual human is to the race: a mere speck in the continuum.

To achieve such a sense of existential triumph, however, as we know from our exploration of tragedy, requires a tremendous inward achievement, of love over hate. As we know from our experience of Shakespeare's *King Lear*, this necessitates the rediscovery of the 'total acceptance' of love such as has been known in infancy, but lost in separation. As Diether concludes:

> The dissolving into *nirvana* at the end of the *Ninth* even hearkens somewhat back to the oblivion of the end of *Lieder eines fahrenden Gesellen*, under the snowfall of blossoms from the lime tree of childhood where 'all was good again: love and grief and the world and dream'—*'Lieb' und Leid und Welt, und Traum.'* But this is the reconciliation of childhood through the mind and heart of a man. This symphony which began with the distant tread of death, and which examined every aspect of its proximity to life, ends as nearly and truly reconciled to both as it seems possible for a man of Mahler's tremendous and clear-sighted intellect to become.

Mahler's regression is not however merely nostalgic, but rather a rediscovery of what Eliot calls 'The voice of the hidden water-fall': in the face of death it penetrates to the springs of potentiality.

Thus, while we take in the reality of death in the symphony, we emerge from it, as after a great tragedy, full of a joyful sense of human *potentia*. So, the end of this funereal and valedictory symphony points towards 'life'—how can we explain this in musical terms? Diether's analysis of the *Ninth Symphony* is profoundly illuminating, not least because this critic is aware of such existentialist problems symbolized in the music, and in the course of following his analysis (together with the analysis made by Stiedry and Newlin) we have, in fact, already seen how the music enacts Eliot's theme, 'in my end is my beginning'.

We saw, as we set off, how the symphony *begins* with a reference to the end of *Das Lied von der Erde*. But this reference is not only to the note of farewell: it picks up the theme of the apprehension of eternity achieved in music and, *continuity* (in relation to the problems of

---

[10] In Diether's essay Example 19. In this book Example 17. The cadence quoted by Diether here is Example 5 (above, p. 101).

gratitude and envy). Significantly, as Deryck Cooke points out, the words which chiefly symbolizes eternity are Mahler's own:

> The lovely earth, everywhere, blooms in spring and grows green again, everywhere and for ever shines the blue horizon, for ever, for ever.

Thus, *Das Lied* transcends the recognition of mortality and the brevity of human life by the discovery of gratitude in Melanie Klein's sense: what contrasts with this is envy, hate, the devouring ghost in daemonic animal shape which mocks at life and meaning.

Gratitude and continuity are expressed in the *'ewig'* theme which is in a sense being rocked and crooned to by the mother, as well as a falling yielding to Eternity. Diether explores the origins of this falling figure, and says that he believes it to be one of Mahler's chief motto-figures from the *Second Symphony*. It has, as we have seen, affinities with the *'Lebewohl'* figure in Beethoven's *Piano Sonata*, Opus 81a. But while it expresses 'farewell' it is also used to *begin* vocal phrases in *Der Abschied*. Thus, as Deryck Cooke says, it can become 'at once glad, peaceful and sorrowful', 'yearning' but yet valedictory. For an atheist, how can these elements be understood, except in terms of *subjective resignation*? The *'ewig'* theme culminated in the 'celebrated tonic chord with added sixth' which so haunted Alban Berg, and persists for no fewer than seventy-four final bars—the 'perfect musical picture of eternity'—in *Das Lied*: (Example 26 above, p. 149 and overleaf).

Throughout, the emphasis is on the sixth, and its yearning for union. The 'outline' indicated by the structure, landing on the sixth, expresses the possibilities of integration only finally realized and only finally possible at the end. The essential structure here is discussed by Deryck Cooke in *The Language of Music* (p. 79) in his passage on the meaning of the major second. He quotes it beside the opening phrase of the 'love' or 'peace' song from the *Ninth Symphony* (see overleaf and p. 123 above).

Discussing the interval of the second, Cooke points out that there is no clear-cut antithesis between the major and minor second. The minor second is painful, and his examples show it used in situations of hopeless anguish as when Strauss's Don Juan sings, 'the fuel is burnt out, and all is cold and dark upon the hearth'.

> Its tension is obviously akin to that of the minor sixth: it is an acute dissonance in relation to the minor triad, but whereas the sixth is drawn by semitonal tension down to the dominant, the minor second is drawn by semitonal tension down to the tonic. This means that whereas the minor sixth is an expression of anguish in a context of flux, *the minor second is an*

expression of anguish in a context of finality: in other words the minor sixth expresses an active anguish, *the minor second a hopeless anguish* . . .

The Language of Music, p. 78

Since he was under the shadow of death, we might have expected Mahler to have used the minor second in such contexts. If the keynote of his work were 'world weariness' he might well have done.

But he uses the *major* second, and, as Cooke points out, the major second 'is rarely isolated as an expressive tension':

It is largely a neutral note, common to both major and minor systems, bridging the melodic gap between the tonic and the third, and strengthening the context, but not functioning expressively in its own right.

Yet this 'neutral' interval takes on a special function in Mahler's *Das Lied von der Erde* and the *Ninth Symphony*.

In latter times it actually has been isolated, and is found to function similarly to the major sixth.

As we have seen, the major sixth Cooke associates with pleasure, from the *Hallelujah!* chorus to *Roll Out the Barrel*: and it is found in *Das Lied von der Erde*, at the 'infinitely yearning' and:

EXAMPLE 131

A mild dissonance in relation to the major triad, drawn towards the tonic by the tension of a whole tone, it has the same 'longing' quality as the major sixth's tension towards the dominant; except that, being connected with the 'fixed' and 'final' tonic, its longing is not in a context of flux, but in a context of finality.

p. 79

The major sixth, not, like the thirds, fixed as concords in the triad, has to 'resolve': so, it expresses a sense of *pleasure* in a state of flux: in my terms it expressed the *possibility* of joy in gratitude, by the *acceptance of needs*. Can we here perhaps speak of that acceptance of dependence which can bring a true sense of independence, in that it marks an awareness of the object as real, released to be its independent self, so that the self can feel real and independent too?

229

The feeling is thus not one of possession or acceptance, like the third, but of *non-possession, non-acceptance, need.*

p. 69 (my italics)

Mahler combined this with 'longing in a context of finality', as we have seen.

As Cooke and Diether point out, this same procedure is carried forward into the main theme of the *Ninth Symphony* and the *Tenth*. The musical structure thus indicates that Mahler's concern is with seeking, in a context of *finality*, the *acceptance of needs, yearning* for an integration and 'encounter' that will at once bring peace, gladness, and yet sorrow. This is surely in quite another direction than what is implied by 'world weariness'? Mahler is in fact in courageous pursuit of existential security from the first.

In this analysis of Mahler's *Ninth* I have tried to extend the range of psycho-analytical and existential concepts which have been applied to Mahler, and to make this kind of approach more *positive*, in the recognition of his originality and creative genius. As one does this, I believe, one can begin to see that Mahler points in a very different direction from that of the 'intellectual pastimes' of the musical *avant-garde* such as those discussed at the end of Donald Mitchell's *The Language of Modern Music*.

By contrast with one major trend in contemporary music, a move towards schizoid coldness, intellectual preoccupation with mere structure and form, and a 'diminution of affect' in music, Mahler's last works are essentially and outstandingly 'heart-rending'—yet this capacity to rend the heart is by no means mere self-absorption. Mahler's song is of 'the sorrow of the earth' and his most poignant moments are moments of a compassion for man in his predicament which, by their very sorrow, imply a deep attachment to the joy of living experience, a reverence for life, and a high and noble sense of human value. Nothing could be further from today's fashionable nihilism and cold sense of futility, than the magnificent agony of pity in such moments as that 'new cry of overwhelming grief and desolation' for example: Example 115 (above, p. 218).

But this is no vague cry from a hopeless Romanticism. The disciplines by which such compassion is expressed are exacting and belong to a structure by which Mahler achieves his sense of meaning in life, accepting our nothingness but asserting the *Dasein* against it. A parallel courage may be found in D. H. Lawrence at best:

230

Piecemeal the body dies, and the timid soul
has her footing washed away, as the dark flood rises.
We are dying, we are dying, we are all of us dying
and nothing will stay the death-flood rising within us
and soon it will rise on the world, on the outside world . . .

We are dying, we are dying, so all we can do
is now to be willing to die, and to build the ship
of death to carry the soul on its longest journey . . .

It is the end, it is oblivion . . .

As I tried to indicate earlier, what we are concerned with when we engage with death while still living is the problem of hate: building our ship of death is at one with accepting our essential ambivalence, so that we may achieve the I AM feeling. Not to feel I AM is worse than death, because it threatens to become the feeling I HAVE NEVER BEEN, or I NEVER WAS, or IT WILL BE AS IF I HAVE NEVER BEEN. It is against this feeling that all religious cosmologies are erected: in Dante's *Inferno* individuals are given an exact place in Heaven, Hell or Limbo: thus they 'matter' to the universe to a meticulous degree. No-one in Dante's Hell has been annihilated out of existence altogether. Yet our fate now appears to the atheist as one which ends in nothingness—as does the end of the world. The Christian cries, 'Let me never be confounded'—the worst eternal torments of Hell are preferable to utter extinction, since the fact that God has prepared such torments shows that 'Thou God seest me'—He cares. But to the man who has no God, no-one cares and no-one confirms him by seeing him. He exists in an indifferent universe, only to become extinct when he dies. His basis of a sense of confirmed identity can only be in whatever sense of meaning in his life he can find during it, and, retrospectively looking back at it. This sense of meaning he can only find in his relationship with others: they confirm him: 'It is from one man to another that the heavenly bread of self-being is passed.'

Thus, finding a true sense of meaning in one's existence, in the face of death, requires the recognition of the existence of others and of what one shares with them. It thus involves not only the discovery of one's own reality, but also *concern*—a recognition of one's responsibilities to others, and the joy of reparation, in giving to them. As Lawrence wrote:

Be kind, oh be kind to your dead
and give them a little encouragement
and help them to build their little ship of death . . .

231

Oh, from out of your heart
provide for your dead once more, equip them
like departing mariners, lovingly . . .

All Souls Day

In *The Houseless Dead* Lawrence adds:

O pity the dead that were ousted out of life
all unequipped to take the long, long voyage . . .

O think of them, and encourage them to build
the bark of their deliverance from the dilemma
of non-existence to far oblivion.

Mahler's latest work was the building of this 'bark', in the quest for deliverance from the dilemma of distinguishing between 'non-existence' and 'oblivion'. Since this involves the insight that all human beings both yearn for a sense of confirmed existence, but yet must inevitably forfeit their identities on physical death, Mahler discovers the essential problem of union and separateness. His impending death seemed to isolate him as a 'lonely wanderer': but in seeking deliverance from his dilemma he discovers ruth—the deepest pity and concern for all man—and so expressed and defines a profound humanness in his sense of at-oneness with all, whose anguish he shares.

Over and over again in his work there are moments when an inexorable progress of death sweeps away someone who is loved, and all meaning and joy seem extinct. The same horror menaces him when a love dies. In his music he re-enacts time and time again, the overcoming of this torment, and the search of the wounded heart for ease and reconciliation. This is a deeply moving feature of the most passionate son in *Lieder Eines Fahrenden Gesellen*, No. 3, '*Ich hab ein glühend Messer, ein Messer in meiner Brust*', and it is clearly a central theme, even in his early work. As Jack Diether says, the tonic-dominant *ostinato* bass-tread in quarter notes is a major stylistic feature linking three words—*Waldmachen*; the *Klagende Lied*; and *Lieder Eines Fahrenden Gesellen*. In the text of his very interesting notes on Mahler's *Juvenilia*, Diether traces elements in the *First Symphony* to the *Gesellen* cycle which is its starting-point. One major common element is this 'tread bass' which stylistically links the *First*, the song-cycle and *Das Klagende Lied*. The first three songs in the *Gesellen* all begin with prominent fourth intervals. The last song brings in the tread bass for the second stanza, and restores the melodic prominence of the fourth interval in the third stanza:

232

EXAMPLE 132

Diether then discusses the influence of the fourth in the *First Symphony*.

Here, musically, we penetrate to the depths of Mahler's anguish. The funeral march on *'Frères Jacques'*, which is a dirge for his dead brother, has the fourth tread-bass beneath it—as Diether says, it 'seems to mock the unchanging bass itself with waggish duplication'. This 'mockery' belongs to the world of the ape—that is, here we have the pressure of that *sense that life has no meaning* which struck Mahler so powerfully when his brother died. *The loss of those eyes echoed for him the failure of creative reflection in the eyes of the mother*: it evoked the dread of non-being.

We have the same failure of the light of life, in the *Kindertotenlieder*. We know it in the *Gesellen* songs, in the references to a yearning for encounter in *Das Lied*, in Mahler's anguished quest to 'find' Alma at the heart of these touching works of art is the whole question of how failures of encounter (by the failure of love, or by death) menace one's whole hold on life.

As Diether points out, the music of the moment when the young knight lies down to sleep under the willow tree, to the words *'zur Ruh'* . . . *'zur Ruh'* is echoed in the final page of the *Gesellen* to the words *'Lieb' und Leid, und Welt und Traum'*: the peaceful interlude from the funeral march of the *First Symphony* is drawn from *'De zwei blauen Augen von Meinem Schatz'*, at the lines about the linden tree.

EXAMPLE 133

EXAMPLE 134

In his notes on the *First Symphony*, Bruno Walter quotes Mahler as saying, 'imagine before the Third Movement a catastrophic happening which is the emotional source of the funeral march and finale'. In 1909 one-and-a-half years before his death, Mahler wrote to Walter from New York, after a performance of his *First Symphony*, 'I was quite satisfied with this youthful venture. I am strongly affected when I conduct one of those works of mine. There is crystallizing a burning pain in my heart. What a world is this that casts up such sounds and *reflections of images*? Things like the funeral march and the outburst of the storm which follows it seem to me like a flaming accusation of the Creator' (my italics).

Walter says, 'Mahler rebelled against God when he wrote this symphony.' But it might be more accurate to say that in it he began to explore the relationship between encounter with the 'significant other', and one's sense of life's meaning: 'secretly and bashfully he watches for a Yes which allows him to be . . .'

What was the 'catastrophic happening'? Evidence from unpublished music seems to suggest that the existential agony in the Third Movement of the *First Symphony* was associated with earlier agonies of his childhood. As Diether says,

> Through this music, he seems . . . to have been unconsciously reliving the emotional trauma of his off-again-on-again affair with Johanna Richter, or something very much like it (footnote in the original: 'This in turn would, of course, be etiologically related to the traumatism of Mahler's infancy . . .')
> 'Notes on Some Mahler Juvenilia', *Chord and Discord*, Vol. 3, No. 1, p. 89

Bruno Walter says that the 'Funeral March in Callot's manner' refers to a drawing by the French engraver Jacques Callot which showed a procession of gaily dancing animals accompanying the body of a dead hunter on its way to the grave.[11]

> But I am sure that Mahler's imagination, when he wrote this revolutionary piece of music, was haunted also by the demonic figure of Roquairol from Jean Paul's *Titan*. In him he found the terrible inner dissonances, the scorn and the despair, the vacillation between heavenly and hellish impulses which for some time may have invaded also his wounded heart . . .

Walter speaks of 'the foe in the breast'. The march, he says, is 'interrupted by a moving lyric episode' then the march starts again with increased bitterness, and *it ends in a mood of annihilation*. The 'foe in the breast' is the feeling of being overcome with nothingness—total extinction of meaning. The march is the unappeasable march of the disease which swept away the brother, despite all the play, songs, love, and care he bestowed upon him: it is the triumph of death over reparation.

So, too, the failure of a love affair is like a death, a triumph of nothingness. Diether traces the word *'Blumine'*, which was the name for the section deleted from this symphony in its final form, to the title of a work of Jean Paul, the author of *Titan*. Without any too-literal recourse to the actual works of Jean Paul, says Diether, the emotional connotations are clear: Mahler has in mind Joanna Richter, the 'blue-eyed sweetheart' of the *Gesellen* cycle and the Cassel opera, 'I have written

---

[11] The figure of the ape on the hurdy-gurdy surely lurks among these?

a cycle of songs dedicated to her'. Mahler wrote to Fritz Löhr on New Year's Day 1885:

> 'she doesn't know them, but they cannot tell her more than she already knows . . . [in them] a man is condemned by his fate to become a wanderer over the face of the earth . . .'

'Ich geh', ich wand'-re in die Berge. Ich suche Ruhe, Ruhe für mein einsam Herz! Ich wandle nach der Heimatt meiner Stätte! Ich werde niemals in die Ferne schweifen. Still ist mein Herz und harret seine Stunde!'—the wanderer has come a long way by the time of *Das Lied von der Erde*—which is the song of the earth's *sorrow*.

Whether Diether and others are right or not, or whether *'Blumine'* was Mahler's pet name for Johanna, and whatever the significance of his strange ambivalence about *'Blumine'* music—what we can say is that these autobiographical fragments give us a clue to the association in Mahler's feelings between love and death. As he knew from his experience of his brother's death, love cannot conquer death, though it can find a meaning that triumphs over nothingness, in the swallowing of tragic despair. *(Lieb und Leid, und Welt, und Traum!)*. The failure of love, of encounter (in those reflecting eyes) is like death: and one way of resolving the dreadful pain in one's breast *('O weh!')* is to learn from the natural world, and to seek solace in the forest, or under the linden tree. *'Mein Gesell' war Lieb und Leide'* modulates into *'Auf der Strasse steht ein Lindenbaum, da hab' ich zum ersten Mal in Schlaf geruht . . .'*—we may recall the young Mahler left alone in the forest all day: the Pan theme in the *Second Symphony*: Mahler listening to the breathing of the Earth: the deep draughts from the regenerative cycles of Spring in *Das Lied*: the 'learning' theme in the *Ninth*; the brother under the tree in *Das Klagende Lied*: *'Wie ein Naturlaut'* and *'Was spricht die tiefe Mitternacht?'* These are indications that in his existential agony Mahler turned not to God, but to the *ahnung* in the natural world, partly influenced by Nietzsche's philosophy, to 'hear' some possible source of balm, for the spiritual emptiness occasioned in him, by the intolerable loss of objects of his love.

This accounts for much in the development of the structure of his music. He must go on and on in repeated engagement with the same basic existential themes until these themes become sufficiently transformed to be reconciled and integrated. It is not that we have conflict between modes of approach to experience so much as the engagement with elements which threaten to *undermine* all positive meaning.

236

This explains the links between death and the lullaby, end and beginning—and the continual exploration that is the basis of the structure of these last works:

> We shall not cease from exploration
> And the end of all our exploring
> Will be to arrive where we started
> And know the place for the first time . . .
> *Little Gidding*

By this continual exploration, moreover, these disruptive threats are gradually discovered to be not only aspects of the same anguish of existence needs, but actually sources of strength. Even suffering and despair themselves become of the greatest value, because it brings the capacity to discover what one shares with others. As Kierkegaard said:

> One must really have suffered very much in the world, and have been very unfortunate before there can be any talk of beginning to love one's neighbour. It is only in dying to the joys and happiness of the world in self-denial that the neighbour comes into existence. One cannot therefore accuse the immediate person of not loving his neighbour because he is too happy for his neighbour to exist for him. No one who clings to earthly life loves his neighbour, that is to say his neighbour does not exist for him.
>
> Sören Kierkegaard, *The Journals of Kierkegaard*, quoted by Leslie H. Farber, in *The Ways of the Will*, p. 181

As Leslie H. Farber and Viktor Frankl have argued, existential despair is not a merely 'morbid' or 'unhealthy' state of mind. If we try to place it as this, we may be 'refusing to conceive it as belonging inescapably in some measure to our lives as human beings' and this may be 'more malignant than despair itself'.

> [It was Kierkegaard's belief that the worst of all despairs is that in which one does not know he is in despair.] It sometimes happens that despair itself provides the very condition of urgency that brings a man to ask those serious —we might call them tragic—questions about his life and the meaning and measure of his particular humanness. When despair is repudiated, these questions go unasked, and it may be exactly here, in the failure to confront these questions, that there occurs a turning in one's development that is false.
>
> *op. cit.*, p. 196

In his *Ninth Symphony* Mahler turns his despair into a discovery of humanness. In the *Ländler* (Second Movement) Mahler preserves the gravity of his despair which he has established in the First Movement against 'the joys and happiness of the world' to which he is dying anyway. In the Third Movement he is engaged with an even more false 'turning in his development' which is the temptation to reject with bitter irony even the value of confronting the questions aroused by despair: a deep insecurity about being creative, even. But having begun to ask the tragic questions about 'meaning and measure of his particular human-ness', and having gained insights into these things *in himself*, he preserves these, against manic denial, against destructive doubt, and against temptations to fall into the even worse despair of not accepting despair. Then he triumphantly declares the meaning and measure of all human life in the Fourth Movement—albeit with a voice rich and sombre with knowledge of mortality and our deepest sufferings.

I have tried to show how one of the main tasks in the *Ninth Symphony* is the resolution of the complex figure of hate—which means, resolving and overcoming menaces to the very capacity to feel that one's existence is meaningful. Or, to put it another way, the symphony is a means to maintain sanity in the face of the threat of utter dissociation.

Deryck Cooke refers to the chromaticism in a song of Schubert and uses the phrase 'a journey from which no-one ever came back': it is something like this that the symphony engages with. In the end Death is accepted as a journey from which no-one comes back, but by creative effort Mahler has overcome the fear of annihilation of meaning which is a dread of something far more terrible than merely dying—it is the utter extinction of having ever been, the forfeiture of the *Dasein*.

Or in other terms, he preserved his humanness, and his authenticity of being, against violation, even by death. In discussing the secret and non-communicating core to the human personality D. W. Winnicott says:

> Rape, and being eaten by cannibals, these are mere bagatelles as compared with the violation of the self's core.
>
> 'On Communication', *The Maturational Processes*, p. 187

We have to make some such distinction as this, between fear of death, and fear of a violation of that which is 'sacred and most worthy of preservation'.

10

The Art of Being Human

I began my essay on Mahler knowing intuitively what it was that he was attempting to do. I have read a great deal since, and have been startled to find how many critics have also been exploring the same themes, and have moved towards similar conclusions: Robert Still, Deryck Cooke, Jack Diether and Donald Mitchell have each approached existential problems around Mahler. What then might be my contribution?

What I hope I have shown is how we can learn from Mahler not only in music but in the other arts. We can, for instance, explore the implications of the obvious fact that Mahler's influence can be found in other composers. As Mitchell says, 'The influence of Mahler on Shostakovitch requires, I think, no detailed substantiation' ('Gustav Mahler: Prospect and Retrospect', *Chord and Discord*, 1963, p. 143). But, if we were to follow Wilfrid Mellers' explanation that the source of Mahler's despair was in the crash of Empires—how is it that we find the same anguish and sense of futility in the music of the most popular composer in the new Soviet State of the Socialist Revolution?

The implication is that we need to look at man in society, and the artist in society, in a new way. The artist speaks of fundamental and universal problems of identity which are only minimally affected by society. He may suffer these problems of existence in a deep way through accident: by the culture he shares with all other men he is able to communicate possible answers to these problems to other men who have them to some degree in themselves. But these are questions of *being* for which one cannot legislate. In facing the ultimate questions of his existence, the 'New Soviet Man' is no different from old bourgeois man, and the communist organization of society provides no more adequate sense of identity, and no richer sources of 'being', than capitalist society. Man still dies, and all his acts on earth are ultimately futile: they are only 'attachments to self and to things and to persons', while 'what is

only living can only die'. The optimism of socialist reorganization cannot solve the existence problem posed by our essential nothingness. The
inner feeling of ontological insecurity remains, and must be worked on in
terms of inner needs—for confirmation, and for ways to overcome the
threats emanating from the hungry regressed libidinal ego. Of course
Shostakovitch has these problems too! (Cf. his *Fourteenth Symphony*.)

The new musical modes in Mahler belong to a whole new movement
of enquiry into the nature of humanness—as here when the Envy theme
is explored, and turns out to be existence hunger, so that 'when the
tongues of flames are infolded' (as the suffering is endured) 'the fire and
the rose' become one—and what was Envy is now gratitude, while hate
is seen as the inversion of love. So there can be joy, and a new security
and *potentia* of spirit. This transformation is achieved by the particular
form he develops, the episodic progress of returning again and again
persistently to the same, or to related themes, transforming them by
experience, as intractable inward elements.

Here a good deal more needs to be explored, so that we can understand the potentialities of that art which persistently explores the human,
and makes a quest for authenticity. Perhaps the traditional forms, and
traditional diatonic music, belong to manic-depressive symbolism, and
a kind of conflict, resolution and synthesis which no longer satisfies our
existential needs. It sustained the sense of meaning merely by 'acting' and
'doing'. Much of our art today is schizoid, as I have argued elsewhere.
It tackles genuine schizoid problems of existential emptiness, but has
also gone schizoid in the sense that it has chosen to turn its back on the
human, in favour of what I would call False Solutions. It has attached
itself to moral inversion, and hate—and so to 'false male doing'—which
can achieve nothing, however desperate it becomes. Mahler's art, though
it originates in the schizoid problem, points in another direction, seeking
to synthesize a sense of identity, from the beginning, in a new way and in
a new form, towards human meaning, by using the energies of 'female
element being'.

There have been changes in musical form before. The same kind of
change comes about in Beethoven's last piano sonatas and his string
quartets. As Wilfrid Mellers says, discussing *Sonata*, Opus 111:

> The reconciliation of sonata conflict and fugal unity flows into the oneness of
> the arietta with variations. The *adagio* of Opus 106, though it no longer
> sounds like a dramatic conflict, is still a sonata movement; in this *arietta*
> the tonal conflict of the First Movement is stilled in heaven.
>
> *The Sonata Principle*, p. 73

The variations in the *arietta* of Opus 111 'are the continuous flowering of melody . . . resembling the sixteenth-century principle of divisions on a ground . . . Finally the divisions become so rapid and so ecstatic that there is nothing left except dissolving trills. The soaring trills of Opus 106 have found their rest *in the unity of being which is sometimes called Paradise*. Something similar happens at the end of the greatest of all works in variation form—the *Diabelli Variations*, Opus 120.'

Mellers sees the transition from 'sonata conflict' to 'the continuous flowering' as having to do with the turning of concern from engagement with the external world to an inward engagement with the *life of the spirit*.

> In his last works Beethoven has given up the struggle with the external world so typical of the middle-period symphonies, because he has fought and won a more important battle in his own spirit. He had wished to conquer himself in order to conquer life. 'Even with the frailties of my body my spirit shall dominate.' But now he says 'O God, give me strength to conquer myself, for nothing must bind me to this life'. This is the profoundest sense in which his deafness is both a physical fact and a spiritual allegory. While Beethoven lay dying a thunderstorm was raging. Just before the end, he raised himself from the pillows and shook his fist defiantly at the heavens. Then he fell back; on his face was an expression of infinite beatitude. His death, like his life, is a parable which complements his music.
>
> Against the theme which is stated in unison at the beginning of the finale to his last quartet, Beethoven wrote the words: *'Muss es sein? Es muss sein'* (Must it be? It must be) . . . the words are . . . metaphysical. The question summarizes Beethoven's years of revolt against destiny; the answer summarizes his new-found humility. In his last work question and answer have become one. Like Blake, Beethoven knew that 'without contraries there is no progression'.
>
> *op. cit.*, pp. 78–9

Professor Mellers here gives a most valuable indication as to the kind of progress towards 'acceptance' that music can make at its greatness. We may, however, question the matter further: in what sense can music, which is surely all 'inward', turn *from* 'the external world' to detachment from the world? What does 'conquer life' mean? What is a 'revolt against destiny'? What becomes what answer to what question?

I am not quibbling over terms: nor do I wish to imply that Beethoven's concern with the heroic difference between 'the God-King of eighteenth-century autocracy' (and) 'the man of strife who is the architect of a new world' is a purely subjective dilemma. There are real political and social aspects of Beethoven's concern to explore the 'alternation of

Life and Death' in the sphere of the 'primarily subjective', because (as
Mellers says) 'social regeneration can spring only from what used to be
called "a change of heart" '. What I do want to press is a closer examination of the nature of the subjective conflict and development, for surely
the social issues only have meaning in music in that they belong to an
engagement with existential problems—'what is it to be human?' and
'what is the point of life?'

Mellers indicates this when he quotes T. S. Eliot's *Little Gidding* at
the end of his essay on Beethoven. The acceptance of the nature of the
external world, and of our own imperfection and mortality, depends, as
I have tried to show, upon our capacity to accept the nature of ourselves,
and on certain inner formative dynamics in us, in our symbolic engagement with these. Moreover, these dynamics belong to being, and require
(as Beethoven's last works required) a different dimension. This does not
mean, however, any kind of dissolution, or retreat from the world, into
the *id* or some primitivism, or relinquishment of reality.

In the present study I believe I have only one major point to make—
or, rather, I am only trying to do one thing, which is to shift an emphasis.
Jack Diether, despite his most penetrating insights into Mahler as an
existentialist composer, can still try to tell us:

> Now modern psychology teaches us that the subconscious mind is *primitive,*
> unsubtle, intellectually *moronic*. Like all our greatest human achievements,
> our musical edifices, straining towards the clouds, are built up slowly and
> painfully out of the *common mud* we inherit . . . the explanation lies buried
> somewhere within that great *unknown primitive mass* we call the un-
> conscious . . .
> (my italics)

It may be true, as he says, that

> we suspect that our private responses are formed by early experiences and
> identifications, perhaps by accidental sound connotations both musical and
> extra-musical, and we may even deliberately set out to explore this ground;
> but we seldom get very far, for we are floundering about in the dark.

Perhaps my inept musical analysis may seem to bear him out! But what
I want to try to change is the picture of the 'unconscious mind' as something 'primitive', in quite the sense in which Diether uses the term, that
is, a *moronic mass*. This sounds too much like something primal and
Caliban-like, beyond our capacity to do anything about, except to live
with it, as a brute within us. *The unconscious mind, after all, produces
the music*: it is by no means moronic, primitive and unsubtle—as, surely,
we discover, when we dream, or wake with a creative problem solved?

At the depths of our being is not something 'moronic' and mud-like, but, as Mahler found, the 'formative principle' of creative being—the need for meaning: the most primary formative principle in our souls—our quest for meaning—is what created civilization.

There are, of course, primitive forces within us, of aggression, hate, and ferocious fantasy. But these in the light of object-relations psychology and existentialism are but manifestations of the essentially *human* urge to find and assert our hereness and nowness, the *Dasein*. They are primitive only insofar as they regress to infantile modes of dealing with the world, by schizoid-paranoid modes. When explored and examined, as Mahler explored and examined them, they are capable of yielding up their poignant secrets, and of being transformed by maturity into essentially human, and positive, qualities. Even the ape, hate and envy, are distorted ways of pursuing *meaning*. Somewhere here lies the secret to those problems of the future of music, which Diether discusses, but which I am not competent to discuss. Was Mahler 'wading deeper' into the primitive moronic mass? Was his work completed in a 'union of poetry and death'? As Diether says, some

> ... find a complete statement and rounding-out in his existing works, ending with his 'farewell to life'. They think of his death as an involuntary suicide, coinciding with the real completion of his artistic life-work.

Or was his later work the beginning of a re-discovery of the sources of identity in 'togetherness'—in the creative dynamics of *liebende Wirheit*? In going out from the self? For if we forgo the analogy of 'primal mud' (with the Caliban-like Freudian *id* as its basic reality), we may discover another kind of image—which is that of the psychic matrix, in the mother's arms, reflected by her face. In the primitive unconscious is also the energy of *being*, and man's wish 'to have a presence in the being of the other'. This exists within us all, by identification, as our internalized experience of mother, as the female element, and our essential humanness. From this centre springs 'life longing for itself', to quote Gibran (in *The Prophet*) speaking back to the ghost of Mahler. As Diether himself says, the emphasis with Mahler should be on the word 'integrate'. *'Where we started'* was in that state of primary identification in which our sense of being was formed, and from which, by tentative unfoldings of love as finding and creating we began to explore our own identity. We did not start in the moronic mud! We began in the creative mystery of 'encounter'.[1]

[1] See Marjorie Grene on Buytendijk in *Approaches to a Philosophical Biology*, and D. W. Winnicott, *Playing and Reality*.

It is these primary processes that Mahler re-explores in the opening of his symphony. He achieves, later, the held moment 'half-heard in the stillness', as I have indicated above, and such tenuous moments occur frequently in Mahler—'quick, now, here, always'—and mark the extreme concentration of his perception, directed at prising open the door of 'Paradise', to find a glimpse of 'unity of Being'. It is not a glimpse of God, but of peace and meaning without an external God.[2]

While Wilfrid Mellers is illuminating about the philosophical implications of Beethoven's development, he is surprisingly disappointing over Mahler, and I believe this is because he too finds the '*id*-instinctual' as primary, and consciousness a burden. His observation of the nature of the music is accurate enough: what seems to me a crux is his negative interpretation. The moment he quotes is (after all) followed on the next page by that significant most triumphant passage on the horns, a statement of immense joy:

EXAMPLE 120

Molto adagio

In truth, Mahler sweeps and soars from triumph to triumph, out of the deepest heart-searching and poignancy as we have seen, to 'construct something upon which to rejoice'. How can this be called 'world-weariness' and *the vanishing of a mode of belief*? Isn't it rather the discovery, not of a new mode of belief, but a new way of developing 'belief in the value of having lived'?

Unless we can respond more gratefully to Mahler we may well misinterpret the direction of the New Orpheus and follow it into unprofitable metaphysical or psychological directions (which indeed is what has happened among the nihilistic *avant-garde*). Misunderstood, his kind of triumph in the inner world could be taken to imply a withdrawal from the outer world and from time in a world-weary sense of futility. Such a

---

[2] Here I believe a good deal more could be said, round the attitudes of Kierkegaard and Nietzsche (see Rollo May in *Existence*, pp. 29ff). See also Tillich on 'The God beyond God' in *The Courage to Be*. The point of Nietzsche's 'God is dead' was that deteriorated theism and emotionally dishonest religious practices had to go so that man's dignity and humanity could be established. Mahler's music belongs to this movement, as we can see if we read May's excellent historical survey.

withdrawal might well include a withdrawal of sympathy between men, since it could involve a denial of dependence and hence of *social* needs and needs for relationship. This is, in fact, happening in the arts, so that today these have even become enemies of society, promoting degradation and egoistical nihilism, along with the forfeiture of consciousness in commercial 'pop'.

In Mahler we do not have this development towards egoistical nihilism: there can be little music as deeply compassionate in going beyond the self as Mahler's last works. It moves in the opposite direction from a desperate encapsulation in the self and serves a life-task of pursuing meaning in 'meeting' and responsibility, a true *Dasein*. It *gives*, and is full of gratitude: the strength is of one who has accepted his own weakness and needs. And though Mahler himself was too broken and doomed ever to allow his profoundest spiritual discoveries to flow fully back into his own life there is every indication that he was making his way towards a new sympathy, a new touch, and a new capacity to relate and accept 'inner responsibilities'. That is, there is every indication that Mahler had discovered the meaning of love, in its relationship to the reality of the 'other' and the world, and that, despite the break-down of his own life, nothing could be more misleading than to read this break-down as being simply reflected in his music, as a 'withdrawal' merely into self-pitying nostalgia. In his art he won victories over dread from which we can profit in our search for meaning and 'that which we have in us to become'— our *potentia*. He conveys a monumental hope for man and belief in life, because he found his own essential human value, and the meaning in his own life.

Wilfrid Mellers' account seems tinged by a feeling that to be pre-occupied with the 'meditations of the spirit' must necessarily mean a withdrawal from the world, because it is a withdrawal from Time. It is, of course true that like Beethoven Mahler 'found his solution if Europe did not', since Europe was plunged into an orgy of hate once more: but the music is not merely the 'madness of a world that burns itself out'. It will not do to imply that to find one's own solution is in any way a treacherous act of *sauve qui peut* since, as Beethoven saw, any growth in European culture depends upon 'a change of heart'. Mahler, far from merely recording 'falling masonry' records the perception that the collapses of civilization come from *within*: the thuds of percussion are less masonry than the murderous blows of hate, within the identity— destructive consequences in the world that come from distorted manifestations of the need to survive. What Mahler records above all is the triumph of a subjective integration that releases gratitude in the world, not mere valediction, or envy of the living.

Mellers' conclusions therefore I find strangely negative, for all that he recognizes the 'seed' in Mahler's achievement:

> In the passages of linear polyphony in the *Ninth Symphony*, and still more in the last movement of his symphonic song-cycle, *Das Lied von der Erde*, Mahler attains a translucent texture that seems in some ways more Eastern than European. The cycle sets Chinese poems without superficial Oriental-isms. But in the 'Farewell' appear strange linear arabesques—sometimes pentatonic, sometimes in chromatically inflected modes, sometimes almost as non-tonal and inhuman as bird-calls: while in the ineffably protracted suspensions on the word *'ewig'* music strains to relieve itself from harmony and metre. Beethoven, we saw, had to free himself from Time and the Will if he was to preserve his sanity. He found his salvation, if Europe did not. In the dying fall of Mahler's last music the madness of a world burns itself out. The obsession with time, which has dominated Europe since the Renaissance, begins to dissolve into Asiatic immobility; and the process is a laceration of the spirit. Mahler lingers on the life he loved with all his richly attuned senses; while the hollow reverberations of percussion sound like falling masonry, thudding through an eternity of years. The chord on which the 'Farewell' finally fades to nothingness is a 'verticalization' of the pentatonic scale; and of all melodic formulae the pentatonic is most void of harmonic implications. Yet out of harmonic disintegration grows a new seed. The linear principle of twelve-note music already is inherent in the texture of the music of Mahler's last years.
>
> *The Sonata Principle*, p. 131

Mellers seems to be applying a worldly and temporal interpretation to the escape from preoccupations with the world and time, as if for Mahler to utter his *'ewig'* were to crawl into a monastery, into a private world, or the grave. The effect of Mahler's music is tragic but positive. It may move one to the deepest sorrow and tears, and even terrify us, but the ultimate effect is of elation: 'we have been through all that and more': *we feel invulnerable*, because we are now in possession of tested meanings. But he is not going back to the baby's cry in relinquishment. His triumph is achieved in his art by re-experiencing of the springs of being, of mother-child relationship, and of the adult authenticity of being that grows from these elements. There are, too, sounds and rhythms from within the self—the rising of anger, the threatening beat of over-excited hate, the quiet heart. And there are *sounds of the earth* which, since the earth is the ultimate object are also 'sound from the object', as of a mother's voice. When Mahler's relationship with his wife was threatened by infidelity he lay sobbing on the floor, as close to the earth as he could get. On p. 56 of the full score a melody like bird-song exerts a healing power:

EXAMPLE 135

Plötzlich bedeutend langsamer (Lento) und leise

These earthly sounds are symbolic of the healing power of that close contact which can yield a sense of cosmic at-one-ness which echoes the primal at-one-ness experienced in infancy.

Mahler's 'listening' (as we have seen) was a philosophical principle, as Paul Stefan (quoted by Mitchell, p. 113) makes plain:

[Mahler] also laid the foundations of the proud edifice of his general knowledge. He became acquainted with the philosophers, especially Kant and Schopenhauer; later [G. T.] Fechner [1801–87], [R. H.] Lotze [1817–81], and [H. L. F. von] Helmholtz [1821–94] were added. In Nietzsche he admired the hymnic vein. Philosophy, in particular the boundaries that touch the natural sciences, always attracted him . . . for instance, he . . . followed the researches of [J.] Reinke [1849–1931], to whom he was led, as to Fechner, by his religious instinct. Goethe, Schiller and the Romantic School were already his precious possessions, his favourites being [E. T. A.] Hoffman and Jean Paul [Richter], especially the latter's [novel] *Titan*. History, biology and psychology held his attention always. As psychologist and poet, Dostoievsky was for Mahler a discovery.

We have here literary tastes and a bent for philosophical enquiry that remained, for the most part, constant throughout Mahler's life; he had, indeed, already revealed the strength of these inclinations at school and university. Bruno Walter writes:

. . . he was interested mainly in those phenomena of natural history that furnished philosophy with new material for thought. Friends of his, professionally occupied with natural science, were hard pressed by his deeply penetrating questions. An eminent physicist whom he met frequently could not tell me enough about Mahler's intuitive understanding of the ultimate theories of physics [cf. Freud's observation on Mahler's intuitive understanding of psychoanalysis!] and about the logical keenness of his conclusions or counter-arguments.

It is of interest to note that the 'philosophers' mentioned by Stefan above were also, almost exclusively, men of science. Such was certainly the case of Helmholtz: Fechner was both experimental psychologist and animistic philosopher, while Lotze's aim was 'the reconciliation of science with art, Literature and religion'. Reinke was a philosophically inclined botanist. All these men, however diversely, pursued lines of investigation which—to put it very crudely—tried to knit the universe together, to demonstrate its unity (Fechner, for example, believed that even plants and stars were animated); some of these thinkers, moreover, were marked by strong religious susceptibilities. That Mahler was so interested in philosophy of this character, which, as it were, took rational, scientific account of intangibles and attempted a comprehensive explanation of the cosmos, throws light on his own philosophy, one never defined, to be sure.

Gustav Mahler, 'The Early Years', p. 114

However, the relationship with the natural world was a symbolic (or phenomenological) matter with him. His music can be seen in relation to philosophical biology in this sense. Dika Newlin writes of the 'symbolic significance' in Mahler's work of 'bird-song', and continues:

Oddly enough, its value for him was only symbolic; actually, he found the singing of birds around his *Komponierhäuschen* in the summertime so disturbing as to be intolerable, and even used to shoot some of them to discourage their fellows.

Perhaps it was in the light of an incident of this character that Mrs Mahler remarks that her husband's 'love of animals was theoretical only'.

Bruckner, Mahler, Schoenberg, p. 115

But in the *Ninth Symphony* obviously, the man's voice and heart follow the bird as if *being taught*, by 'natural being'. We find the same interest in natural sounds in Messaien and in Shostakovitch: what is surely being symbolized is the need for man to listen to his *own* nature and the nature of his world.

In the progress of the work, every exploration discovers further bitterness and loss. And each consequent threat requires a return to the original processes of 'creative reflection' by the mother. Only by such 'controlled regression' can the adult anguish be overcome and the existential security found.

This explains the 'growing' structure of the work, to which Mellers draws our attention. For the matter is not that a conflict between the will and the world has to be resolved in terms of action and doing. It is rather that there has to be a deepening of contact between subjective and objective, by the discovery of the 'unity of being' through the resolution of envy and hate by love and creativity. Since this is a process of growth in the context of regression (like psychoanalysis) it takes the form of continual repetition, elaboration and melodic extension. Significantly this symphony is still a song-cycle because what it explores essentially is voice speaking to voice—mother to child and child to mother, mother earth to man and man to mother earth in paean, the voice of the heart and the voices of hate, the man to his beloved, and man to man, in compassion. This structure which follows the processes of encounter is explained well in the notes of the 1935 recording by Henry Boys:

> It will be noticed that Mahler's melodies here owe their extreme pliability and plasticity to their being built about the same harmonic of unity and relatedness. Thus all accompaniment figures are, if not sections of, highly related to, the main themes; a clear example is the way in which the opening melts into the first theme. The polyphony, apart from its function as accompaniment, is used, as it were, to give hints as to the possibilities of the melodic line. What makes the main lines distinct in face of this method is, first, the clarity of the orchestration—nothing is more studied—secondly, the transitional passages which, although they echo their sighing cadences, are clearly recognizable as transitions, so that the sections become clearly separated. This relatedness of the themes also enables Mahler to achieve variety by joining a section of one theme to a section of another. And he is master of melodic extension. The whole technique is based on principles of variation. From this it will be seen that to call Mahler's symphonies inflated song cycles simply because his melodies are long rather than short epigrammatic themes is quite beside the point.

The need to go over the same ground is perhaps explained by Eliot's line, 'After such knowledge, what forgiveness?' Whatever has been gained has to be continually tested. This new mode of progress is disturbing and painful, because it is a process of real reparation: as the schizoid problem of the fear of love is dealt with there emerges the problem of concern—the fear that one's hate may destroy the world, and from this emerges a heart-rending pity. This, I consider, explains the resistances his music encounters, even among admirers.

For instance, Dr Hans Redlich speaks from an academic point of view somewhat slightingly of the *Ninth Symphony*: of the First Movement he says:

> None of the succeeding three movements is a match for it, and the whole structure shows a certain top-heaviness . . . it is this movement's failure (the *Ländler* movement) that it cannot obliterate the memory of its predecessors within Mahler's own creative work . . . the movement is . . . like the work of a Mahlerian rather than Mahler himself . . .
>
> *Bruckner and Mahler*, p. 227–8

This is surely a form of resistance to the ferocity of the manic denial and doubt to which Mahler exposes his gains by the recognition of envy?

Although Professor Redlich speaks of the 'almost unbearable contrast' of the *Adagio* to the 'defiant harshness and garish hilarity' of the *Rondo-Burleske*, there is a deeper unbearableness perhaps this critic would not accept, because it hovers on the verge of utter loss of meaning? Redlich seems to misunderstand the nature of Mahler's development and the originality of the form, which arose out of the necessity for continual re-examination of gains achieved.

Redlich's reaction is that of a musicologist who perhaps fails to recognize that Mahler was 'arguing' like one of R. D. Laing's schizoid patients, 'to preserve his very existence' (*The Divided Self*). Significantly, Dr Redlich overestimates in a sentimenal way the part Alma played in Mahler's life.

> There can be no doubt that Alma completely transformed Mahler's whole life . . . deeply understanding and sympathetic critic of his music . . . a woman . . . of originality of mind . . .
>
> p. 134

In truth Alma may be said to have been devoted but, looked at dispassionately, she seems not to have truly 'found' Mahler any more than he 'found' her. In a sense the couple failed utterly to find one another: she related to him as a father, he to her as a mother, and perhaps both tended to relate to projected idealizations. In many ways they failed to 'meet', even disastrously, until towards the end, after the *Ninth Symphony*, Mahler took an interest in her songs, listened rapturously to her breathing, and dedicated his *Eighth Symphony* to her. By then she had become merged, as it were, with the world-as-object.

It would seem that Mahler did gain in his relationship from his re-enactment of primary being, and his wrestle with hate in his music. But such gains in the world of expression make little impression on the stubborn intractability of psychic reality. It is more important to acknowledge the failure of the Mahlers' relationship and thus to be obliged to understand the poignancy of his creative striving. If we do we shall perhaps be better able to understand the structure and meaning of the *Ninth Symphony*. Seen as a massive exploration in the quest for the capacity to find a sense of secure identity through painful steps towards integration, it is by no means 'top-heavy', but rather contains the seed of the future, as the harmonic 'disintegration' evolves into the linear principles of later music, while the episodic progress and moments of counter-progress enact stages of the growth of the integration of being. The tenacity in working over the same ground is a recognition that we shall not cease from exploration, and can never achieve our goal, 'For us there is only the trying'. The vast subtle and complex structure of the work is an attempt to hold an identity together through a period of recreative regression.

The positive human quality of the work is especially due to the song-like quality of its melodic and choral-polyphonic nature which suggests the frail human voice striving against the whole reality of experience. But the voice is not alone: it is answered as a mother answers, and as the world-as-object responds. By re-finding this state of identification with the subjective object before it became the objective object Mahler found a position from which the 'questions (of life) seem to cease to exist': as we have seen, Mahler said,

Or rather, I feel quite clearly that they are no question at all . . .

The music *is* the sanity Mahler could not find in reality: it is an over-coming of the threat of dissociation, which threatens annihilation because of the hungry ego-weakness.

What Mahler discovered and created was a peace which knows hate to the core: which is strong enough to live with fear. And this end is still heart-searching, and anguished, for the sense of loss consequent upon disillusion can never be wholly overcome: man's predicament is eternally tragic. Even when resignation is achieved, despair is still an element of the triumph. So, the end is both triumphant but with agonized under-currents, and no analysis can do justice to its richness, And although Diether characterizes this close as 'not of this world', in its achievement of that 'inner peace' and security of identity, it is of a very human kind, and so, it is easily possessed—and indeed if it could be widely possessed it could perhaps help save the world from the devastations of hate. Here we need to reverse the view of the sociological critic, that culture 'reflects' society: such a regeneration of consciousness could change our world.

For we urgently require such contributions to our reintegration. As Rollo May says, the 'psychological and emotional disintegration' which Kierkegaard and Nietzsche described 'was related to man's loss of faith in his essential dignity and humanity'. Nietzsche's emphasis on the 'will to power' was an 'ontological category': 'it is the individual affirming his existence and his potentialities as a being in his own right': It is the 'courage to be as an individual', as Tillich remarked. May quotes Kaufmann:

Man . . . should cease letting his 'existence' be a 'thoughtless accident' . . .
'Wie man wird, was man ist'—how one becomes what one is . . .

May goes on:

> The fundamental drive . . . is to live out one's *potentia* . . . Health [Nietzsche
> sees as] the ability to overcome disease and suffering . . . The human being
> can lose his own being by his own choices . . . if you do not have 'courage
> to be' you lose your own being . . . in Sartre's contention, you are your
> choices.
>
> *Existence*, p. 32

These phrases indicate the kind of anguished struggle which Mahler was
enacting—and they indicate philosophical problems we are only just
beginning to understand. Our achievement of a sense of meaning in life,
as Frankl indicates, is bound up with our 'intentionality':

> What man has done cannot be undone. I think that this implies both
> activities and optimism. Man is called upon to make the best use of any
> moment and the right choice at any time, be it that he knows what to do,
> or whom to love, or how to suffer. This means activism. As to optimism,
> let me remind you of the word of Lao-Tse: 'Having completed a task means
> having become eternal.' I would say that this holds true not only for the
> completion of a task, but for our experiences, and last but not least, for
> our brave suffering as well.
>
> *Psychotherapy and Existentialism*, p. 31

These words link the suffering of Mahler, in trying to make sense of
his existence, and the suffering of Viktor Frankl himself, who went
through the ultimate hell in human life, of the concentration camp, and
survived, to promote humanness at large, and to help restore 'intentionality'.

*

Then even at the end of one's interpretation, one has to add—and now
let the work stand for itself. The creation of the work, and our response
to it are both manifestations of the 'eternal feminine'. To overinterpret
may be to attempt to subjugate her to 'the male way of knowing'.

Let Mahler himself have the last word—in an extract from a letter
to Alma about Goethe ('Letters 1909' in *Gustav Mahler*, p. 320–1). It
shows his immense intelligence, his profound insights, his creative confidence: also his contempt for 'commentary', such as I have found it
necessary to make of his work:

Your interpretation of the final stanza[3] than those offered by the learned commentators (whom, I confess, I have never read, but I know that this passage has kept them busy for the last hundred years). It is a peculiarity of the interpretation of works of art that the rational element in them (that is, what is soluble by reason) is almost never their true reality, but only a veil which hides their form. But in as far as a soul needs a body—which there is no disputing—an artist is bound to derive the means of creation from the rational world. Whenever he himself is not clear, or rather has not achieved wholeness within himself, the rational overcomes what is spontaneously artistic, and makes an undue claim on the attention. Now *Faust* is in fact a mixture of all this, and as its composition occupied the whole of a long life the stones of which it is built do not match, and have often been left simply as undressed stone. Hence, one has to approach the poem in various ways and from different sides—But the chief thing is still the artistic conception, which no mere words can ever explain. Its truth shows a different face to each one of us—and a different one to each of us at different ages; just as Beethoven's symphonies are new and different at every hearing and never the same to one person as to another. If I am to try to tell you what my reason at its present stage has to say to these final verses— well, I'll try, but I don't know whether I shall succeed. I take those four lines, then, in the closest connection with the preceding ones—as a direct continuation, in one sense, of the lines they follow, and in another sense, as the peak of the whole tremendous pyramid, a world presented and fashioned step by step, in one situation and development after another. All point, at first dimly and then from scene to scene (particularly in the Second Part, where the poet's own powers have matured to match his task) with growing mastery, to this supreme moment, which though beyond expression, scarcely even to be surmised, touches the very heart of feeling.

It is all an allegory to convey something which, whatever form it is given, can never be adequately expressed. Only the transitory lends itself to description; but what we feel, surmise but will never reach (or know here as an actual happening), the intransitory behind all appearance, is indescribable. That which draws us by its mystic force, what every created thing, perhaps even the very stones, feels with absolute certainty as the centre of its being, what Goethe here—again employing an image—calls the eternal feminine—that is to say, the resting-place, the goal, in opposition to the striving and struggling towards the goal (the eternal masculine)—you are quite right in calling the force of love. There are infinite representations and names for it. (You have only to think of how a child, an animal, or persons of a lower or higher development live their lives.) Goethe himself reveals it stage by stage, on and on, in image after image, more and more

[3] *Alles Vergängliche ist nur ein Gleichnis;*
Das Unzulängliche, hier wird's ereignis;
Das Unbeschreibliche, hier ist's getan;
Das Ewig-Weibliche zieht uns hinan.
From Goethe's *Faust*, the text which Mahler used for Part Two of his *Eighth Symphony*, the *Chorus Mysticus* (D.M.).

clearly as he draws nearer the end. In Faust's impassioned search for Helen, in the Walpurgis night, in the still inchoate *Homunculus*, through the manifold entelchies of lower and higher degree; he presents and expresses it with a growing clearness and certainty right on to the *mater gloriosa* —the personification of the eternal feminine!

And so in immediate relation to the final scene Goethe in person addresses his listeners. He says: 'All that is transitory (what I have presented to you here these two evenings) is nothing but images, inadequate, naturally, in their earthly manifestations; but there, freed from the body of earthy inadequacy, they will be actual, and we shall then need no paraphrase, no similitudes or images for them; there is done what here is in vain described, for it is indescribable. And what is it? Again I can only reply in imagery and say: The eternal feminine has drawn us on—we have arrived—we are at rest—we possess what on earth we could only strive and struggle for. Christians call this "eternal blessedness", and I cannot do better than employ this beautiful and sufficient mythology—the most complete conception to which at this epoch of humanity it is possible to attain.'

I hope I have expressed myself clearly. There is always the danger of an exuberance of words in such infinitely delicate and, as I said above, unrational matters. That is why all commentary is so disgusting.

So, we must return to the music itself.

Appendix:
The 'Holy Mary' Syndrome

Im Rhein, im heiligen Strome,
da spiegelt sich in den Well'n,
mit seinem grossen Dome,
das grosse heilige Cöln.

Im Dom da steht ein Bildniss
auf goldenem Leder gemalt;
in meines Lebens wildniss
hat's freundlich hinein gestrahlt.

Es schweben Blumen und Eng'lein
um unser liebe Frau;
die Augen, die Lippen, die Wänglein,
die gleichen der Liebsten genau.
                                    Heine

> (Set to music by Schumann in the Song-Cycle
> *Dichterliebe*)

The 'Holy Mary' complex was a term used by Freud for the intense idealism of the feminine which he found in Mahler. Mahler, as we have seen, worshipped the Eternal Feminine, his lofty, idealizing conception of the *mater gloriosa* being matched by a neglect of his actual wife, of which he was unaware. As Reik says (*The Haunting Melody*, 1953), he 'withdrew his libido' from Alma.

Freud diagnosed that in the background of the problem was the fact that Mahler's mother had been 'careworn and ailing'. The consequence was that in his infantile experience developed a split, between the object as he willed her, restored and radiant, and the actual woman, whose ill condition threatened his existence. Yet where any actual woman was concerned Mahler felt that he could only love her *if* she was sick and ailing. The complex effect of this on Mahler was that he wanted his wife to be 'more ailing' and yet at the same time wanted to make her into a Mary-ideal; his mother was called 'Marie' and he obliged his wife to be called 'Marie' too: as Alma Mahler writes:

255

Gustav Mahler's mother was called Marie. His first impulse was to change my name to Marie in spite of the difficulty he had in pronouncing 'r'. And when he got to know me better he wanted my face to be more 'stricken'— his very word . . . he told my mother that it was a pity there had been so little sadness in my life . . .

Freud's analysis of Mahler, however, stopped short at the Oedipal level. I believe there are underlying factors which we need to explore, to explain such disastrous splitting of the object as that of Mahler's, combined with the intensity of his feeling of existence anxiety—in which are the springs of his art.

The presence of the ideal object in art is often associated with a child-like purity, and here I propose to invoke for the purposes of comparison a play by Sir James Barrie in which the ideal woman or Virgin Mary ghost is predominant. Here the ideal object is a woman become child again. Mary Rose becomes an infant girl on the lap of her own adult son at the end of the play. As we know, Mahler treated his wife like a girl-child, and she related to him as a father: her father was a painter— *ma(h)ler*—and she admits this paternal element in her relationship from the first. It seems highly likely it was in Mahler a fear of adult sexuality in woman, which made him impotent.

Mary Rose has to remain a Virgin. In *Mary Rose*, as Goitein says, 'we are fairly clearly given to understand that the marriage is never consummated and as far as earth is concerned Mary remains a virgin'. Her son is born of the *father* who 'fishes round her island' and is represented by 'The Call'. In Mahler's earlier work his intense adoration of the Virgin, as in the *Ewig-Weibliche*, is at the far extreme from eroticism, while eroticism in his work is always associated with pain.

Mahler was deeply affected by painful scenes in his childhood, in one of which he was 'involuntary witness of a brutal love scene between servant and son of the house'. His father also 'ran after every servant, and flogged the children'. After another brutal scene of violence between his mother and father he fled from the house. From his background, as Diether says, he developed

a strong unconscious identification of pain with sex, as exemplified in the relationship of his mother with his father.

Mahler and Psychoanalysis, p. 7

There is, however, a yet deeper element which we need to approach, which is the area of *confirmation of existence*. The most disturbing moments in the three works specifically under discussion are those when *existence is threatened*. The split off ideal object must be removed from harm. Mary Rose actually goes out of existence for periods. In Mahler's work, from music of rising passion, emerges the surge of hate: and his work elsewhere alternates between adoration of the Holy Mother, the celebration of childhood innocence, and the exploration of annihilation as the consequence of love (as in *Das Klagende Lied*).

Following recent psychoanalytical thought about the origins of the confirmation of identity, and our sense of existence-security, I believe we can say that the origins of these feelings lie in infantile experience in family situations in which it was impossible for the mother to offer her child a satisfactory experience of Primary Maternal Preoccupation, and also impossible for her to complete the processes of psychic weaning. The consequence is an extremely weak sense of identity at the core of being, together with a confusion of distinction between *me* and *not-me*, lack of integration, and that 'existential despair' which is the basis of their art. Fear of ego weakness is a fear of the female element—and so this must be split off and projected away.

Having written a great deal about Mahler in this vein, I was glad to find others who had independently arrived at the same problem. Robert Still, for instance writing in *The American Imago*, says of Reik's study:

> . . . taking Mahler's vast *Eighth Symphony* as his example he writes, 'For the context into which we put this analytic fragment of the composer's biography it is important that here the last and most important psychological link between the *Veni Creator Spiritus* and the idea of the last Faust Scene becomes recognizable. Here emerges from the darkness the secret substructure of the stilted arch which bridges the passionate artistic zeal with the sublime concept of the Eternal Feminine. At the bottom of that proud and lofty building we recognize the contours of a familiar emotional constellation: the invocation of the Holy Spirit, that pleading for creative power, finds its answer and reward in the appearance of the *Mater gloriosa* of the untouchable mother-image. The zeal for highest achievement is followed by the redemption, by the grace of the Holy Virgin. In the storm to the heights of the Divine Father, that passionate request is met with a response of the mother in her most idealized shape. Freud realized that secret emotional connection between Mahler's striving for the highest achievement, and his 'Holy Mary Complex', the infantile pattern behind the philosophical façade of the 51 years old artist.' Reik concludes by saying that Mahler worked far too hard in his search for the absolute and did not really allow himself to live.

Now, all this is an improvement in the sense that the 'Feminine' and the 'Creative' are identified, but Reik's whole concept is still in terms of mother-object. Identification with the mother is scarcely hinted at, nor are the obsessional symptoms very clearly defined in relation to what they are supposed to be masking, and the very vagueness of the writing suggests that he is having great difficulty in trying to explain everything in terms of the Oedipus Complex, which is hardly surprising when we reflect that so much of its character is determined by the simple two body relationship of the infant to the mother, necessarily of earlier origin.

Beneath any 'Oedipal' explanation of Mahler's 'Holy Mary' complex, therefore, we need to seek problems arising from *primary identification* as the source of beginning to be and its effect on later life. As Still points out, Mahler identified with his wife and was so much concerned to deny her separate existence and reality that he must forbid her creativity, demonstrating that as far as he was concerned, she was part of himself, or confused with himself. He also confused himself seriously with his sister. Alma Mahler speaks of him having been 'in a sense married to Justine. He regarded himself as bound to her by vows of fidelity, and deliberately eluded all temptations . . . He exacted without mercy the same self-denial of Justine.' When Justine embarked upon a love affair and Mahler detected it he refused to speak to her for weeks, told her he regarded himself as entirely free and 'His love of her, great as it had been, was now done with for ever'. On his death-bed he failed to recognize her, saying 'Who is this lady?'—yet he recognized his next visitor. Still says:

> . . . we get a feeling that Mahler imagined he was actually part of his sister, and that he suffered from a physical sense of shock when he realized that she was not, in that he behaved as if some kind of disaster had happened to him, and yet, by not recognizing her, as if it had not really happened to him.

Still ponders whether this reflects the 'dismay at the discovery that he was a separate entity from his mother' ('the shattering of primary identification') or 'whether the introjections and projections at the anal stage . . . coupled with the arrival of the brother' was responsible for this state. Whatever we conjecture, we can see certain significant schizoid aspects of Mahler's earliest experience indicated here:

1. A confusion of identity to do with looking and being looked at.
2. A tendency to split off his female element, because of a weak sense of being at the core and to project it over a woman, in whom he seeks to 'control the female factor' obsessionally, and to exert over her denial, hostility and jealousy.

In the light of these insights, strange as it may seem, we may find in Gustav Mahler psychological dynamics similar to those in the Barrie of *Mary Rose*. Each of these artists had the greatest difficulty in becoming able to accept the full nature of adult sexual relationship. They were unable to express love as the capacity for an integrated individual to relate to a whole object: in their attitudes to the problem of love, the object must be kept split between ideal and libidinal, which parallels splits in the self.

The origin of this problem would seem almost certainly to be in the failure of a facilitating environment—in large, poverty-stricken families in which the mother was not freed by love and support to be able to 'forfeit her self-interest' sufficiently and *be for* her baby, at the particular moment of his psychic parturition. Consequent problems of identification with the mother were confused by the presence of siblings in the same predicament competing fiercely for the same preoccupation. The Oedipal problem would become exacerbated by the father's sexual role in actually making the whole situation less hopeful— and especially by the death of other siblings. Often we find large families in which there is a 'Holy Mary' syndrome, the mother had become 'resigned', which suggests some kind of loss of psychic energy and perhaps depression. Mahler's family life was appalling:

> Gustav was born into utter squalor, in a 'pitiful little house, whose windows did not even have glass. *Six of the children died in infancy*, and after the death of the parents the remaining five all became dependent on him . . . Then one of the brothers shot himself, while another became notorious as the village half-wit . . . Mahler grew up in an atmosphere of death and near-madness . . . The *Kindertotenlieder* . . . are not so much an anticipation of the death of his little daughter . . . as an unconscious memory of his identification with his own parents' sorrow.
>
> Diether, 1958, p. 7

Reik says:

> The sensitive boy Gustav must have unconsciously experienced the mourning of his parents . . .

This 'experience of mourning' seems to me the most significant experience of all, underlying the attitudes to life of Mahler and Barrie. What is 'mourning'? If we refer to our earlier discussion of death and hate, we can see that mourning is an experience in which inward feelings of guilt and loss become intense, not least because the hate within us threatens to swallow up our whole identity. Reparation becomes seemingly impossible, since object-loss seems so overwhelming: that is, we feel as though the hate we at times bore the object has in fact now annihilated the object—and so our identity is threatened by object-loss, by the withdrawal of a regard that confirmed our existence. Hence in mourning guilt is bound up with existence anxiety.

So, where a child already suffers from existence anxiety, and is not adequately confirmed by the mother's reflecting role, mourning in the mother will bring the profoundest threat to contining existence, and cause the child's reparative capacities to be exaggerated to the limits of his powers—and beyond, which takes him into the realm of magic. He can only cope with his agony by believing in his own omnipotence. In order to keep the mother alive he must somehow separate her from the realities which seem to threaten her existence and his with it: he must idealize her.

I have discussed elsewhere over Dylan Thomas the way in which loss of a sibling can evoke Oedipal guilt.[1] So has the father. If a sibling dies it seems as if the Oedipal envy, which has an intense sexual significance, has 'worked'. So, it seems as if the sibling-rival has died as a consequence of oral-sexual feelings, which are feared anyway for their threat to existence (since sex is felt to be a form of dangerous eating).

Now perhaps we can see why the ideal object, who becomes split off, as the *eternal* feminine, must necessarily be *pre-sexual*, without libido, a child-girl, virginal, ethereal, unreal, heavenly. She is the object restored by manic reparation, without the recognition of loss and guilt—and in the denial of the subject's dangerous sexual feelings which unconsciously wished for the death of the father—and which seem to have caused the death of the sibling. Moreover, though they have not caused the death of the mother *they have caused her removal from the role of confirming and reflecting* (by her withdrawal state)—and this feels terribly like the most dreadful episode in which she failed to offer confirmation of identity at the stage of Primary Maternal Preoccupation.

The schizoid child thus suffers, at a time when it is more aware of the risks, the agonies of feeling 'let down' and threatened with extinction as when his mother failed him in the first few months of life. He experiences the deepest agonies of being forced to be alone when he cannot bear to be alone: he loses ego-relatedness, and yet cannot find sufficient support within the ego because of the earlier failures in ego-relatedness. So, he casts around for all the magical powers he can summon, and he must try to believe in his omnipotence as best he can. He seeks to escape from reality and to deny it, and to try to find from elsewhere these mysterious forces of psychic confirmation which have been inaccessible in his mother, or cut off by her grief.

The solution which Barrie was working out symbolically was that

---

[1] See *Dylan Thomas: the Code of Night*, Athlone Press, the University of London, 1972.

which Mahler explored: the need to regress in order to find a way to begin *to be*. In Mahler's *Ninth Symphony* it is expressed by the combination of crooning lullabies and rocking rhythms as if the mother's lap, in contrast with the surge of passion, the thudding omens of the funeral corteges and the howls of hate. The success of the creative work on such a problem needs to be judged according to its capacity to relinquish magical solutions, and discover truly reparative, creative ones—as Barrie never could.

The problem is the discovery of humanness in all its mixed, weak mortality. The individual with very serious schizoid (or 'existence') problems often cannot find the human reality of his woman, because he cannot find the human reality of himself. The individual who suffers from the 'Holy Mary' Syndrome vacillates between adoration of a split-off ideal, and loathing of the fleshly woman. James Joyce, for instance, alternated between one and the other, yet, identifying intensely with his wife, said, 'My love for you is really a kind of adoration'. If she refused to share his mood, however, she became an enemy.

Thus the 'adoration' is revealed as the mark of a desperate need to be reflected and confirmed—at the expense of the object's self-interest and independence. The Virgin Mary is a symbol of utter and eternal selfless Primary Maternal Preoccupation: every man to her is the Infant Jesus, omnipotent and infinitely to be adored in return.

Alas, to remain in such a relationship would mean never to be disillusioned, so as to become able to face the realities, and to experience the satisfactions, of independent adult living in relationship to another adult. Very often in a work of art, where the Holy Mary symbolism is predominant, there is an overpowering barrenness in consequence, and only that manic reparation which achieves no lasting gains in our exploration of experience.[2] By contrast, Mahler's achievement of integration through the anguish of true reparation seems very great indeed.

[2] I discuss manic reparation and the failure to find love in *T. F. Powys: Love Under Control*, in preparation.

Bibliography

BALINT, Michael. *Primary Love and Psychoanalytical Technique* (Tavistock, 1952).

BARRIE, Sir James. *Mary Rose* (1920).

EINSWANGER, Ludwig. *Being-in-the-World* (Basic Books, 1963).

BOWLBY, John. *Child Care and the Growth of Love* (Penguin, 1960).

BOYS, Henry. *Mahler and His Ninth Symphony* (The Gramophone Company, 1938, issued with the H.M.V. recording).

BUBER, Martin. *I and Thou* (T. & T. Clark, Edinburgh, 1958). 'Distance and Relation', in *The Knowledge of Man*, ed. Friedman (1964).

CAGE, John. *Silence* (Wesleyan, 1961).

COOKE, Deryck. *The Language of Music* (Oxford, 1959).

DE LA GRANGE, Henry. *Mahler*, Vol. One (Gollancz, 1974).

DIETHER, Jack. 'The Expressive Content of Mahler's Ninth', in *Chord and Discord* (U.S.A., Vol. 2, No. 10, 1963).

— 'Mahler's Place in Musical History', *ibid*.

— 'Mahler and Psychoanalysis', in *Psychoanalysis and the Psychoanalytical Review* (U.S.A., Winter, 1958).

ELIOT, T. S. *Four Quartets* (Faber, 1944).

FARBER, Leslie H. *The Ways of the Will* (Constable, 1966).

FRANKL, Viktor. *Psychotherapy and Existentialism* (Souvenir Press, 1971).

KIERKEGAARD, Søren. *The Journals*.

KLEIN, Melanie. *Our Adult World and its Roots in Childhood* (Tavistock, 1963).

— *Envy and Gratitude* (Tavistock, 1957).

GRENE, Marjorie. *Approaches to a Philosophical Biology* (Basic Books, 1968).

GUNTRIP, Harry. *Personality Structure and Human Interaction* (Hogarth Press, 1961).

— *Schizoid Phenomena, Object-relations and the Self* (Hogarth Press, 1969).

HARDY, Thomas. *Vestigea Veteris Flammae*, Poems 1912–3, in *Collected Poems*.

JONES, Ernest. *Sigmund Freud, Life and Work*, Vol. II.

LAWRENCE, D. H. *Poems*.

LEAVIS, F. R. 'Justifying One's Valuation of Blake', in *The Human World* (No. 7, May 1972, p. 42).

— *Now Shall My Sword* (Chatto and Windus, 1972)—on the 'nisus' and the 'ahnung'.

MARCEL, Gabriel. *The Philosophy of Existence* (Harvill Press, 1948).

MAHLER. Alma, *And the Bridge is Love* (1946).

— *Gustav Mahler, Memories and Letters*, ed. D. Mitchell (John Murray, 1968).

MAHLER, Gustav. *Lieder Eines Fahrenden Gesellen*.

— *Das Klagende Lied*.

Bibliography

— *Kindertotenlieder.*
— *First Symphony.*
— *Second Symphony.*
— *Sixth Symphony.*
— *Eighth Symphony.*
— *Ninth Symphony.*
— *Tenth Symphony.*
— *Das Lied Von Der Erde.*
MASLOW, Abraham. *The Psychology of Being* (Van Nostrand, New York, 1968).
MAY, Rollo. *Existence: A New Dimension in Psychiatry* (Basic Books, 1958).
— *Love and Will* (Souvenir Press, 1969).
MELLERS, Wilfrid. *Man and His Music: The Sonata Principle* (Rockliff, 1957).
— 'Mahler as a Key Figure' in *Scrutiny* (Vol. IX, pp. 343–51).
— *Music in a New Found Land*, on Charles Ives and Mahler, p. 62.
MITCHELL, Donald. *Gustav Mahler, the Early Years* (Rockliff, 1958).
— 'Some Notes on Mahler's Tenth Symphony', *Musical Times* (December 1955).
— 'Gustav Mahler, Prospect and Retrospect', *Chord and Discord* (1963, p. 143).
— 'Some Aspects of Mahler's Tonality', *Monthly Musical Record* (Nov.–Dec. 1957).
— 'On Mahler', *The Listener* (25 October 1962).
NEWLIN, Dika. *Bruckner, Mahler, Schoenberg* (King's Crown Press, 1947).
POOLE, Roger. *Towards Deep Subjectivity* (Allen Lane, 1972).
REDLICH, Hans. *Bruckner and Mahler* (Dent, 1955).
REIK, Theodore. *The Haunting Melody* (Farrar Straus and Young, N.Y., 1953).
SEGAL, Hannah. *Introduction to the Work of Melanie Klein* (Tavistock).
SHOSTAKOVITCH, Dimitri. *Fourth Symphony.*
— *Fourteenth Symphony.*
STEIN, Edwin. *Orpheus in New Guises* (1953).
STIEDRY, F. Notes to the Recording, *Ninth Symphony* (Hawkes and Co., 1944).
STILL, Robert. 'Gustav Mahler and Psychoanalysis', *The American Imago* (Fall, 1960).
VAUGHAN-WILLIAMS, Ralph. *Sixth Symphony.*
WALTER, Bruno. *Gustav Mahler* (1958).
WINNICOTT, D. W. *Playing and Reality* (Tavistock, 1972).
— *The Maturational Processes and the Facilitating Environment* (Hogarth Press, 1965).
— *Therapeutic Consultations in Child Psychiatry* (Hogarth Press, 1971).

GLOSSARIES

RYCROFT, Charles. *A Critical Dictionary of Psychoanalysis* (Nelson, 1972).
LAPLANCHE, J. and PONTALIS, J. B. *The Language of Psychoanalysis* (Hogarth, 1973).

Index